Adventures in
Consciousness:
An Introduction to
Aspect Psychology

Books by Jane Roberts

HOW TO DEVELOP YOUR ESP POWER
*THE SETH MATERIAL
*SETH SPEAKS: The Eternal Validity of the Soul
*THE NATURE OF PERSONAL REALITY: A Seth Book
*ADVENTURES IN CONSCIOUSNESS: An Introduction to
    Aspect Psychology
*DIALOGUES OF THE SOUL AND MORTAL SELF IN TIME

Novels

THE REBELLERS
BUNDU
*THE EDUCATION OF OVERSOUL SEVEN

*Available from Prentice-Hall, Inc.

Adventures in Consciousness: An Introduction to Aspect Psychology

by *JANE ROBERTS*

PRENTICE-HALL, INC.
Englewood Cliffs, New Jersey

Printed in the United States of America
Prentice-Hall International, Inc., London
Prentice-Hall of Australia, Pty. Ltd., Sydney
Prentice-Hall of Canada, Ltd., Toronto
Prentice-Hall of India Private Ltd., New Delhi
Prentice-Hall of Japan, Inc., Tokyo

10 9 8 7 6 5 4 3 2 1

Library of Congress Cataloging in Publication Data
Roberts, Jane.
    Adventures in consciousness.
    Includes index.
    1. Psychical research.   2. Consciousness.
I. Title.
BF1031.R63   133.8′01′9   75-8610
ISBN 0-13-013953-X

Preface

I don't know how many hours I've spent in various trance states during the past ten years. At least twice a week I've turned the focus of my consciousness away from its usual orientation and spoken for a personality called Seth—who is clairvoyant, writes books, relates to people with great understanding, and displays different characteristics than mine.

In 1972 a whole new development appeared in my life. I discovered many other levels of awareness, each distinct and bringing its own kind of perception and experience. Some provided me with excellent creative products as well. Yet nowhere in past or current theories could I find any acceptable explanations for my own experiences. They were relatively unique, intense, and extraordinary enough so that I was driven to find my own answers.

This book is the story of some of those events, and an introduction to what I call Aspect Psychology. I offer it as a framework through which previously denied psychic elements of life can be viewed as proper, beneficial, and natural conditions of our consciousness.

Such a theory is sorely needed. My correspondence shows me that many people are in a quandary as they try to understand their own psychic experiences. Those curious enough to allow their consciousness unconventional freedom are often labeled "emotionally disturbed" by psychologists, or considered "possessed" in the light of religious beliefs.

For several years I've also been involved with a group of people, my students, who embark with me upon adventures in consciousness. We give ourselves freedom to perceive the reality of the moment as it appears through the lens of other, alternate, states of awareness. I began to develop the ideas in Aspect Psychology precisely because my experiences and those of my students and readers raised so many questions.

So-called psychic events happen within the framework of normal life. They are not something apart from it. Only because we've been taught to isolate them from normal concerns do they often appear so unnatural, separate, and odd. Aspect Psychology is an attempt to correlate our psychic abilities with our other emotional behavior, and particularly to enlarge our concepts of the nature of personality.

Any psychology worthy of the name must be large enough to contain all of our psychologically vital, valid experiences, whether or not they fit into conventional ideas about the characteristics of consciousness. Aspect Psychology, then, accepts as normal the existence of precognitive dreams, out-of-body experiences, revelatory information, alterations of consciousness, peak experiences, trance mediumship, and other psychological and psychic events possible in human behavior.

I don't believe in good and bad spirits, demons, possession, or the power of evil as they're generally described in Christian thought, Spiritualism, Gnosticism, or any other "ism" for that matter. I'm also appalled that some "psychic" investigators without a qualm speak of mischievous spirits who impersonate the "godly dead," move the Ouija board pointer, wield the pen for automatic writers, or just wait to waylay the unsuspecting living in whatever way they can.

As yet, conventional psychology has found no acceptable explanations for such personalities as Seth, trance personalities in general, automatic speech or writing, and other related events. Aspect Psychology at least presents a framework in which these can be viewed as valid psychological experiences, themselves neither good nor bad, but expressions of the personality as it struggles to come to grips with its spiritual and creature nature.

Aspect Psychology begins with the idea that man's consciousness is mobile, focused in the body but not dependent upon it except for three-dimensional life. I do not consider this an assumption, but as a fact of my experience, and therefore as a human characteristic. The theory is based firmly in the importance of our creaturehood and spirituality alike. It examines the basic components of personality and sees them as Aspects of a greater, largely unknown self which is the source of our physical being. As Freud thought that slips of the tongue gave evidence of the subconscious areas of the personality, I see the varius Aspects of our personalities as pointing toward still undiscovered abilities; and our psychic and creative experiences as hints of a hidden, multi-dimensional self.

"Aspects," the second half of this book, is an intuitive construct. Much of it came to me in altered states of consciousness. It wrote itself as it went along. I also consider it scientific in the truest sense of that word, in that I used the best investigative tool to examine consciousness—consciousness itself. I utilize different levels of awareness to examine the nature of the psyche and its reality. The goal is set deliberately at a conscious state, and from that stage I program myself to journey to other portions of the personality, and view "reality" from their viewpoint, and with their own kinds of perception.

To this end, I've also examined my own trance material, and from my side of consciousness scrutinized Seth's reality as it appears in my experience, and in his behavior and writings. To date, Seth has produced two books, *Seth Speaks: The Eternal Validity of the Soul* and *The Nature of Personal Reality: A Seth Book*. Recently he began his third book, *The "Unknown" Reality*.

This "Seth level" has expanded into two other states that I call Seth Two and Three, though I've reached the Seth Three stage only twice. The Sumari development happened in 1972, further enlarging the scope of perception available. This involves several distinct alterations of consciousness, which will be described in this book. All of these experiences gave me the impetus to develop a theory large enough to contain them, and also (fortunately!) provided me with the material to do so.

Our class group experiences also brought me additional "unofficial events." Things happened that couldn't happen, according to official or conventional ideas about reality. Such "reincarnational" encounters, the sighting of "'apparitions," and other events led me to examine the nature of perception and events in a way that I would not have believed possible a few years ago.

An intuitive inside look at the personality may be far less distorted and closer to reality than objective theories that deal with case histories, or view the psychological condition of others from a detached standpoint. The latter originate with the physically and culturally attuned aspects of the mind, and not with the fountainhead of the psyche beneath.

What do the inner levels of the self feel about their own reality? How do they view our exteriorized life? Since our private experience comes from these inner Aspects of the self, at least they deserve a hearing. Our intellectually based theories stress the parts of the personality with which we are most familiar and ignore deeper experience, which they cannot reach alone.

If you're working to obtain scientific data in objective terms, then you utilize the part of consciousness that analyzes exterior phenomena. If you're looking for answers about the inner nature of personality, then you must use those parts of it most familiar with the psyche.

While my own experiences are relatively unusual, they are different only in quality and degree. Each man and woman sometimes senses a greater self within, is struck by inspiration, or startled by a dream or premonition that "comes true." Many others have startling psychic experiences that seem inexplicable. Often such events provide the most significant, richest memories of a lifetime, yet they remain like dangling participles—evidence of poor taste at best—unofficial events that can't be denied or explained.

I hope that this book will not only present an introduction to Aspect Psychology, but also show it at work, for the writing method included alterations of consciousness, and the theory came to me one night in the proverbial flash of inspiration.

The theory is workable. It helps us understand ourselves better, or at least provides a framework in which we can accept and view all of our experiences, not just those considered respectable by orthodox schools of knowledge. I am not presenting "Aspects" as Truth, but as an excellent method that will let us discover the truths of ourselves; as a diagram of the psyche that each person can use; as an alternate map of reality for anyone to follow. For we are all on a pilgrimage. I hope that "Aspects" will give us a clearer idea of the rules of the game, and the nature of the search.

JANE ROBERTS
Elmira, N. Y.

Contents

PART TWO:
AN INTRODUCTION TO ASPECT PSYCHOLOGY

PART ONE

ADVENTURES

1

The Class That Went Too Far. Seth and Alterations of Consciousness

The story behind Aspect Psychology began with a series of events that I couldn't deny or explain to my satisfaction. Intuitively I was intrigued. Intellectually I was scandalized. I admit this freely because it was my incessant questioning that finally led me to keep notes of everything that went on in my Expansion-of-Consciousness Class—records that I'm using now in writing this book.

The June 21 class in 1971 stands out in my mind as the turning point. We weren't involved in scientifically oriented experiments that could be checked out in one way or another. Instead, we were dealing with psychological events of a most unusual nature. These were either extraordinary perceptions, or hallucinations in response to group suggestion—or they fell in some strange area in between the two.

I'm a private type person. For the first year of my class I wouldn't even go into a Seth trance. Now I really enjoy such spontaneous sessions. One minute I'm me, sitting there, and the next minute I sense an opening, like a psychological door, and I walk into it. And become Seth. It's something like an astronaut's launching window in a way: My reality lines up with something else, and an exchange takes place. I step aside to an invisible holding position, and Seth is where I was.

This particular class was small, about fifteen people. Seth "came through" early in the evening and led them in an exercise in alteration of consciousness. Speaking for him, my voice often becomes quite deep, and sometimes it's of considerable volume, so it can be quite a shock for people used to quiet-voiced "spirit guides."

In previous classes, Seth had given arbitrary names to various levels of consciousness, just to help us pinpoint the different subjective states involved. Each seems to have its own characteristics and accompanying alterations of perception. That night the psychological journey was to be Alpha Two, which is the second stage adjacent to normal consciousness.

While Seth gave the simple instructions, students' recorders buzzed and traffic sounds rushed up from the corner intersection below. The living room lights were on, but people put down their wine glasses and cigarettes and closed their eyes. Listening to Seth's voice, they focused less and less on the smoky room and exterior environment. Instead they peered into inner landscapes and turned corners of consciousness that intersect only in the world of mind.

Seth comes through as a very energetic personality, so while he gave his instructions, "his" eyes were open and "his" voice was strong and emphatic. First he told students to think of Alpha Two as a door. "I want you to realize that your perceptions at this point are limited only because you have chosen to limit them," he said. "You are in the midst of other realities, but you are in the habit of blocking them out. You are now beginning to release your perceptions, to open doors that have been closed. Therefore, imagine Alpha Two as a doorway adjacent to your normal consciousness, and see it open."

Seth went on to say that each person would interpret the experience in his or her own way:

Beyond the door are other realities and people with whom you have always been acquainted. I want you to freely open your inner eyes. Walk with joy within these other realities that exist as surely as this room does.

Open your inner senses and direct them along these lines. The physical body will not hamper you; in fact it will help you, for hidden even within the flesh are mechanisms that aid the inner senses in their functioning. I want you to realize that you are getting glimpses of a reality that is instantaneous, and as much a part of you as your own heartbeat. You can learn to manipulate in that environment.

Then Seth asked students to pause awhile at that threshold of consciousness, and to imagine still another door, "or, if you prefer, a path, avenue, landscape or alley, but still another reality that opens up adjacently from your present level. From this new viewpoint you can sense other probabilities that you, yourself, have brought into existence. I want you to feel their strength and vitality and to realize that they also reinforce your own life."

Seth continued to explain this level of consciousness for a few moments and asked students to pause there. Then he said:

Now, I want those of you who can to follow still further, for we will travel beyond these fields of probabilities in which all times are born, into another in which times are not manufactured and hours or years of any kind do not exist. Here, in your terms, all probabilities are as yet unborn, while in greater terms they are already accomplished and yet coming into fresh existence. You also have a reality here, and this dimension nurses your own world, reaching down into your system. These realities are still only those at the edge of the one in which you have your present existence. For beyond are others, so alien [to you] that I could not explain them. Yet they are connected with your own life, and they find expression even within the smallest cells of your flesh.

I've only given the general highlights here of Seth's instructions. He spent quite a bit of time guiding students back to their normal stage of consciousness, for example, and teaching them to retrace their mental footwork. Still, the entire episode took less than a half hour. I came out of trance easily—as usual—and the students told me what happened. I rarely remember exactly what Seth says. Though I think that I'm aware of each word as Seth speaks it, the word exists in a special charged Now, so that when the instant is gone, so is the word or any sense of continuity.

Everyone reported feelings of refreshment and relaxation at the Alpha Two level, but several people had vivid, even startling experiences. Two in particular impressed me and sent up a whirl of questions.

My friend, Sue Watkins, hesitantly described seeing a man very clearly. She seemed to be standing with him on a flat plain. She saw a lake and some buildings beyond, and as she listened, she heard Seth's voice as if it were coming from a great distance. The man told her that his name was Jason, and that he had known her in past lives.

All the while, Sue was conscious of the directions that Seth was giving. When he said to imagine Alpha Two as a doorway, Sue saw a door that opened, and a three-dimensional pyramid of light. Sue was securely *in* this scene, not viewing it from the outside, and everything seemed physical and real. Suddenly Seth's voice seemed even further away, and she realized that he was ending the exercise. What would happen, she wondered, if she tried to bring Jason back with her? The two of them retraced their steps back to the door. But when she went through it, Jason was gone.

When she was fininshed telling about the episode, Sue said, almost defiantly, "He wore a long robe or gown, too," but we grinned at each other. Sue's much like I am in one respect: We give ourselves a lot of intuitive or psychic freedom, and then end up trying to make intellectual sense out of what's happened. Yet both of us were disquieted. Long-robed spirit guides? It was somehow too pat, and the name "Jason" was suspiciously romantic. Yet it was Sue's experience. It had happened whether we approved or not, and at that level of consciousness, the experience was valid. We'd yet to understand the terms of that validity.

The other dramatic event happened to a young man I'll call Joel. In the Alpha Two state, he found himself involved with a band of Christians heading south across Europe on the way to the Crusades. They came upon a group of wandering Moslems, and Joel found himself in the middle of a fierce battle. He was quite white-faced as he told us about it. "It was terribly clear, too clear," he said. "In the beginning, the fields were fresh and green, and when it was all over, the ground was gouged up, with blood everywhere. I saw horses just cut up—" Somewhat shaken, he added that the Christians had fought with savagery, and at the end of the experience he'd seen a monk come out of a nearby monastery and stand there, grieving.

All of us knew that Joel had recently left the ministry. Was this a symbolic statement of his own feelings dramatized at another level of consciousness? Was it a legitimate glimpse into his own reincarnational past? Or was it a brief backward look into history, a psychological snapshot of a vanished time? We discussed the various possibilities, then took a half hour break.

I intended to continue the discussion when class resumed, but changed my plans when I felt that Seth wanted to speak. This time one of those odd transitions took place in which another level of activity is triggered, and I speak for Seth Two. In our terms, this is a "future" Seth, or Seth at another stage of development. Seth Two comes through rarely, maybe four or five times a year.

Just before this transition, Seth said: "I want to give you a brief moment in which you sense, to some extent, the vast distances in which your own reality has its meaning, and the other dimensions of existence in which you also have your part."

Then my face emptied of all the characteristic Seth expressions. His normal gestures stopped. There is an emptiness about my body at such times. I always feel that I leave it, moving quickly toward a pyramid shape that extends above me to some vast distance. Contact seems to take place "out there." Then there is a moment or so before the voice starts—this one light, very faint, and unemotional. Students say it reminds them of what mathematical figures would sound like if they could talk.

After Seth Two speaks, it takes me a few minutes to come back, while with Seth the transition is almost instantaneous. But this time I returned easily, as if down a chute of consciousness. Class was obviously excited and impressed, but when the students told me what Seth Two had said, I had mixed feelings. This is the part of the message that bothered me:

> *Certain translations are being made for you so that these communications make sense. Our energy forms worlds. We help you maintain your lives, as you help maintain other existences of which you have no conscious knowledge. We watch you as you watch others, yet so vast is the distance that communication is difficult.*
>
> *We do not watch as human forms. You perceive us that way in distorted view. In your terms our forms would be geometrical. We do not understand the nature of the reality you are creating, even though the seeds were given to you by us. We respect it and revere it. Do not let the weak sounds of this voice confuse you. The strength behind it would form the world as you know it and sustain it for centuries.*

The Seth Two voice went on to say that we were being observed, but that there was nothing to prevent us from "observing our observers" in whatever way we could. In fact, we were being invited to do so. Students played the recording of the message back for me. As always, I was struck by the difference between Seth and Seth Two. The very sound of the emotionless, faint words suggested the distance between me and whatever it really was that I contacted.

There was no time for quiet analysis just then, though, because everyone was talking at once. Two students had seen a pyramid over my head, saying that it had vanished only when I came out of trance. Several persons insisted that during the entire performance, they'd seen three-dimensional blurred faces around the ceiling of the room. Others reported sensing the faces but not actually seeing them. Everyone was emphatic about one thing: Seen or unseen, the room had been crowded with other consciousnesses besides our own.

The room was in mild uproar. Some people were writing down their impressions on the spot. Others were checking with their neighbors. I heard someone say, "I don't care. I saw what I saw." I was disconcerted, wondering what had actually happened. Quickly I called class to order, and said that we'd better ask ourselves how much suggestion might have been responsible for the faces on the ceiling and the related phenomena.

I got a rather indignant response. For one thing, as several people pointed out, the lights had all been on, and everyone's eyes had been open. No one had said a thing until afterward. The people who saw the faces didn't know that other students sensed faces in the same place—or anyplace, for that matter. Certainly many were in an altered state of consciousness, and it's precisely at such times that our perceptions can show us data that isn't usually perceivable.

I was still questioning the students when something else caught my attention. First dimly, then more vividly, I began to sense the presence of an invisible personality beside me. That is, I didn't see him, but felt his emotional reality quite as strongly as physical vision could ever show it.

I'd "met" this same person in several previous classes when he told me mentally that he represented a past life of mine. Then, supposedly, I'd been some kind of jealous leader, demanding utmost loyalty. My friend Sue had been one of my followers. Now he wanted to confront her, feeling that she was going her own way this time and not following in his footsteps, as he thought she should have.

What to do? I try to be spontaneous in class, at least within reason, so I said, "Sue, that other-me is here." I laughed—only to me it wasn't my laugh but his, richly sardonic, indulgent, and amused all at once. I felt a strange facial expression from the inside and realized that my features were adapting it.

Sue just stared at me. "Yeah, I know he's here, and I wish he'd go away," she said.

At the same time I began to feel much bigger and stronger than I am, physically, as this other personality really began to rouse himself. An anger against Sue—*that* certainly wasn't mine—rushed through me. He wanted to confront her directly, speaking through me. That wasn't fair, I thought. If he had a score to settle, he should contact the person Sue *had* been. Sue and I as ourselves would have nothing to do with it. So, firmly, I tried to hold myself aloof, and to end the matter I called out, "Time for a class break, everybody."

But I didn't quite make it. As people began to mill about, I heard that laugh that wasn't mine directed at Sue again. "I've looked at you with this expression on my face many times," 'I' said. "You should know it well."

Sue cried out, of all things, "I've got a two-year-old defender this time," meaning her child, and 'I' answered scornfully, "That's one of the most foolish remarks you could have made to me."

But now I decided that the affair had gone too far. I didn't approve of this other-self's grand manner or the tricky way he'd tried to come through, when my attitude toward him was plain. So this time I closed off completely—it's just a matter of really saying "no" and meaning it—and I realized that earlier, I'd only half-wanted to end the confrontation. I'd wanted to close the personality out enough to prevent his speaking, but not enough to prevent me from probing into *his* reality. Now he just disappeared entirely.

"We're going to have to work that through sometime," Sue said.

"Yeah, but let's wait," I answered, and we grinned at each other, both content to let the episode rest.

The post-break dialogue only lasted a few minutes, and during break, the students were discussing what had happened earlier. Some were still finishing the notes they began before.

It was getting late. When class resumed, Seth came through, apparently just to say good evening, but even he allowed himself to become sidetracked. "I do indeed bid you good evening," he said, "The experiment continues, and it will continue as you go about your daily chores this week. Now, there is nothing to prevent you from watching the watchers. In fact, you should find this most intriguing."

According to class, Seth was about to close the session when a student I'll call Ron interrupted to ask a question. Somebody made a mock moan: Ron was known for getting tangled up in his own questions. He also considered himself quite an intellectual, took himself very seriously, and loved to "pose" questions for Seth. He was really a very nice young man with a lot to learn, though, and Seth usually treated him kindly, with an amused tolerant air.

This particular evening, however, the whole class was still highly curious about Seth Two's message and their own impressions. They were particularly intrigued by the implications of the "experiment," and by now they were all in a very serious mood. When Ron asked his question, Seth "took him on" with the kind of humor that instantly cleared the air. There's nothing like a good laugh to return us solidly to the world that we know and plank us back onto the firm framework of our own emotions.

Ron's actual question was voiced like this: "Do you see, in other words, when Jane is speaking . . . can you see the room? Or do you only see the room . . . ?" Ron paused and wet his lips then said, "Do you see what I'm getting at?"

Seth said, "When I am speaking, I cause myself to concentrate on this minute portion of time and space that you think of as this room. Otherwise, I can look at you, seeing your reincarnational existences, for example, and I am not limited to perceiving only the one self you imagine yourself to be."

"Would you be aware of, say, the pot on the table?" Ron asked.

"Only if I were interested in the pot on the table." As Seth, I was smiling broadly.

"But how would it appear to you?" Ron persisted.

"As a pot on the table," Seth said, sardonically.

Ron frowned. "The same way it would appear . . . ?"

Seth said, "When I use perceptions in your reality, then I automatically translate inner data into physical terms. Otherwise, I am not limited to that kind of perception." Smiling, speaking very slowly for effect, he added, "I need not perceive that object as a pot, but I can perceive it as a pot. You must perceive it as a pot. And *now* I am saying good evening."

"But you didn't answer my question," Ron said, stubbornly.

"I did indeed. You did not listen to the answer. Your questions obsess you, and you do not listen."

Ron came out with another garbled version of what he was trying to say. He was growing red-faced, but even more determined.

Seth said, with a note of finality, "The reality of the pot on the table—as you know it—is a portion of my entire perception of it."

Very soberly Ron said, "You answered the question. I understand." "Thank you," Seth said, so dryly that the students all broke out laughing. Even Ron started grinning. He didn't feel put down either, but vindicated because he felt that he'd held his own just the same. Seth made a few general remarks, then said, "Now *again* I bid you a fond good evening. And remember that the experiment continues."

People were still excited, but the dialogue between Seth and Ron had put the evening back into a more normal perspective. Yet by the end of class, I didn't know what to think. At least a part of me wished that Seth Two hadn't come through at all. Most of all, I wished that people hadn't reported seeing faces on the ceiling. I just didn't believe that "beings" from another reality were peeking into my living room. I didn't like the emotional confrontation with Sue either, particularly since I wasn't sure if I regarded reincarnation as a fact or as a symbol for something else.

Yet *something* happened. People perceived certain data. Even in terms of altered perception alone, the evening's events were significant. At the time though, those events seemed so intellectually unrespectable to me that I put the class notes aside, unable to grapple with their implications.

What bothered me was the lack of a suitable framework in which to assess what happened. What we had was a group of psychological events and perceptions that would be treated with scorn by many people. Yet this was human experience. Joel would remember the frightening battle on the grassy plains long after he forgot the facts of the day, such as what he'd eaten for breakfast or what suit he'd worn. Sue would recall her memory of Jason and her attempt to bring him back into the room long after other more "valid" events had been forgotten.

Why should we be afraid of our own experience because it seems strange in the eyes of the world, or because we're afraid that it might? Why are we so worried about an intellectual respectability when it implies limitation of perception, or when we must scale down our own experience to fit preconceived notions? I think we react this way, many of us, because we've been warned so often since childhood not to trust our imagination or intuitions, and to judge our perceptions constantly against a definite world of facts. And this world of facts was set before us as the *only* criterion of reality. A lie, after all, is an untruth—something said that did not happen in the world of facts. So, by implication almost, there's a moral connotation connected when we see something others don't see: Someone must be lying.

If we can say that suggestion operated, then we're at least half safe, for we mean that we were lying, but not on purpose: We thought we saw what we did, but we were mistaken. Of course suggestion operates! But no one is really sure what suggestion is. Besides, perceptions directly caused by suggestion in usual terms may still be as valid as any others. Our very perception of the physical world is caused by suggestion given to us by our senses. Even a slight alteration of consciousness causes us to experience events in a different fashion.

On the one hand I knew this, but on the other hand I was still trying to relate my experiences to a framework too small to contain them. I kept going over the events in my mind. The emotional power and interchange between Sue and "my" other personality was definite. Were Sue and I unconsciously acting out inner feelings toward each other that needed release? Was that all—a dramatized encounter with both of us unaware, consciously, of the inner mechanisms involved? If so, the episode was certainly therapeutic and creative. Why wasn't that enough? Because it purported to be something else, of course.

Was all of this true or false? Did Joel relive a portion of a past life experience, or didn't he? Were there *actually* faces on the ceiling or weren't there? So the evening's events sent me into a whirl of intellectual questioning, in which it seemed at times that my intellect and intuitions were at odds. It took a while before they began to merge in a new synthesis that would lead me to Aspect Psychology, and a framework in which such events could comfortably be considered; a framework large enough to contain the meaning of all of our experiences.

As my intellect and intuitions worked together, they led me to discover an inner order of events and introduced me to alternate realities, each with their own laws, so that the facts in one system may seem quite senseless in the other. But I didn't know that then. I only knew that I would insist on allowing myself psychic and intuitive freedom, while using my intellect to criticize the results. Because, until a short time ago, I still shared with many others the belief that the intellect's main function was a critical one, operating separate and apart from intuitive levels of the self.

The volumes of Seth Material, all dictated in trance, should have taught me otherwise, since there the intellect and

psychic are so beautifully blended. But even in 1971 I was scruti-
nizing Seth from the standpoint of True or False, and to a large
extent I was blinded to his greater reality, by trying to understand
it in too small a context.

2

A Reincarnational Drama, and Other "Unofficial" Events

The energy from that one class seemed to spread outward into my students' private lives. During the week, Sue Watkins called to tell me that she'd had an experience that she was positive was connected with Seth Two's experiment.

"I was getting ready for bed," she said. "The lights were all on. Suddenly my arms and legs felt huge, and much heavier. I looked down, and I swear, they *were* that way. At the same time, this curious wonder flashed through my mind, like: How fantastic bodies are! What amazing machines, and I was full of this appreciation of how bodies work. But it wasn't me. It was the most alien sensation. It was . . . someone not used to living in a body at all."

Dorothy, another student, called to tell me that she'd seen three-dimensional triangles around the ceiling of her dining room in the morning, three times in a row. And ·if *my* intellect wanted something to work on, my intuitive self was seeing to it that it got what it wanted, because the next class once again presented me with perfect examples of the kind of experiences that so intrigued me, yet threw me into a critical quandary.

Five students reported having "class dreams" in which they attended a class at another level of reality, with Seth as teacher. Such dreams, with many variations, are now a regular part of the class's extra-curricular activities. In them, I'm convinced that students develop themes and experiences begun in class. Often Seth is used as a symbol for the individual's own greater consciousness.

In a class only last week, for example, a young man, Larry, told of a dream in which he saw Seth's face close to his own. Seth looked physical and real and appeared looking exactly like a portrait that my husband, Rob, painted of him several years ago. The painting hangs in the living room where class is held and it has also been reproduced in *The Seth Material*. In their dreams, many students see Seth in that guise.

When Larry finished telling his dream, Seth came through with one of the best sessions to date. It began with the question: Who is Seth? The first part was directed to Larry, the dreamer. I'm quoting a few paragraphs from the session here because they contain information that I didn't have back when class first started reporting class dreams.

What Seth said the other night to Larry was this:

> *Who is Seth? I put this question to you. And what magic is worked here [in class] that you work and that we all work together? Now I will tell you this: On the one hand, I am someone you do not know, lost before the annals of time as you understand it, lost in the annals of the past and the future, as you understand them. On the one hand, that is what I am. And that is a loaded sentence.*
>
> *On the other hand, I am yourself . . . so through me do you view and meet the selves that you are; and so I rise, in your terms, from the power and antiquity and the glory of your own being, projected outward into the world of time from a universe in which time is meaningless.*

In 1971, though, I was upset by the implications I saw in Seth as a "spirit guide" popping in and out of people's dreams —particularly since they took this as proof of Seth's independent existence in a way that bothered me. That particular night, then, I was fascinated by the dream events reported, but refused to accept pat explanations. And yet I couldn't find any others that satisfied me.

But the dreams were merely the beginning. As I listened, I suddenly felt Seth Two's pyramid above my head again, not physical but just as real. I could feel my consciousness rushing upward, seeping out gradually at first, then faster. Even as I thought with mixed wonder and skepticism—"Bodiless observers from another world; triangles appearing from nowhere on dining room ceilings;" and "Here I go again," I was gone.

After a certain point, whenever Seth Two is involved, there's an emptiness through which I sense I must travel, then a live spot of contact. Then that atonal voice begins to speak. As always, students told me afterward what was said, and the session was recorded.

"The experiment continues," the voice began.

"We are trying to appreciate the nature of your present existence, so those of you who are curious about the nature of nonphysical reality may then follow us, using this voice as a guideline into existence that . . . knows neither blood or tissue. Follow then beyond the knowledge of the flesh to those domains from which flesh is born, Feel the kernel of your consciousness rise beyond the knowledge of the seasons.

For you there may seem to be an unbearable loneliness, because you are so used to relating to the warm victory of flesh, and [here] there is no physical being with whom to relate. Yet beyond and within that isolation is a point of light that is consciousness. It pulses with the power behind all of the emotions you know; it feeds them and sends them sparkling and tumbling down into the reality you recognize.

This is the warmth that forms the pulse of physical existence, and yet is born from the very devotion of our isolation; that is born from creativity; that is beyond flesh and bone; that forms fingers without feeling fingers; that forms the seasons without knowing summer or winter; that creates the reality you know, without itself experiencing it.

From that devotion and creativity comes all that you know;
and all of that has also been given to us. For the energy that we
have is not ours alone, nor are we the source of it. It flows through
us as it flows through you.
The experiment, then, continues as it always has. Only in
your past you were not aware of it.

The voice stopped. I started my downward climb, getting lost and disoriented for a moment, then suddenly, surely descending through many levels of awareness.

Almost every student had experienced some expansion
of consciousness while Seth Two spoke. Rog, an engineer, felt as
if he were alone in space, with nothing to "act against," and
overwhelmed by loneliness. To one extent or another, many of the
students felt the same kind of suspension and isolation. Joel (the
young man who found himself involved in the Crusaders' battle
the class before) also felt himself surrounded by space. He seemed
to be bodiless, drawn toward a gigantic flower. As he fell headlong
into the open petals, the inside of the flower expanded so that it
seemed bottomless. He felt as if he could fall through it forever.

His experience made me think. When Seth Two came
through, was I switching to another level of consciousness and
observing physical reality from that viewpoint? Were Seth Two's
"beings" an unconscious dramatization of that level of awareness
itself? Or did these beings exist in some other way, like Joel's
flower? Was the flower Joel's own interpretation of another kind
of consciousness too?

In other words, how literally could we take Seth Two's
message? If Seth Two was a representation of another portion of
our own psyche, dramatized, then couldn't the message be interpreted to mean that other nonphysical parts of our present selves
watched our reality, couched in our own psyches? And were we
being encouraged to experience to some degree the vast portions
of our own souls from which our physical reality springs?

The difference between Seth and Seth Two was dramatized that night too, because when the students finished discussing

what happened, Seth came through. With Seth Two, students had to strain to hear the quiet, unemotional, almost colorless tones; my face was expressionless and my body slack. But Seth's voice boomed out; my body took on a more muscular, active air, and Seth was there, speaking and looking about. He often looks at particular people and singles them out, so there's no doubt about whom he's talking to.

He spoke to Joel at once: "Your flower was an excellent image, and in your terms, it represents the characteristics of space as you might relate to it. Specifically, it is your symbol for the physicists' black hole. These [black holes] are other dimensions of actuality in which the reality that you know is automatically translated in different terms; not annihilated."

Then he told the class that they were learning to manipulate at other levels of awareness. I knew that they were, of course, but I wasn't prepared for what followed. We were discussing class events and Seth's interpretation of Joel's mental adventure, when I became aware of loud voices in one corner of the room. I heard the word, "Indian." Then people turned toward Joel and Bette.

Their manner told me at once that they were involved in what I call a Reincarnational Drama. That is, they were convinced that they were acting out a definite episode from a past life.

Again, these dramas intrigue me, but I'm always aware of how little we know about the nature of consciousness or memory. Now I see reincarnation in a much broader context than I did then, as you'll see later in this book. Certainly the following episode, among others, had much to do with the intense questioning that led me to "Aspects."

Bette wore one of the long ankle-length skirts then coming into style. Her legs were spread out beneath it, her arms on her hips. It was easy to imagine a rifle lying across her knees. Her smallish eyes were furious. She looked for all the world like the nineteenth-century pioneer woman she thought she was at that moment. "You only killed my whole damn family, kids and all." She hissed at Joel, and her eyes never left his face.

"You killed your own husband," he said. To all of us the normally slight Indian characteristics of his face seemed now exaggerated. His voice was tense, but didn't have the emotional force of Bette's. Then he said slowly, "*You* killed him. We didn't. What did you do it for?"

"Because he was a coward. Because I had a bunch of crying kids, and I didn't need a crying husband to boot. Yes, I did it, and I'd do it again. Is that what you want to know?" Her voice was fiercely calm.

The class was quiet. We were alert, ready in case Joel and Bette really got into it.

I was having my own difficulties. In my mind I saw the scene they'd been describing; Bette squatting in this hut of a house, on her hands and knees almost, handing out guns to the kids while the Indian band came rushing over a hill toward the clearing. For an instant, through Bette's perspective, I heard the bloodcurdling screams—howls really, and felt her fury. Her cries rose in my throat. I pulled myself together. I had the class to think of, and I wanted to monitor Bette and Tom's experience, not fall into it with them.

But Joel was backing off some, I could tell. He said, "You were taking our land. We were just defending it. Didn't you care what you were doing to us?"

"Hell, no!" she cried, staring back at him. "Why should I? I didn't give a damn what happened to the Indians. I just cared about my own, my kids. And I protected them, I'll tell you that. I knew when you were on the warpath though. That I knew." Now her eyes were really beady. She leaned forward threateningly. Her emotional belligerence filled the room.

There was a moment's silence. Then as we watched, the intentness began to leave Joel's broad features. A smoothness seemed to fill in the contours of his face, and he started to speak as a personality called Dave. I'd heard Dave speak once before but class hadn't, though they knew about him.

I stayed where I was, watching Bette and Joel and the

class's reactions. All attention was riveted on Joel's face as students searched for differences between this speaking-for-Dave Joel, and the Joel they knew.

My reactions were mixed. I sensed the class's strong pivoting toward the new personality; the awe, the hope that perhaps here was the answer. Maybe Dave had the answer to life's problems and could explain them simply. They wouldn't have to work for their own answers—someone else would do it for them.

Great, they've learned a lot, I thought sardonically. There they sat, teachers, business people, college kids, listening to another voice, another "guru," someone else who might have the answers and be flattered or cajoled enough to give them up. But I was being unfair, I told myself, and to some extent I was. The phenomenon of speaking for another personality is unusual and startling enough to capture anyone's attention, and brings to mind all of our old legends of gods speaking through mortals; spirits looking out of human eyes; gods, devils and sprites cavorting through the fields of the human psyche.

Dave's voice was much like Joel's. He spoke intently but dispassionately, while Bette stared back with a mixture of awe and defiance. She was still furious—but at Joel, not at Dave.

"You knew that Indian men and women were dying," Dave said. "Didn't that affect you at all?"

"All we knew was who was on the warpath and when," Bette said in a hard voice.

"Did you know when your *own* race was on the warpath?" Dave asked calmly, as if translating or as if speaking to a child.

"No!" Bette yelled angrily. "I was in my own existence. All I cared about were my kids, and you took care of that . . . " She stopped, glowering, because Joel had been replaced by Dave, and from then on, when she answered Dave, she called him "Sir" in a tone that neatly mixed deference with sarcasm. After a rather lengthy discussion though, Bette said that she felt better toward Joel now; that she realized his people had been caught up in their own passion, and were only trying to defend their land. She grinned and said, "Don't fight with me anymore, either. Just be nice."

Her attitude was so different than it had been that a few people laughed.

"I mean it," she said. "I learned a lot from that lifetime, and in this life I'm a regular crusader when it comes to Indians . . . . I have great feeling for them. Whenever anyone mentions the blacks as the downtrodden minority, I remind them of the Indians—so I must have forgiven them for what they did to me." When Dave answered, though, Bette couldn't refrain from saying, "Oh, thank you, *sir*," and that hard look came back into her eyes.

The entire episode took nearly an hour. Part of the time Dave spoke alone or answered Bette's questions. Now and then I asked a question, but all the while I kept myself focused on the objective room, because whenever I let my consciousness stray I was back in that hut with Bette. I kept feeling her screams in my throat and was determined not to give voice to them.

For one thing, I didn't want to interject my own perceptions at that point: This was primarily Bette's and Joel's experience, and I was curious as to what they'd do with it on their own. For another thing, I had the whole class to think of, and I wasn't about to unleash all that emotion in the room, particularly when I sensed that I'd be thrown into the event myself and unable to monitor it properly.

There were no dates given for the Indian attack. Dave mentioned a name, Kewate or Kewata, but without giving its designation. When asked for the name of the tribe, he said, "It was an offshoot of a larger nation or conglomerate of tribes, and the language is not familiar to *me*, but it was something like Shu . . . Shu shon ack."

When it was all over, Bette said that she'd felt animosity toward Joel since he came to class, and that now she understood the reason for it, and also for her habitual passionate defense of the Indians. The emotions that had swirled around us just dissipated. As this happened, Joel shook his head, coughed, looked dazed for a moment and said, "Hey, what's been going on?"

What indeed?

One thing was instantly apparent to me. Dave had come to Joel's aid precisely when Bette's belligerence was strongest. Moreover, he nicely took the wind from Bette's emotional sails, a fact I'm sure she recognized and resented. Dave was not Joel— in the framework they were working in—and Dave's "loftier" attitude changed the immediacy of the earlier encounter to one in which Bette "lost her equal status."

On Joel's part, this was excellent psychological footwork at the least. Three levels of activity were involved—the usual Joel, Joel-as-Indian-in-past-life encounter, and Joel-as-David, a personality who was supposed to contain the knowledge of the other two.

Yet the phenomenon itself bothered me. There was a strained quality about it, as if one part of Joel's personality didn't know what to do with the other part. The performance was . . . cracked in a funny fashion, as if somebody was trying too hard but with the best of intentions. Some sensed contact wasn't quite made.

I didn't accept Dave as a "spirit" in usual terms, but then, I didn't look at Seth that way either. The whole affair, of course, made me wonder again about the nature of Seth. But he is a fully rounded personality in a way difficult to explain, and he arrived in my experience that way. There was never any strain involved. While I appreciated the levels of consciousness being utilized by Joel, I was also struck by a certain feeling of grotesqueness, of ability that struggled to be used and yet was also caught in a dilemma of psychological duplicity.

But all of this was quite aside from questions about the reincarnational material itself. Did Bette and Joel actually live the event they seemed to be remembering so vividly? Was I mentally hearing the piercing screams of a woman about to see her children slain? I'd felt as if I could have lost myself, for a while anyway, in that other time and place.

Yet Bette, I knew, was filled with belligerence at *this* particular time in her life. Had the entire episode been a creative emotional drama that freed her from that pressure, in a safe framework? Joel, then, would have had his own reasons for participating. Certainly the entire class seemed released, purged. Had the two "main actors" dramatized the combined withheld aggressive energy of the entire group?

My questions were endless, it seemed. Most of the students took it for granted that a definite reincarnational event had been re-experienced. I admitted that the entire episode was valid, but I also suspected that its validity might straddle our concepts. Again, I felt that reincarnation was something far more significant than usually supposed, and that by accepting it, per se, we might prevent ourselves from discovering its "real" meaning.

A short time later, as you'll see, I was to be presented with a unique example of a "past life personality," in a suprising encounter involving Sue and my husband, Rob—an experience which would also throw light on Joel's performance in class as Dave. As it was, I knew enough not to interpret our experiences in old dogmatic ways (the dogma of spiritualism—or reincarnation—can be quite as limiting as any more conventional church dogma), yet I was unable to see another framework. So I kept knocking my head against mental walls.

From Seth Two to Indian war cries was quite enough for one evening—from bodiless observers from another system of reality to the emotional power of Bette's belligerence against a man she believed had wiped out her entire family over a century ago—but whatever was going on, we all had to get up early in the morning. So I ended class.

Yet as people filed out of the room, I thought: How great that we all feel free enough to explore the nature of our own consciousnesses together. Who knows what we might discover? And I still feel that way.

The next day, though, I spent two hours writing down my impressions of that class and trying to sort out my own attitudes. I just put a piece of paper in the typewriter and started writing whatever came to mind, without questioning. I find this an excellent method of releasing pertinent ideas. In fact, until I read what I'd written, I didn't realize that I'd actually chosen one main direction from several others that had also attracted me.

I'd found the "spirit guide" designation more and more hampering. At the same time, that's exactly how people related to Seth. Whenever I objected, they became confused. For one thing, many people want desperately to believe in life after death, and "spirit guides" automatically offer them proof. Besides this, however, the concept presents a framework in which a spirit can be encountered in any medium's living room, without other intermediaries, to bring comfort, solve problems, and provide an intimacy with spiritual realities that the churches have long forsaken.

Even in the beginning of my own experiences, I didn't think it was that simple; nor, for that matter, did Seth describe himself in those terms. But up to this June class, I'd suspected my own doubts. Maybe my intellect *was* getting in the way, I thought. Maybe Seth *was* a spirit guide—just as people said, and in exactly those terms. And maybe reincarnation existed the way others thought it did, too.

After reading over my own notes the next day, though, I saw that I wasn't going to let Seth be stereotyped, and that I had to allow my own experience to expand in its own way. My attitude toward Seth was pretty well expressed in the following paragraph:

> *Last night, Seth Two led us into adventures in consciousness that are liberating, creative, and valid. I think that they certainly increase individual perception, and may be forming a group class level of awareness that overlaps into the dream state. But I dont want to feel 'forced' to visualize a disembodied spirit peeking in*

on us. I think we're really on to something, but I don't know what it is yet. If we take it for granted that everything we can't explain is the result of 'spirits,' then we're just left with dogma again.

About the Reincarnational Drama, I wrote:

Again—a terrific adventure in consciousness for those involved, in which the participants experienced reality in a different way and set up new gestalts of relatedness. They looked at existence from an entirely different focus than usual, and to some extent or another, this let each class member do the same thing. As such, I think that this was constructive, dynamic, and exciting. I don't know whether or not Joel and Bette were reliving definite past events, or whether the idea of reincarnation provided a framework through which these experiences could flow, releasing them from usual life roles

Maybe it doesn't even matter. But I think that there is strong pressure from people involved in the psychic field, amateurs and professionals alike, to accept such events at their face value. Sometimes from their remarks and letters I think that people want to believe in something so badly that they feel threatened when I question my own experience, or that they want me to write a kind of Bible from which all uncertainity is removed—for them. But then I'd be caught up in a dogma that I'd be sworn to protect, and I'd never have the guts to examine my own ideas again. I just can't go looking for neat little cliché symbols to tuck my experience in.

Because underneath it all, there's something invaluable, that as a people, we've always overlooked. And just maybe I can get a few clues as to what it is—

I wrote those paragraphs vehemently, certainly exaggerating to some degree, but at least I felt clearer about my own attitudes than I had in some time. Considering my feelings, you can imagine my reaction to Martin Crocker, who attended my next class. The appointment had been set up some months earlier. Martin, I found, personified all the ideas that I'd just decided I could do without.

3

A Spirit Guide is a Spirit Guide is a...?

Mr. Martin Crocker was a masseur and healer. His wife sat beside him on the couch; quietly, as if trying to be invisible. Martin himself was a crisp, dapper, precise gentleman in his fifties, in a dark suit and white shirt, neat as he could be, with a smallish pale face and old-fashioned glasses and red hair—a little rooster of a man, as it turned out, well able to hold his own.

But as he talked in class, I grew more upset, and if the truth be known, outraged. Again, because he was so sincere, so good, spoke about love and threw around the name of God, I felt my hands tied to some extent. To his way of thinking, love was balanced by "a-tooth-for-a-tooth" and "an-eye-for-an-eye"; by repentance, punishment, and the just God that no one in his right mind would want for a Father, much less a friend.

He told us about cups flying through the darkness of musty seance rooms, "whizzing through the air so that you wanted to duck. But they didn't hit you, of course, because they were being controlled by the other side." Controlled, all right, but from a more mundane place than Heaven, to my way of thinking. Yet Martin Crocker believed what he believed. His beliefs were part of him, wound up with all his tissues and thoughts, so that to take even one of his beliefs away would be to unravel everything else. And I'd never do that, even if I could.

But I couldn't sit there in seeming acceptance, saying nothing, while one student who should have known better, Audrey, stared hopefully, credulously—if cups really did fly someplace, thrown by a ghostly hand, then why not here? And all the while Martin sat primly, yet determined to hold his own—the good Christian amid obvious infidels—nice infidels, perhaps, though I don't think he was sure of that either. But like Daniel in the lions' den, he dared to speak his truth no matter what we thought. And for that you had to give him credit.

I don't really fit the lion image, though half the time I wanted to roar, but I wasn't going to lap up all that stuff like a kitten, either. So it went, back and forth. Class took it rather well, until Martin said that he didn't understand how women could be mediums or healers. Everyone knew that women were negative, where men were positive; that women drew illnesses and bad influences, while men were closer to God and naturally good. Or at least, better.

Listening to this, Martin's wife nodded her docile head, while something like a roar did rise up then, from everyone else in the room. The sounds of protest sounded great to me, but I put them down, like an idiot, out of concern for Martin; bending over backward because he was so "good," if misguided.

Which was stupid. Anyone with the laws of the universe on his side didn't need me to help him out. And they *were* on his side, as far as Martin was concerned. Trying to be very open-minded but firm, he explained why he didn't "touch a drop," how liquor of any kind dulled the senses and ruined the spiritual vibrations. "And I sort of enjoyed a glass of beer now and then in my youth," he said wistfully, and I felt myself smile at him almost fondly—the upright man offering up his glass of ale to the Lord.

I sipped my wine and smoked a cigarette, and listened

to him talk about the evils of the flesh. So be it. The poor body, though, such a splendid God-given mechanism to be called sinful by those who insist upon God's goodness. If the body's so sinful, what did their God give us one for? Why do so many systems of thought try to make man ashamed of his own image? But I let Martin sit there for a while, shining in his righteousness, explaining his theories—to make sure that he'd have equal time.

The students were divided in their reactions. Sue and I were least sympathetic. But the hope was there, the magic, the questions. In his world, cups did whirl through the darkness. The saints and dead prophets did visit, kindly and indiscriminately, with scores of sitters in the dim parlors of numberless mediums. Wouldn't it be great? But would it?

"The intellect has nothing to fear from truth," I said. "If a cup went flying through this room right now, with all the lights on, I'd be the first one to accept it. I'd never deny the evidence of my experience. But if the lights were off, I'd be the first one to turn them on. And if a cup *were* zooming through the air, thrown by anyone or anything, it would continue on its way. The lights wouldn't stop it."

Martin half closed his eyes and pursed his lips. "Then listen to this," he said. "Once I heard a voice in a seance room, a direct voice speaking just out of nowhere. It was very loud and husky, and belonged to a spirit called Charles. Now Charles said that he'd go through the floor and the voice would prove it. So the voice started at the ceiling, then went lower, then lower still. Then it was coming from beneath the flooring. Now what do you say about *that?*" His question was spoken in the slyest, most triumphant manner. He had me at last.

"Were the lights on?" I asked, gently.

"Of course not. They'd ruin the vibrations," he said. He thought that I was stubborn, more skeptical than a medium had any right to be. I thought that he was, at best, credulous.

"I don't deny that such things may be possible," I said.

And I don't. But when such reports are brought to me by people whose common sense I already suspect, then I do take them with a grain of salt.

I didn't say that. Instead, I asked him about his healing work.

"I don't heal," he said. "I can't. A person can't do a thing on his own. The Holy Spirit heals through me. I'm just the channel—"

"I suppose it's just a matter of each of us using different terms," I said, hopefully. "But since God made us, then we must be able to do *something*. We must be sacred and great and meaningful on our own—"

"We are," he said. "But just the same, we can't do anything on our own. Only the Holy Spirit heals."

"And we're a part of what the Holy Spirit is," I said.

But he just stared stubbornly at me, sure that I was trying to trick him with words. I looked at the clock; it was time for a class break. After I announced this, Martin came over to me.

"I hope you'll forgive me if I leave early," he said. "I can tell that I'm holding the group down. I know how it is when you're trying to work with a group . . . to have someone who doesn't fit in."

Instantly I felt I'd been unsympathetic and ungracious. Martin had come all the way from Ohio for this one class. "Of course you're not holding the group down. They like you," I said. And they did, for that matter. So did I, on one level. I tried to hide my impatience and irritation. After all, I thought, I should be big enough, understanding enough—

Martin smiled (smugly?) and sat down. At once I wished I'd let him leave. So I really wasn't honest. His honesty and mine might have cleared the air, but I was too afraid of hurting his feelings. And just as Martin sat down, Seth came through. He addressed himself first to Martin. As Seth, I leaned forward, smiling broadly:

"I do not want our friend, here, to feel that he is

cramping our style." Then, nodding at Martin: "There is an incident in your life that had to do with inner perception. It was not an ordinary event in your terms. There was another person connected with the affair who telepathically knew what was happening, helped bring about the events, and communicated them to you."

Then, to class:

> *Now Martin is a good man, as Ruburt [Seth's name for me]* *said earlier, and besides, I like him. He may not approve of Ruburt's habits but then Ruburt does not approve of his. That is* *between the two of them. There are distortions in Martin's thought, as there are in* your *thoughts. He thinks of vitality in different* *ways than you do, but he uses it very well.*
>
> *Open up the doors of energy. Do not close them down. All* *of the myths will float away. A man's myths are like his clothing. They are his own affair. Beneath the clothing is the person and* *his reality.*

Seth expanded on the above ideas briefly, then I came out of trance. Class members were smiling. Martin looked vindicated.

Great, I thought, and I asked what I'd said as Seth. Before anyone could answer, Martin grinned with the oddest mixture of timidity and smugness. "Seth told me something that no one else in the room knew," he said. "In the beginning of the session, he mentioned something about an incident in my life and the use of inner perception. I believe I know what he means."

Martin paused, wet his lips, and eyed class members dramatically. Then he continued. "At a circle last week, I said that I was coming here and asked if Seth could say something ahead of time to me from the Spirit world. He came through the medium, sounding much as he did here tonight." Martin paused again, this time reverently. "No one here knew about that, what Seth told me. I didn't even tell my wife. So I'm satisfied," he said, and he smiled that prim, secret, triumphant smile.

I was speechless for a moment, and I suppose my indig-

nation was funny—my Seth muddling around such spooky gather-
ings. Not likely. Besides though, as mentioned earlier, I just don't
think that Seth exists in those terms. That night, Martin represented all the ideas about spirit guides that I found so disturbing.
About him I felt an invisible tangle of religious superstition. I had
a class member read back Seth's first statements. They were quite
indefinite, as far as I could see.

But Martin Crocker was taking them as his proof of the
night; showing Seth's independent nature . . . the secret told that
no one else knew. Seth had spoken through two separate mediums,
obviously proving his own separate existence. It was almost useless,
I thought, to try to unravel the misunderstandings. So for the
moment I just told Martin that I doubted Seth had been at his
meeting. Martin only smiled at this further indication that the
medium herself had no knowledge of the affair.

I've had this sort of thing happen before, where people
will take the flimsiest of "evidence" to prove this or any other
point, then go on merrily from medium to medium, spirit to spirit,
grasping at any straw. That's one game I refuse to play. Seth's
existence is a demonstrative psychological reality. That reality
should make us question the nature of human consciousness as
we know it, and wonder about our own abilities. To think of Seth's
reality being at the mercy of such "proof" as Martin's filled me
with deep sadness. Yet I still had one foot in Martin's framework,
because I was still trying to squeeze Seth into the confines of a
limited true-or-false world.

But I didn't realize that, then. I should have, because
Seth came through again, this time leading students in an exercise
that was to focus their consciousness toward probable realities.

Seth not only maintains that probable worlds exist, but
also that we can perceive our own "probable selves" under certain
conditions. These ideas, like Seth himself, are impossible to place
in one neat category. Certainly, however, they do not fit in the
framework of conventional Christian thought. How would a theo-

logian suggest saving a probable soul, for example? And many atomic scientists who would accept probabilities wouldn't grant the existence of the soul in the first place.

Seth's instructions and the exercise took about twenty minutes. Again, he asked students to use the image of a pyramid as an aid:

> *Concentrate on the feeling in the back of your skull. The feeling itself is the important thing, for from it the pyramid shape will form. The pyramid may appear differently to each of you, because it is your own personal path into probable realities. It may appear as a path or as a ray of light or in some other form, but follow it with full confidence and freedom. Use my voice simply as a thread to accompany you, but concentrate upon your own feelings and sensations.*

Seth went on to explain the various ways in which the pyramid might open—into paths or rooms or dooways. "Learn to use the mobility of your consciousness joyfully," he continued, "and follow even further into the pyramid, which is a channel between your world and others that also exist. I want you to draw energy and power from this voice, and use it your own way. Let it become whatever you need it to become, in the particular probability system in which you find yourself.

"If you find worlds that you do not understand, look upon them with wonder, but send your consciousness as far as it can go, with great vigor, with freedom and joy . . . "

I've just quoted a few passages here to give an idea of how the exercise was conducted. As usual, he spent some time "returning" the students to their usual orientation.

When I came out of trance, students reported their experiences. Again, several were particularly interesting. Sue Watkins said, "I seemed to be in a probable system, not like ours but enough like it so that I could relate. I met a humanoid in a weird stunted forest. He spoke to me, but now I can't remember what he said."

John, another student, had seen miniature people who symbolized energy. They made a circle, dancing around him. As Seth's voice grew louder, these miniature people led John to a pyramid. There was a man inside, and John greeted him as a long-lost friend, though by the time he reported the episode, he'd forgotten who the man was.

Another student said, "This may not make sense, but I saw a man. He went into Nothing . . . split the side of Nothing . . . and saw the physical universe."

When I asked Martin Crocker if he'd gone along with the exercise, he shook his head emphatically and said, "Nothing happened at all Absolutely nothing. I didn't see or feel a thing. Nothing." I had to laugh at myself, because Martin obviously found our ideas of probable selves and probable realities as improbable as we found his world of good and evil spirits, the just God who threw people into hellfire, and the whizzing cups that flew through the night.

But there is a vast difference and an important one, I think, between the two approaches. All of my students accept such exercises as adventures in consciousness. They delight in turning the focus of their awareness in different directions, and in exploring the nature of reality from different subjective viewpoints. But no lables are stuck onto the mental events. We feel that we're taking mental snapshots of an interior landscape, and realize that we're probably bound to distort them to some degree by our own preconceptions.

Martin Crocker, and all the Martin Crockers, presuppose that the world and any afterlife exist in certain, definite, known fashions. They program themselves to interpert their experience according to rigid expectations, and ignore anything that doesn't fit. There are Martin Crockers in every line or human endeavor. Yet often those who are convinced that they have the truth, the "whole truth," usually have least of all.

But people are people; and Martin was a unique, cocky little man, impossible to pigeonhole as all of us are. He came to class secure in the knowledge that there were "spirit masters," and had his faith reinforced. He managed to interpret everything that happened so that it fit into his preconceived ideas. Perhaps all of us do this in our own way, as we experience the events of our lives. I've thought of Martin Crocker many times, uneasily. He was distorting his experience to fit his ideas; granted. To what extent was I doing the same?

4

Probable Selves and More Questions

Even while I was trying to figure out Seth's position in *our* world, he was leading us further into the dimensions of our own consciousness and enlarging our concepts of what *we* were. Even so, the results of the next class exercise caught me by surprise. It was the class following Martin Crocker's visit. Even before Seth began to speak, I felt an odd sensation in the back of my skull, as if a long pyramid extended from this point to some immeasurably distant vanishing point. (This wasn't above my head, as with the Seth Two experience, but parallel to it.)

At the same time I "knew" that at the other end the pyramid opened up again, and was somehow connected to a Probable Self. I also sensed these same psychic extensions behind each person in the room.

I never know what I'm going to say on such occasions. As usual, I just spoke spontaneously, explaining what was happening. Then I suggested that each student try to sense his or her own pyramid structure. Here, Seth began to speak, so smoothly that there was hardly any transition between my last words and his first ones. He began giving instructions much like those given in the last class. For a brief instant, I felt a shock: Rob's painting of Seth hung behind my chair, but suddenly I felt inside it, looking through the portrait's eyes out into the room. My chest and arms felt sturdier, bigger, and more compact than they are.

As Seth continued to speak, the feeling at the back of my neck grew more noticeable. It throbbed and continued to expand. At one point (as I learned later) Seth said that another, probable class was also experimenting, and that we might be able to glimpse our probable selves. A few minutes later, he suggested that everybody open their eyes, look at the room, and immediately close their eyes again.

When I came out of trance, I was more disoriented than usual. More than this, the students seemed in some strange way different, and unlike themselves. As I looked about, rather confused, I was greeted by at least ten people, all trying to talk to me at once. One student, Brenda, said that she felt as if her features were changing, just as I noticed that she looked really odd. Her face was puffy, not firm in some way, as if the muscles weren't sure what form they were supposed to take. At the same time, Sue, Bette, and a young college girl, Anna, all pointed to Brenda at once. Sue shouted, "Wow, that's not Brenda," while Brenda just sat there, breathing heavily. Her eyes watered, and her features kept . . . sliding around, like rubber.

People kept talking; everyone had something to report. Lora, a young housewife, said that Margie, an older woman, had turned into an Egyptian; that when Lora looked about the room as Seth suggested, the Egyptian had been in Margie's place. Bill, a salesman in his forties, looked dazed. He'd found himself walking through a dark corridor inside a pyramid. Someone shouted, "Don't let him in. He knows," and a door that had been before him suddenly shrunk in size and disappeared.

Helen, usually a very serious woman, sat laughing, her face full of vitality. "Boy, do I ever feel like dancing. I've got so much energy, I could dance all night," she said, and I thought, "I could swear that's not Helen." Before I could say anything, another young woman, usually very quiet, suddenly began talking in a rush. Words seemed to slide out of her mouth effortlessly. "It's so easy to express yourself," she said, smiling. "It's so joyfully simple. How did I ever think it was difficult?"

She sat there, looking for all the world like a twelve-year-old, though she was in her early twenties. In that moment, her face was as completely smooth as a child's.

In the meantime, Helen kept swinging her legs back and forth, wiggling her feet, and asking other students if anyone wanted to dance.

Roger, an accountant, was still dazed as he told what had happened to him. First he'd seen five versions of himself. Then, inside a pyramid he found himself looking at a very plush apartment with a dark green carpet, a couch, and above it, gold-framed paintings. It was here that Seth asked students to open their eyes for a moment and look about the room. When he did so, Rog nearly jumped a foot, because he still saw the same room!

These are only some of the experiences; others were just as startling. I kept on, asking each person what had happened in turn, but all the while I was having trouble orienting myself to what was going on. Each time I questioned someone, my voice grew weaker. Disquieted, I found that I wasn't concentrating on what was said as much as I should have. Instead, I was focused on a strange sensation in my right hand and arm.

I was sitting in the rocker, my arms on the arms of the chair. But my right hand felt very boney, the fingers almost like thin claws. To my dismay, the sensations spread until my whole body felt fleshless. I knew that if I looked down, my normal body would be dressed in its blouse and skirt, yet it made no difference. Mentally, I looked out of skeleton eyes.

A calm detachment and understanding quickly vanquished a momentary sense of nostalgia: I had left this physical room and this reality long ago, and so had my students. I sat inside a skeleton, in a rocking chair, addressing other skeletons who sat on chairs and couches in a room that itself had long since disappeared. So, I knew, had the town and the civilization in which it had its being. All of this, the class and students, had happened millions of years in the past. Even the skeleton images, that now seemed the only right ones, were only mirages. Yet I wasn't sad, or even curious. Only the sense of vast distances briefly held my attention. So with a strange new . . . courtesy, I continued to address my questions to those in the room.

Gradually, the feelings began to vanish. As they did, Seth came through:

> *Examine your own feelings at this time. If you have ever learned to examine the nature of your own consciousness, do it now, for to one extent or another, you have made an exchange with your probable selves. Some of you are in the wrong room.*
>
> *I want you to follow that channel backward, and reverse your journey. Now, the selves that you know are returning to their rightful places. Therefore, collect yourselves, and return to this time and place.*

I came out of trance and looked around the room. We were all ourselves again. Ourselves? Or were we just the selves we'd been told to think we were?

My own experience with the room of skeletons came back to me. What did our experiences mean? How were we to interpret the results of our alterations of consciousness?

From the beginning I'd known that the Seth phenomena offered me a unique opportunity to study the nature of consciousness. These class experiences were throwing the whole question of perception out in the open. True or false again: How valid were our experiences, and in what terms? Had there really been faces around the ceiling a few classes back? Did we literally make an exchange with probable selves? Now and then I'd wonder: Did it make any difference? The experiences were enriching our lives. As a result of our reincarnational dramas, for instance, students were relating to their families and friends with far more flexibility and understanding. Did it matter whether or not those remembered lives really happened?

I know that many people experiment in mind control classes, learning to change the focus of consciousness. But few seem propelled by the need to fit their altered perceptions into the normal world, or wonder what they suggest basically, about the nature of being. As our classes continued, I was beginning to see that our world of facts was extremely limited. The fact was, the framework of "facts" couldn't explain our experiences at all.

This actually became obvious with the publication of *The Seth Material* in 1970, when I made my private experience public, and therefore gave it reality in the normal world where people could say, "Is it true? Did it really happen?" Those who accepted Seth and my experience often did so in a structure of reference that literally drove me up a wall. Seth made perfect sense to them in a framework like Martin Crocker's—that included good and bad spirits, religious dogma, punishment, and possession. There, Seth had instant status. I had a good spirit to protect them from bad spirits.

As some of these people wrote or came to class, I soon discovered that my ideas didn't fit that framework any more than they fit into conventional psychological or scientific dogma. With serious reservations, I still trust the physicists most of all. Several physicists obtained excellent data from Seth that expanded the range of their own investigations. As time went on, though, I saw that I certainly wasn't going to achieve any respectability in their eyes either. While they might chat about Seth among themselves and use his ideas, they certainly weren't about to use his name or mine as a reference for an official scientific paper.

I didn't even realize that I wanted to be "respectable," but it was still difficult to admit that I didn't really fit into any particular field, because I was placing Seth and my experiences in a context in which such things had never been considered—at least to my knowledge.

After leaving the Catholic Church years ago, I was deeply suspicious of organized religion, but at least the Church had only one god and devil to worry about. After *The Seth Material* came out, people began to send me some occult or "Gnostic" literature. To my horrified amazement, I found an even more rigid dogma. There were a definite number of levels of existence. The number varied according to the school of thought, but each level had its own lord or guardian, out to discourage the unwary mental traveller.

A few days after Martin's visit, for example, one leader of such a group called me. He told me that he had found himself in a particular realm of existence in an out-of-body journey. The lord of this level commanded him to make certain ritualistic motions that included kneeling and bowing. Otherwise, he'd be annihilated. So he knelt and bowed as prescribed.

I thought he'd used good sense, with his beliefs and under the circumstances. But this man never questioned his experience. I knew very well that out-of-body travels were possible and I experimented with them often. I also knew that out-of-body doesn't have to mean out-of-mind, and that in body or out of it, we find what we expect to find.

But this "spiritual master" was calling *me* a white goddess, insisting that Seth and I were saying the same thing as he was saying, only in different terms. He wouldn't allow his students to read my books until they'd reached a certain level. How had I ever found myself even remotely connected with such a frame of reference?

Other "leaders" of the psychic field thought that I was dangerously leading the public to the Ouija board—when any good responsible psychic knew that evil spirits waited for such unsuspecting dabblers. The dead didn't have much better sense than the living, it seemed, and even a lower idea of amusement.

Good God!

While these summer classes were going on, the mail started coming in. I began to hear from my readers—from *people,* people in all kinds of trouble, people brought up to believe that they couldn't solve their own problems, yet who believed that almost anyone else could solve them for them. Amazing, vital people, with the ground cut off under their feet by all kinds of psychological and religious dogmas that said the same thing: You can't trust yourself, your own abilities or knowledge; theories that constantly put the individual down.

Their reality became part of mine. I'd be getting supper, the table set, meat in the broiler, for instance, and the phone rings. Suddenly I'm speaking to some frightened stranger who is going to commit suicide if Seth doesn't give instant help.

This kind of thing knocked me for a loop. Where did my responsibility begin or end? Seth was to be a healer, a marriage counsellor, and a mentor, and I was to be his handmaiden—a Jane to his metaphysicial Tarzan. Many psychics, I discovered, specialized in just such activities. If you can help people in that way, why not do it? Don't you have the responsibility?

Yet I found that many psychics also encouraged people to use them as crutches; that some people I tried to help kept coming back for *more* help—and in areas in which they were quite capable. And I knew I had more to offer than that. Even from the beginning, I felt that my experience could lead toward a concept of being that could untangle religious and psychic experience from superstition, and literally free our consciousness, at least to some extent, from its present practical limitations.

Would the concept be true or false? If I ever got outside of that framework, it wouldn't matter, because even in 1971 I could feel the still unborn concept working for me and my students. Our ideas about consciousness *were* changing our private experience of what consciousness was.

But we are taught not to trust ourselves. Even during these 1971 classes, for instance, the more doubts I had, the more intelligent and critical and balanced I thought I was. The scientifically oriented congratulated me on my objectivity. The spiritualistically oriented cautioned me that my intellect was running away with my psychic experience, but they *meant* that it was blinding me to the reality of good and bad spirits, and all the rest of the baggage usually considered part of the mediumistic adventure.

So I was in a quandary. My skepticism was not in the validity of the spiritual world, but in the superstitious nonsense with which that reality is interpreted. Seth's concepts and my own lead me far beyond those limitations. Yet, in a way I'm at a disadvantage, because Seth's theories and my own are still open. Seth is still having sessions, and only the other night he began delivering some material that significantly enlarges the scope of his concepts on the nature of being. This book itself will present only an introduction to the theory of Aspects; it too is still in a state of becoming.

Nor, important point, do I deny the reality of life after death or the existence of personalities so vast and complex that they *seem* to dwarf us. It is precisely because I sense their greater reality that I can glimpse, at least, those greater human abilities that make such perception possible. We often assign to spirits those abilities that are rightfully ours, simply because we have been taught that we ourselves are so inconsequential.

One of my students in particular tells me that I'm overly concerned: If I were broad-minded enough, I'd realize that all the symbols mean the same thing. Often, I've been tempted to agree with him. And I appreciate the beauty and utility of symbols. The trouble is that people often forget what symbols mean, or even that they stand for something else. Truth can wear out its symbols, just as people can wear out clothes.

But why not just call Seth a spirit guide and let it go at that? In other words, why not let other people's interpretation of my experience blot out my own? Because that's a great way to lose personal vision. Who needs more conventional dribble from spirits alive or dead, handing out the same dogmas in different clothes, only minutely altered to fit the circumstances? Yet most spirit communications do just that. People have been taught to structure their unique revelationary experiences through definite pre-packaged ideas. Thus they are neatly robbed of their own vision, and the world is poorer for it.

By "original vision," I mean that which is felt by an

individual in his or her own way; it can belong to no one else, because it can't be experienced in the same way by another. It can be recorded and translated. But only by being true to our private visions can we really learn anything at all, much less hope to teach others.

This isn't to say that healing, or helping other people isn't important. God knows, it doesn't mean that I don't feel their need. It does mean that I know that the old frameworks of therapy are vastly limited. I know that we create our own reality, privately and jointly, and this greater truth has to be *my* framework. Only by telling others that they form their own experience can I help them in a way that no one else can.

To do this, I have to let Seth write his books. I have to be peaceful and energetic enough to follow my own mystical nature, and try to show others how to recognize their own abilities. This means that I can't take great amounts of time to answer mail or hold sessions on individual problems. Many other psychics as well as doctors, psychologists, and ministers provide assistance of that nature, and all in the same basic framework.

I knew that I had to stay clear of many accepted ideas and practices connected with psychic work, then, but I was faced with them constantly. Even with Rob's help, it was a lonely way. How much easier, for example, to go along; to pretend that I was saying the same thing as the spiritualists, the Gnostics, or the eastern religions? There are similarities, but the importance of my work lies precisely in the differences. Those differences will become apparent throughout this book.

With Aspects, I'm still groping in the dark. I've only taken my first few steps, but at least I feel that I'm going in the right direction at last, and that I've avoided many pitfalls that could have held me back.

Again, we're taught to doubt ourselves most of all, and doubt becomes our measure of our stability. We've been taught to squeeze our individual vital experience and vision into old concepts, until we no longer recognize them as our own. Too many people are afraid to disagree with mass ideas, afraid that their private vision will make them appear vulnerable, odd, or even fraudulent in the eyes of others.

Not that there aren't a thousand cults, set up against the better organized establishment; but here, too, people are often blindly following dogmas that differ from the main ones only by appearing more exotic or colorful. Seth says simply: You form your own reality. People aren't encouraged to follow him; but themselves. He hopes to give them faith in their *own* existence and meaning.

5

Reincarnation Hits Too Close to Home. Nebene and Shirin

The summer of 1971 went quickly. Monday and Wednesday nights after supper, I'd do the dishes, take a short walk, and then around nine, have a Seth Session. Seth was finishing his own first book, *Seth Speaks: The Eternal Validity of the Soul.* The last few chapters contained some material dealing with biblical times. Neither of us knew much about the Bible, so Rob spent a good deal of time studying reference books, so that his own commentaries in *Seth Speaks* would be correct.

To his surprise, he discovered that biblical authorities differed considerably on the dates of even important events. To *my* surprise, I discovered that Rob got quite irascible when he was poring through the reference books. At first, I thought little about it: After all, he wanted his notes to be accurate. Gradually, though, I became more and more aware of his increasing irritability.

Several times I came upon him, muttering to himself as he searched for some date or another. An intense yet subdued fury seemed to drive him. He stood one night, really scowling, a book open on his drawing table. His face was white, drawn, and angry in the light from the long-armed table lamp.

"Hon, you're going to so much trouble," I said. "Do your notes really have to be so detailed? I guess they just don't have definite dates for lots of biblical events."

"But *why* don't they?" he demanded. Then he said sharply, "Do you *know*? When was John the Baptist born?"

"How should I know?" I answered, half laughing.

"Well, *somebody* should know. These so-called experts don't know anything." He turned abruptly back to his notes, ignoring me completely, and puzzled, I went back to my own study.

The next night, the whole matter came to a head. Sue Watkins came over, bringing some reference books. *The Dead Sea Scrolls* and Will Durant's *Caesar and Christ*. Sue had a friend with her, a young man we'd met a few times before. Our voices carried to Rob's studio, I knew, so I expected him to come out to join us, particularly since Sue had made a special trip over to give him the books.

But Rob worked for more than an hour on his notes before finally coming into the living room. Then, instead of greeting Sue and her friend, Tim, as he usually would, he turned to the books instead and leafed through them impatiently. He'd read a few passages, then stare haughtily at Sue or me and say, "See, they don't know. The so-called experts contradict themselves constantly." He kept this up, reading a few passages then remarking in this way, for nearly an hour. I kept staring at him: Rob, of all people, practically pinning Sue and Tim to the couch, while he force-read them portions of religious history. I couldn't get over it.

I'd never seen Rob act that way before. Usually he's a most considerate host, but whenever anyone tried to change the conversation, he'd just look up rather coldly, then continue with his reading and comments. I caught Sue's eye. She looked over and shrugged comically.

"Hon, why don't you tell us about the records, and

straighten out all those wrong dates?" I laughed, thinking that my joking question would snap Rob out of it.

Instead, he turned to me and said seriously, "Don't you understand? I'm concerned because of the stupidity involved. It's a simple enough thing to keep records—"

Sue and I broke out laughing. I tried to tell Rob how differently he was behaving than he usually did, but he couldn't see it. Not only that, but there wasn't a shred of humor in his attitude. Twice I started to say something, and he cut me off so rudely that I felt confused and humiliated.

I'm very good at picking up Rob's feelings, though, and *he* simply wasn't angry at me. Where was the anger I felt coming from? Was I upset at Rob, hiding it, and then projecting it outward? No, I was sure it wasn't that. Yet Rob *was* displaying strong disapproval . . . and that disapproval somehow made me want to bait him. Finally Sue and I both started asking Rob about records again, with a mock seriousness.

Just at this point, I suddenly "saw" a sharp and brilliant mental image of a tall man in a long robe standing behind Rob's chair. He wore a pointed hat, and looked very formidable and disapproving indeed. His presence was unmistakable. Sue sat across the coffee table from me, facing Rob. Something made me glance over at her, as soon as I saw the figure. Sue literally shrank back on the couch, her face bright red, and her eyes wide open, staring. I hadn't said a thing about what I was seeing.

Involuntarily I said, "Sue!" meaning, "What's wrong?"

"Why I'm really . . . afraid of Rob suddenly. Intimidated is a better word." She kept staring at him, obviously astonished by her own reaction.

"Really?" Rob spoke so innocently that I swore he didn't realize what was happening. But when I said, "Hon, I think you know more about those biblical records than you realize," he answered in quite a normal voice, "Yes, I do."

I didn't know why I made the comment to begin with,

and I still saw the man standing behind Rob's chair. I didn't want to mention my vision, hoping that others might become aware of the figure without any clues from me. I knew that the man in the robes was somehow connected both with Rob and the records.

"Tell me what you know," I said to Rob, keeping my voice as neutral as possible. "Or I'll ask questions, if you want, and you try to answer them automatically." As I spoke, I felt that the figure behind Rob wanted to speak, and thought that Rob might find himself effortlessly expressing the other personality's ideas. Suddenly I realized that Rob *had* been doing that all night.

"All right," Rob said. Sue hadn't taken her eyes off his face. Her friend, Tim, hadn't said a word.

"What do you know about the records of the time?" I asked.

"I kept them." Rob spoke quietly and evenly.

"Is that why you've been so upset?"

"Yes. I was there."

"Did you know Christ or Paul?"

"No, but I heard of them . . . I kept records."

"What was your name?"

"Naz . . . Naz . . . something. I can't get the rest."

Sue was staring at Rob with the most intent expression, so I said to him, "Do you have anything to say to the girl on the couch?"

Again, I didn't know why I asked that particular question either, except for Sue's intentness. Rob looked directly at Sue then and said, "You were quite a problem." He spoke quietly, in his own voice, but there was an alien quality to it, too. I barely had time to notice this, though, when he and Sue began speaking at once, so quickly that the conversation was difficult to follow.

They both began describing an identical scene, a school in Rome, agreeing on everything from the building's construction to the seating arrangements of the students. Sue spoke much more emotionally than Rob, but the two of them interrupted each other frequently. Rob would mention some detail; Sue would say impatiently, "Yes. Yes, of course, and do you remember—" and off they'd go again. According to the conversation, Rob had been a teacher named Nebene in a school run by Sue's parents at that time.

I was surprised for several reasons. Rob's "psychic experience" till then had centered on his paintings and various kinds of internal or exteriorized images that he used for models. Outside of that, and some out-of-body experiments, he'd more or less left psychic experimentation up to me. I also knew that he was well aware of my ambiguous feelings toward Reincarnational Dramas in class.

As Sue and Rob talked, I still sensed the man behind Rob's chair. Finally he turned his attention to me. He wanted me to act as a psychic go-between, and now there was no doubt of his identity: This was Nebene. Rob was going along with the experience, but it was obvious to me that he was also cautious and inhibiting some strong emotions out of consideration for Sue. This holding-back angered Nebene. I was having trouble trying to follow Sue and Rob's excited conversation, while at the same time Nebene kept mentally communicating with me, wanting me to make his presence known.

So I interrupted and described the image of Nebene. Then I stood up behind Rob's chair to show where the form was.

As soon as I did this, the "invisible" Nebene yelled at me mentally. "Have him tell her about the clay tablet! Tell her what it meant. Tell her what it meant to the school," he said. He was obviously furious, and now ready to speak through me.

I held off and decided to relay the message instead. For one thing, Nebene's attitude toward me didn't exactly win me over. He obviously considered me frivolous, beneath his notice, and he couldn't understand how such a person could be so psychically gifted. I sensed his strongly disciplined character at once, but his perfectionist tendencies had been allowed to completely dominate his creativity. I didn't like him; and I refused to speak for him, though this took a good bit of effort on my part. My own voice sounded like a whisper compared to his mental voice shouting at me, but I said to Rob, "Tell her about the time she broke the clay tablet—"

Sue yelled, "Oh!" before I finished speaking.

Now all warmth vanished from Rob's voice: "You broke the tablet in half. Deliberately."

"And I ran home. And *you* told my father." Sue was near tears.

At this point, Nebene tried to get me to speak for him again, and again I refused. As I did, Sue looked up and caught her breath and Rob suddenly turned toward me. "Jane's face is changing," Sue cried. And I *did* feel funny; taller, taut, almost cold. Most of all, I felt as if my features were older, the chin becoming very tight, and the lips tucked in and pinched.

"Hon, are you all right?" Rob asked. I nodded, half angry and half amused, because through Rob's concern, Nebene suddenly understood that Rob and I were man and wife. He backed away, scowling. As Rob held my hand for a moment, my features cleared. Mentally I told Nebene what I thought of him. Still, I was struck by the mobility of his reactions, and the fact that our present hadn't been known to him beforehand. At least it didn't seem to be, because he seemed quite surprised to discover that Rob was married. In fact, Rob's concern for me took some of the wind out of Nebene's sails, and finally I didn't sense his presence any more.

Rob, Sue and I were all tired. We decided that we'd each write up our own notes of the night's activities, and called it a night. In bed, as Rob was dropping off to sleep, he turned to me and said, drowsily, "My father was in that class, too. I just saw him as a girl."

Right after breakfast the next morning, the phone rang. It was Sue. She spoke excitedly, but gradually I found out what had happened. She'd started to write her account of the Nebene episode, when suddenly automatic writing took over and she was writing for the girl she had been as Nebene's pupil. Her name then was Shirin. The sheets of paper quickly filled up with Shirin's scrawling script.

When the writing stopped, Sue went about her daily housework. As she swept the floor, however, she was overwhelmed by a deep sense of sorrow. Appalled, she stood there, until she realized that this was Shirin's grief over the death of a brother back in the past. "It's been some morning," Sue said, and promised to bring the notes over to us that evening.

It was a Friday and we also expected our friends, Peg and Bill Gallagher, to visit. As it was, Sue arrived first that night. Blushing, she made a joke reference to a "pie for the teacher," and thumped down a homemade pie and a six-pack of beer. A gesture to Nebene, I thought; but Rob was still painting in the studio. Looking embarrassed, Sue handed me the notes and I read them while we waited for Rob and the Gallaghers.

There were several pages. I'm quoting a few paragraphs here, because the episode mentioned was so pertinent in the relationship between Nebene and Shirin. As I read, I felt Sue's scrutiny. The passage is directed to Nebene.

> *There was something you said in class one day, something you really hollered at me about. You just let go and went up one side of me and down the other, because I wasn't bothering with my lessons or the stupid formulae and rules, and you yelled about my being no better than the illiterate whores in Rome, and that's how I'd turn out.*
>
> *You said that in front of all those other brats, and I grabbed those tablets in a fury, those tablets that you'd gotten the stuff for in Greece when you went there, and I smashed those tablets right against the wall, as hard as I could, smash, smash, smash, right into the wall, and the pieces flew all over the room, and the noise was still ringing in that room when I was running and screaming down the aisle.*
>
> *I ran all the way home and went to my father. I was still screaming with fury, but he didn't sympathize with me at all. He punished me because I'd done something awful to you, and he respected and understood you. My father was a calm, firm man,*

*and the two of you talked a lot. I hated you for a long time after
that, but my father made me go back to that school, but I wouldn't
look at you or listen no matter what you said. But I knew by then
that I'd ruined something very precious to you, and I was sorry
and I didn't like myself much for it, but I was proud, oh God was
I proud and I couldn't say anything to you after that.*

Actually, this entire quoted passage was written almost
like one long sentence, separated here and there with "and." The
words, "smash, smash, smash," were in capital letters and under-
lined. Fresh emotion rushed out of the written words, and seemingly out of the paper itself. I was almost embarrassed to meet
Sue's eyes, but just as I finished reading the notes, the Gallaghers
knocked at the door. A moment later, Rob came out from the
studio. I handed the notes to him.

The room must have been charged because the Gallaghers stopped in the middle of the room before sitting down.
"What's going on?" Bill asked.

"Nothing," Rob said, and immediately he sat down and
began to read the notes. I grinned uneasily and said something
like, "Rob and Sue have this past-life thing going." Sue just
shrugged, and the Gallaghers and I began an innocuous conversation.

In the meantime, in a motion so smooth and easy that
it almost escaped me, Sue slid from the couch and sat in front
of it on the floor. She rested her elbows on the long coffee table,
and looked up steadily at Rob as he read. Instantly I realized that
her body language was important: She'd taken the same sort of
position in relation to Rob, as the one she'd described with Nebene
in the classroom.

Rob went on reading.

"Well?" Sue said, with a touch of defiance.

"I just finished it this minute," Rob said. "The part I
remember myself most is the description of your father. I see him
in my mind so clearly that I could paint his portrait now. I don't
recall yelling at you, though, as you say in these notes—"

And Sue was Sue-Shirin, or Shirin-Sue. Rob had sounded more or less like himself, though he was obviously speaking to Shirin, but Sue seemed much more Shirin than Rob seemed like Nebene. "You don't remember?" she shouted out. "You only called me a whore in front of the entire class. It damn near haunted me all my life, and you don't remember?"

"If that's what I said, then I'm sorry. I mean it," Rob said. "But your father is far more vivid in my memory—if *my* memory is what you want to call it—than you are."

I thought that Sue-Shirin was going to cry. And Rob was blocking Nebene—quietly, stubbornly, but quite effectively. As soon as Rob said he remembered Shirin's father better than he did her, then the Shirin-in-Sue began baiting the Nebene-in-Rob, trying to draw him out. She was just daring him to show himself, while Rob, I knew, was just as determined to keep under control.

Sue said, innocently enough, "It *would* be great though, to find out more about those old records."

"I'm willing enough," Rob said, but his voice was mild and noncommital. Sue scowled, and I realized that Shirin-in-Sue was demanding attention form Nebene as she always used to, while Rob was reacting exactly like Nebene and witholding it, though now for entirely different reasons.

I pointed this out to Rob. When I did, he looked directly at Sue and said, "I'm sorry; and you've changed a lot. But so have I." Then, with no transition, he went into the kitchen for more beer.

He'd no sooner gone through the door when Sue yelled and pointed to the doorway. "It's him, Nebene. Three-dimensional." Bill Gallagher grabbed a pen and scribbled down her description of what she saw. Sue whispered it to us, her eyes never leaving the doorway.

Nebene was solid, not ghostly, about five feet ten. He wore a dark blue robe with huge sleeves, apparently the same one that I saw him in, mentally, the night before. He was thin, his neck chords sticking out. His nose was long and the lower portion of his face sunken. His lips pursed in a clipped, tight smile. He looked about forty-five.

Sue saw him for several minutes, then he disappeared. When Rob returned, the whole thing was over.

Sue's description matched my mental image of Nebene, though this time I hadn't seen anything. Neither had Peg nor Bill. Rob didn't seem a bit surprised either. The conversation returned to biblical times and the Dead Sea scrolls, subjects about which I know little, and that night they just didn't interest me at all. So I just sat there, listening, letting the words go over my head. My glance drifted over to Sue, who still sat on the floor. She wasn't taking part in the conversation either.

Then I did a double take. This girl wasn't Sue. She had the same coloring and general features, but there the similarity ended. Peeking out through Sue's eyes, Shirin showed herself so blatantly that I caught my breath. She struck me at once as unusually alive, immediate and vital, no matter who she was or what was happening. This personality showing through Sue was as responsive and agile as an animal.

As I watched, Shirin "took over" Sue's features completely. The transformation was fascinating to watch. Shirin stared out with belligerent curiosity into the room, studying everything on the table in turn. There was a strong sense of covert behavior, a sly delight in getting away with what she was doing, and a determination to take full advantage of the opportunity. Click, click, click—you could see her file away each bit of information for future use.

To me she seemed to be a greedy, grimy, mean little girl of about twelve or thirteen; shrewd, highly intelligent, loaded with energy, but unloved and furious at the world. I didn't dare to draw any attention to her, for fear she'd vanish. Rob and the Gallaghers went on with their animated conversation. They seemed lost in it.

I sat there, stunned, watching. My heart went out to

the girl, though, because this was the real Shirin, not the little lady suggested in certain passages of Sue's notes (not included here) where she laid great merit on her parents' wealth and social position. This was a little slut of a child, and one bright enough to know it.

In the beginning, her slit speculative eyes just went from object to object. What were those things? What were they used for? You could see the questioning. Then as I watched, the head lowered, the jaw jutting out, and in one swift sideways motion Shirin stared boldly at Peg Gallagher. One full look. Then the head lowered again. This gesture was repeated with Bill and then—triumphantly—with Rob.

Again I nearly gasped. This girl was alive, here and now. I remembered Joel speaking for Dave in class. How counterfeit or one-dimensional Joel's performance seemed in contrast to Shirin's vital legitimacy! While I was thinking about this, Shirin stared at Rob again. This time, involuntarily, I whispered his name. Rob stopped in mid-sentence, turned toward me, and Shirin disappeared in a flash.

I explained what had happened. The Gallaghers hadn't noticed anything. They'd been completely engrossed in the conversation. Rob had sensed Shirin's presence, though, and I think he purposely avoided the situation for Sue's sake. Sue had been aware of Shirin's feelings and reactions all the time. "I could feel her peeking out at a world that was strange to her; getting a first-hand look at Nebene, or at who Nebene is now." Sue grinned and added, "She couldn't get over the fact that Rob and I are friends, or that I wasn't in a subordinate position any more."

But I was staring uncomfortably at Rob, and suddenly making some connection of my own. I knew Nebene too, but in a different way. What about those times in our marriage when Rob seemed taken over by an uncharacteristic coldness? When an implacable insistence on perfection suddenly possessed him? These characteristics would rise now and then, seemingly from nowhere, and then vanish. And I always reacted to Rob, then, exactly as I did to Nebene. What part had Nebene played in our marriage?

I said what I was thinking, and wondered aloud what particular remarks of mine might trigger Nebene-like responses from Rob. Before Rob could answer, Sue spoke up so quickly that one word fell over the other. "Wait. I get it," she said. "Each of us relate to certain past aspects of ourselves, and other people, too. It's like solving problems all across the board; one incident in the present acting like a magnet to attract a personality say, that lived, three centuries back—"

For a moment we were quiet. We teetered on the edge of knowing. Peg Gallagher said, slowly, "Like Nebene and Shirin, working out old problems tonight, in our present."

"But in *their* present, too!" I almost shouted, because I caught another glimpse of Shirin, peeking through Sue's eyes. Seldom have I seen pure emotion as honestly and clearly in anyone's face, reflecting so exquisitely the inner guises of being. Was Shirin "newly born" that night, I wondered, brought to life in response to a Nebene who was a personification of certain buried elements in Rob's being?

Did a Nebene require a Shirin, and vice versa? Were the two personalities bringing themselves up to date with amazing rapidity, grabbing memories literally out of the air? Were we witnessing the birth of personality, seeing in accelerated form a process that might really take place in us constantly, usually showing only in the gradual change we show through time?

Or were we seeing two persons who died in our terms long before any of us were born? If so, then, "Death, where is thy sting?" I thought, because I guarantee that Nebene and Shirin are as alive as I am. I stared at Rob. He seemed perfectly himself. Then where had Nebene gone?

Other selves flickering in and out of our glances . . . ? Other moods (once ours?), rising up the stairs of the molecules? Again, I caught the hint of some knowledge that could vastly illuminate our current concepts, and shed new light upon our own behavior. But it would be another year before I understood that night's significance.

The strong emotions that had charged the room were gone, but we were still riding down invisible psychological hills. Once Sue asked Rob about the records again. He looked up and said in an absentminded way, "I was a cut above the ordinary citizen. I knew a lot about what went on, because of my work. It was about A.D. 30. Some of the records I left in the busy northwest section of Nazareth . . . Zabodee." He paused, blinking. "I don't know why I said that, or where it came from, but there *are* more records. I hid them outside of Damascus, in caves. *She* knows." And he pointed at Peg Gallagher.

Peg just sat staring at him.

"You *do* know," he said.

Peg's eyes widened. "Why, I'm seeing something," she said. "A big tree on a hill; no, it's a flat-topped plateau. It's sort of an orange color. I'm almost getting a name."

"Her—rog—bah," I said suddenly, separating the syllables.

"That's it," Peg answered.

And Sue was suddenly Shirin. She turned to Bill Gallagher, her throat muscles moving compulsively. "You . . . you . . ." The furiously uttered words were all she got out, before Sue clamped down and came back to herself.

"What's the matter?" Bill asked. "Was I there too? Did I rape you or something?" He was joking, but his face was bright red, and he was still shocked by Shirin's vehemence.

Sue was blushing. "You were a soldier; at least, that's what I'm getting. A dirty old man type."

Bill didn't say a thing for the rest of the evening. Very shortly he said it was time to call it a night. Usually he has a special word for Sue before he leaves, but that night he walked past her as if she weren't there.

We'd eaten Sue's pie. I told her to wait while I washed

the dish. Instead, Rob took it into the kitchen, washed it, and returned it to Sue with a particularly gallant gesture. Nebene, I thought, making amends.

The night was over, but its implications rested in my mind, and the questions it presented hung unanswered. We weren't finished with Nebene or Shirin, but I wouldn't be at all surprised if some of the concepts in Aspect Psychology weren't born that night. If so, then Nebene and Shirin did us more service than we knew.

6

"Another" Universe, a Flower From Nowhere, and a Writing Class Goes "Psychic"

As summer passed, life's normal flux and flow seemed to touch us with growing intensity. Rob's father had died the previous winter. His mother now lived alone in the family home in Sayre, Pennsylvania, about twenty miles away. She didn't want to give the house up, and she couldn't wait to get rid of it at the same time. Her health began to fail, and we spent each Sunday with her. Sometimes we also visited her during the week. She spent months at a time visiting the homes of her other sons, where she could have a private room and yet join in family life.

We took care of her at "this end." Numerous small crises came and vanished. Yet Mother Butts was amazingly resilient. She developed an ulcer, and got rid of it in something like three months. We went with her to the hospital for her checkup. There was a wait of nearly two hours in the waiting room, since Mother was to see a new doctor. When her name was called, Rob went into the office with her. I decided to wait where I was.

Finally I grew restless and bored with the month-old magazines that were provided, so I started looking for the doctor's office. There was a long corridor, so I followed it. It was prosaic, gray, and institutional.

I heard my mother-in-law's voice as I went down the hall and approached one of the offices. The door was open. I walked in and paused just inside. Rob and his mother sat at one side of the room. The doctor—a thin, dark-haired young man with glasses—sat facing me and the door. Behind him, a curtain fluttered in the wind, and through the window I saw the street some three floors below.

I'm not sure exactly what happened next. The doctor looked up and saw me. Instantly he put his arm out in the weirdest gesture, making a wide arc with it, as if beckoning me into his arms.

I went blank. Not for an instant did I question him, his gesture, or its meaning. Automatically I walked across the room to him.

From a distance, I heard Rob say, "This is my wife," but I was already past Rob and the chair he'd vacated for me. In that instant, my relationship was with the doctor. Rob and his mother were the strangers. Without a thought, I walked into the open welcoming half circle of the doctor's arms.

Then, just as quickly, I came to. What on earth was I doing? I was in a position I couldn't rationalize or justify. In the same moment, the doctor blinked. He dropped his arm, slowly and awkwardly, as if wondering how it got there. I was left to back away as best I could. There was no way to cover my retreat.

Rob looked up in the last moment. He told me that he'd seen the doctor make some odd beckoning motion to which I'd responded. At the time, I simply accepted the gesture as natural. Later I realized that it was somehow archaic, not at all normal in our time or country. The movement of his arm seemed to be making room for the natural fall of the folds of a robe or long, full sleeve.

Yet after this incident, there was no embarrassment on anyone's part for the rest of the visit. On the one hand, it was as if nothing had happened; on the other, it was as if what occurred was so inevitable that there was no reason to discuss it.

The very ease of my motions and the unquestioning acceptance contrasted so with my usual behavior that I was nearly appalled. Dr. W. and I both had the same body build, thin and small-boned, and we both had dark hair and glasses. Had these similarities simply brought about a kind of instant sympathy and understanding? I tried to tell myself that was the answer, but I'd felt sympathetic with people before and never found myself in another man's arms while my husband and mother-in-law looked on.

Mother Butts, happily, had been looking in her purse for another doctor's prescription when all this was going on, and she never noticed anything. The strange rapport between the doctor and myself went on beneath the normal conversation about Mother Butts' condition. There was nothing particularly sexual about it. Later as Rob and I discussed the episode, I realized that I felt as if the doctor and I were beloved colleagues at another level of experience—or in another life.

Yet I wouldn't ask Seth what was involved, and I didn't try to find out on my own. Laughing, I *did* wonder what the doctor thought later, or how he rationalized *his* behavior. In a few months when the Sumari development began, I understood at least one reason for the instant recognition we'd felt. And now I wonder if that meeting was a trigger, one among others, that would initiate future events. Mother Butts had another appointment with Dr. W., but I purposely stayed home. I had plenty to do there.

We'd lived in the same spacious four-room apartment for years. The large living room had served as my writing area, and we ate our meals at the big table in front of its bay windows. Now the room also served as a classroom on Tuesday nights. Besides that, I had begun a tiny creative writing class. We were running out of space.

Just then, the apartment across the hall became vacant, and we rented it. This gave us nine large rooms, and by closing the hall doors, we had the whole back of the second floor. I took over the new living room and turned it into my studio. We used the back wing as a bedroom. This gave Rob a two-room studio in our original apartment; and except for our joint bedroom, I had what amounted to my own suite across the hall.

Next to my studio is a small kitchen that used to be a sun porch. It's nearly all windows; the old-fashioned ones made up of small panes that open outward. When we moved in, it was July, and those windows were just inches away from the leaves of a huge oak tree. My own tree house! I sat there, drinking coffee, looking out, for more hours than I could tell.

And something began to happen. I felt as if the leaves and I were changing places. I'd feel all sunny and warm and loose, hanging out there; and from a leaf's standpoint I'd see myself through the other side of the open windows, sitting at the table. I knew, inside the leaf, what I looked like, but the leaf perceived my . . . pattern, identifying it according to shape and shadow. This happened time and time again.

The quality of my perception was deepening in some new way. The dimensions of the present moment opened up; so that in any given instant, the normal back yard scene with its trees, lawns, and gardens suddenly came into a new spectacular life; a life that had been there all the time, but with which I was just becoming acquainted. Some of the most joyous hours of my adult life began.

We took our vacation to decorate the new apartment, and suddenly I began writing with new bursts of energy, beginning an autobiography, and a book about our class experiences. The latter was to be called *Adventures in Consciousness,* and much of the material from it is included in the first section of this book. At the same time, I kept questioning everything, from the reincarnational dramas to the nature of Seth. Those whispering leaves surrounded the whole east side of the house, though; and even when I was writing, I could hardly take my eyes away from the huge branches.

I was writing about five hours a day; the ESP class was full; and Seth was finishing up *Seth Speaks* in regular sessions. My pet project at the time, though, was the small creative writing class. It had only two women in it. Class was held in the big living room on Wednesday afternoons—a poor day, really, since the ESP class ran late on Tuesday night, and Wednesday was a regular Seth session night. It seemed I was often rushing, and sometimes on Wednesdays, my own writing didn't get done.

Just the same, the class had a kind of magic. I'd begun it purposely as a diversion; it emphasized writing and the arts, and the goal was to utilize flexibility of consciousness as a writing method. Yet, to my own surprise, I found myself shifting the emphasis more and more to psychic experimentation, and we tried several exercises that were difficult to do with a larger group.

The younger woman, Mattie, began to produce some excellent writing. It developed into a short novel called *Bernard*, about a writer in seventeenth-century England. Mattie had done some writing as a college girl back in the fifties. Now, with her children in school, she wanted to develop her abilities. *Bernard* was what many people would call an automatic script, but we put no labels on it. When Mattie's daily chores were done, she just sat down at her typewriter and the character of Bernard "came through" so quickly that she could hardly get all the words down. The writing was far superior to Mattie's work at a normally conscious level.

Bernard told his story in the first person, and Mattie saw all the scenes he described. Louise—the other student—and I always looked forward to hearing Bernard's latest exploits, yet something happened in one class that made us even more aware of Bernard; and presented me with still another episode too bizarre to fit into the usual framework of concepts and reference.

The setting was prosaic enough: the three of us in the two o'clock sunshine, with coffee and crackers on the table, papers and manuscripts all over the place, and the traffic noises rushing up loudly through the open windows from the intersection below.

In fact, class began on a humorous note, at least to me. Mattie and Louise came bustling in, sounding excited and pleased with themselves. Mattie was in her early thirties, Louise in her late fifties, yet they'd become good friends. I looked up in mild surprise, because they were more dressed up than usual. It turned out that they'd spent the morning together at Louise's Wednesday Morning Club. Louise said that she rarely attended, but the meeting featured a speaker she'd wanted to hear.

They'd gone, feeling somewhat out of place with the more conventional ladies. I think they felt like co-conspirators, but it was all great fun because they weren't "that far out," of course. They just didn't wear hats or gloves, but they wore stockings and high-heels and "afternoon" dresses, and not a hair was out of place on their coiffured heads.

I found all this delightfully hilarious in the light of the rebel roles they'd assigned themselves. If they'd gone to the meeting in dungarees, that would have been something else. But anyway, the meeting made their day, and they were like kids out of school, laughing that the other ladies might consider them daffy, but they didn't care.

Then Mattie read the latest installment of *Bernard*. It dealt with an agonizing masturbation experience, and was written with insight, authenticity, and far greater understanding of basic issues than Mattie usually showed. This from a young woman whose idea of showing freedom was not wearing a hat to a Wednesday Morning Club!

For the first time, I was struck by the significant differences between the usual Mattie and the author of *Bernard*. We began to discuss the whole affair. Had Mattie once lived a life as Bernard? Was an independent Bernard dictating the script to her?

Or was her own creative greater self simply seeing to it that she used her writing abilities, sweeping aside all cultural limitations and freeing her from inhibition? So far we'd been content to let the questions rest, but that afternoon they swirled about us.

How "real" was Bernard? Were we meeting a personality in transit, a personality latent in our own? How did Bernard fit into an entire picture that included Seth, Nebene, Shirin, and the ordinary selves that we know?

Creative writing class began at two and ended at four o'clock because all of us had evening meals to prepare. By three that afternoon, Mattie had read her week's work on Bernard, and Louise had read portions of an autobiographical manuscript. Then I suggested that we go into the "Alpha Two" stage of consciousness to see what creative material we could uncover.

The instructions were simple. I just told them to imagine Alpha One as one step adjacent to normal consciousness. "This time," I said, "we want to go a step further. So imagine taking two steps to your right, if you want, and step over from one to the other. See what happens. Or, go out the back of your head, imaginatively. Just keep your purpose in mind, to exercise your consciousness."

Having given the instructions, I closed my eyes and followed them myself. I could participate in this class more fully than I could in the "psychic" ESP class, since I didn't go into a Seth trance, and there were so few present. So I relaxed, imagined the two steps in my mind, and mentally saw myself step to the second one.

Immediately, I found myself outside the large bay windows. A tightrope stretched from our house to Dr. Sam's house next door. I was dressed like a clown, with big floppy pants, and walking the rope high in the air. Then I let myself fall off, and go rolling gently down.

This is an experiment in consciousness, I thought: so I can fall upward, too. The next instant I went rushing effortlessly up through the air like a wind in an updraft.

Most of my consciousness was in the image of the clown, but part was in my physical body, monitoring the performance. This part commented that the clown still wasn't floppy enough, so I let it go still more. As the clown, I'd been carried high; now I dropped down into Dr. Sam's pear tree and rested. The self in the chair knew quite well that the tree had been cut down the year earlier, while the clown relaxed completely in the treetops. Then, grinning and refreshed, I let the clown just disappear, brought all of my consciousness back to my body and opened my eyes.

Mattie and Louise still sat quietly, with their eyes shut, so I decided to go back into Alpha again while I was waiting. I looked at the clock; less than five minutes had gone by. Usually I allow about ten minutes at most for such exercises, so I still had five to go. I closed my eyes.

Once more I felt drawn to an area just outside the bay windows. This time, though, I lost contact with my body at once. I was in mid-air, looking at Dr. Sam's house, two stories up from the parking lot below.

At first, everything else looked normal. I saw the usual curved horizon over and beyond the house and the afternoon sky, all swirling now with gray clouds that rushed past the dimmed yellow sun. I noticed this particularly since the day had been sunny when class began. Then suddenly, the three-dimensional world behind Dr. Sam's house folded up flat behind it, so that the whole thing was two-dimensional—like a flat piece of cardboard, with the house just painted on the front. At the same time, I shot through the whole flat surface, ripping through to the other side.

Here, to my considerable amazement, was another universe—or at least what looked like one. Velvet black space stretched as far as I could see, with pinpoint stars in an unimaginable distance. I was obviously headed in one particular direction, and I went hurtling onward, never approaching any particular star, or changing course.

This seemed to take a very long time. I had no body,

but seemed to be just a point of light moving at incredible speed. This wasn't a mental image; the space all about me had dizzying depths. Suddenly I slowed down and lost altitude. Very gently, I felt myself drifting lower. The next thing I remember is a glimpse of quite ordinary autumn streets, seen from above. Then, seemingly without any transition, I was sitting on the ground in front of my childhood home.

The first thing I was really aware of was the wetness of the grass beneath me; and the fact that my body felt very odd. Ferns reached above my eye-level, and I was staring at the lattice-work beneath the porch. With a shock, I knew that I was a very young child.

There was a curious familiarity about the touch of wet earth I was sitting on. I was enjoying the sensation immensely. It took me a moment to get my bearings: I was definitely looking out through the child's eyes. Beyond doubt, the child was me. I stood up, unsteadily, but with great enjoyment and the most delicious sense of accomplishment. Then I realized that I was just learning to walk.

Astonished, I looked down to see short pudgy legs stuck into white socks and a pair of children's white shoes. Everything I saw was at the child's eye level. I tottered down to the gutter and crossed the empty street. At the other side, I fell down as I tried to get up the curb. Then I plopped there where I was for a minute, very matter-of-factly, before getting up. I was utterly engrossed in what I was doing. It's very difficult to explain this, but I felt the child's reactions and emotions, not mine. "Matter-of-factness" doesn't nearly describe the aplomb I felt at moving myself about, for example. Falling down seemed to be something the body did all by itself. But getting it up again was something that "I" did, and I was completely absorbed in getting the knack of it.

After this, I walked over to a large sprawling lilac bush and plopped down again—this time with great satisfaction—and stared at a wire mishmash fence. After sitting there for a minute, a plan firmed in my mind to run to the house nearby. The intent was quite deliberate, and I could feel it form in my mind in the weirdest way. Getting from where "you" were to where "you" wanted to be was of supreme importance. In her (my) brain, the child formed a mental image of herself walking, then running from where she was to the house. She projected the image out in space so that I saw it in her mind's eye, sent out in the yard ahead of her. She was going to follow it physically. Then—again without transition—I was back in the living room.

(The oddest thought just hit me now, as I wrote that last sentence. Was there some connection between the child projecting her image out through space in front of her, and *my* return? Did she, somehow, project herself into the future as she moved ahead of herself in space?)

I was certainly disoriented for a moment. The transition between child body and adult body was really startling. I'd felt such a marvelous compactness and corporal intensity. Now I felt tall and gawky. But I was positive of one thing: As children, we learn to move the way I'd just experienced it. We send out mental images and learn to follow them.

Mattie and Louise were sitting there, writing notes when I returned. I started to tell them what had happened, but Mattie had a story of her own to tell. She looked at me in the oddest fashion, tilting her face like a round, brightly lit lantern in my direction. I took notes because she told me ahead of time that she considered the experience important.

"To say the least, it was fascinating," she said. "I went out through the back of my head and saw Bernard. He was dressed like a clown in these baggy pants—"

At this, I yearned to interrupt her, but didn't.

Well, we embraced, a great—I guess you could say, exuberant —embrace. I felt myself flow into him, right through him, and I got scared and pulled out. But he was still there. Then I thought that this was an exercise in consciousness, and I might as well go along with it, not be frightened, and see what happened. I let my-

*self go . . . and I could feel myself flow down to his toes until I
was absorbed by him completely.*

*The next thing I knew, I was standing in a graveyard, with
all sorts of statues and monuments about. I was a little disoriented,
but there was a gate nearby, so I went over, opened it, and came
out on a busy street. Everyone but me was dressed in old-fashioned
clothing. I stood there a minute, trying to decide what to do next,
when all of a sudden I was back here, on the couch.*

Louise's experiences hadn't been as startling as Mattie's
or mine, but she was delighted because they'd specifically given her
information she'd wanted for her autobiography. A series of rich
images had flashed through her inner vision, all consciously forgotten till then, and all relating to her early experience.

We still hadn't done any in-class writing for the day,
so I suggested that Louise and Mattie go into an Alpha state
again, only this time they were to try to write at the same time.
While they were doing that, I decided to see if I could find that
"other universe" again.

I closed my eyes. At once I sensed a person to my right,
but not filled in or substantial. Then I felt drawn to that same
spot outside the windows. At once a hole appeared in the side
of the house that faced me. I could clearly see the edges of the
hole curled inward, as if an implosion had occurred. I was swept
through this hole.

The last time, the world behind the house had turned
flat. Now it stayed three-dimensional, but the hole was a chute
of some sort that went completely through the world we know—
and out on the other side. The journey through this channel also
seemed to take a long time. I saw nothing inside it, as I was swept
through so quickly that I couldn't possibly estimate my speed.

In the beginning, some of my consciousness stayed with
my body, but it was drawn out, bit by bit. With dual awareness,
I could feel part of me being drawn out of my image, and as the
bodiless part inside the chute, I could feel these other portions
catching up or following. The pulling-out process seemed to be

taking too much time, though I don't know how I knew this. Suddenly, the rest of my consciousness that was still connected with my body turned into a series of "bullets" which were shot through the hole. They all went rushing through, one after the other.

The other end of the chute opened up, again, into another universe. I didn't know if it was the same one I'd been in earlier or not. There was limitless black space, and stars ahead of me. The bullets of energy containing my consciousness burst out, exploding like rockets, showering in all kinds of displays of color and design; like firecrackers, giant-sized.

I saw this universe ahead of me as I emerged from the hole; the "last" parts of me seeing the parts that had gone first and were exploding ahead in the distance. The contrast was spectacular—part of my consciousness still in the dark chute, looking out to see the illuminated spread of sparkling energy and color. There was no feeling of danger. I had the feeling that my consciousness departed in lightning, leap-frog fashion from the bullets of energy that composed me, so that I could watch the ones ahead exploding, while not feeling that "I" was exploding.

As the last portions of consciousness burst out into the new universe, the lights and displays began to come together somehow and form a flower of lights. Here the experience took another turn, even more difficult to explain. I'm not sure, but I think that the flower was gigantic in size; a tremendous blossom of energy. My entire consciousness was there, and I was completely unaware of my body.

Then with no warning or sense of travel, I was back in the chair—I presume with my eyes closed—only that gigantic flower was still coming at me with incredible speed, propelled from that other universe. I was positive that it was suddenly in front of me, in the physical room. This was so real and astonishing that I yelled out involuntarily.

It was then that I must have opened my eyes. The flower vanished, and I had the feeling that it disappeared inside of me. I was convinced that the flower followed me from one universe to the other; and represented some kind of intrusion into our space. My shout startled Mattie and Louise who had, of course, seen nothing.

My next experience with the hole in Dr. Sam's house would be in the late autumn and be directly connected with the beginning of a new development. Even at the time, though, I knew that these were not *just* mental experiences. I *was* in some kind of chute that led from one system to another, and my consciousness *did* behave like bullets of energy. I took it for granted, on the other hand, that the hole was not a physical one in Dr. Sam's house for someone else to see. I didn't expect, on coming out of trance, that the walls would show a gap, or that neighbors would stand there, staring.

Yet I stubbornly insisted that in some way . . . a gap *was* there, or had been there, and that I could find it again.

The flower had been so immediate that for a moment I thought sure Mattie and Louise would see it; but in the next instant I knew it existed in the same way that the hole did. It would take me two years before the ideas in Aspects would give me some clues about an inner order of events in which such experiences have great meaning.

Summer vanished and autumn came before I realized it. My correspondence list grew. There were more letters and calls, and I was particularly concerned with all the people who wrote for help in personal and health problems. One day a man and woman just appeared at the door, without calling, and pleaded for an interview. They had a very sick child, who was also retarded.

I'd just washed my hair. It hung wet, down my back. It was creative writing day, and I was in a rush. Yet, somehow, I couldn't turn the couple down.

I told them that I didn't specialize in healing, though, and suggested they write to Dr. Harry Edwards, the English spiritual healer.* "I don't know why we've come exactly," the man said, stubbornly, "except that I'm sure you can help in some way. I'm not sure about healers anyway. I don't want to get mixed up with anything to do with the devil."

"What's the devil got to do with it?" I asked, dryly.

So we had a talk, and the man said, in a rush now, "I thought maybe I was being cursed. When Dottie was carrying the baby, I had a vision of it. It wasn't right and wanted to die. And I told it that it had to live. So I thought that maybe God was punishing me—"

The poor man was plagued enough by the child's illness, but worse, he was haunted by the feeling that God was punishing the child for *his* sins. I was outraged. Again I wondered —and this time aloud—what kind of a god this was supposed to be, anyhow? I was able to give some impressions about the baby; at least I saw him alive and looking normal enough, about twelve years old, but in the yard of some kind of special school.

Mainly, however, I was able to relieve the father of his sense of guilt. If he felt cursed when he came here, at least he felt graced to be a part of the universe when he left. But I was still upset, thinking of all the people whose religious beliefs only added to their own problems.

I was still thinking of the episode later that day when writing class began, and I told Mattie and Louise about it. A few minutes later, I felt that there was a form of some kind in the air above the coffee table. Then I saw it clearly, though I could also see *through* it, so it wasn't entirely physical.

The form was in the shape of a person, but I knew that actually it represented massive energy. It was connected to the help that I had been giving others; as if without knowing it I'd been building up this "form" in another dimension, and now could consciously use it to help myself and other people, too.

I didn't necessarily think of it as a personality; but

*Dr. Edwards' address is: Burrows Lea, Shere, Guildford, Surrey GU5 9QG, England.

more as a force. The word "helper" came to mind. Later I discovered that I could send "Helper" out to people in trouble. The appearance of Helper may also have been another clue; certainly all of these events were smoothly beginning to accelerate. I felt new changes and directions in the air.

On the one hand, I welcomed them, of course. On the other hand I kept straining my intellect as far as it could go. I kept trying to fit these experiences into some kind of acceptable framework, and kept coming up short. Again, I just couldn't place them in the conventional spiritualistic group of concepts—not when it included demons and superstitions that I couldn't accept. Yet the scientific framework was, I felt, intuitively sterile.

So I kept trying. The beginning of Sumari in November, 1971, made me try harder.

7

The Sumari Development

The rich life of the psyche provides the creative ingredients from which we form our daily lives. There are always new possibilities for action and fulfillment just beneath the surface, ready to emerge in response to the events of our days. Such upthrusts of energy and creativity are given precisely when they are needed, if only we are flexible enough to recognize and accept them.

Looking back, it's obvious that such stirrings were rustling just below my consciousness during that entire summer and fall. My other-universe experience happened on November 4. On November 15, Rob mailed the final manuscript of *Seth Speaks*, signalling the end of a creative endeavor; and on November 16, my father died. The Sumari development began on November 23 —at the time, seemingly out of nowhere.

I didn't know my father well. He died at sixty-seven, quickly. I hadn't seen him in several years, so he actually seemed as alive, dead, as he had ever been, except that no more occasional letters came. Yet I think that his death had something to do with what happened a week later. In fact, all of the events of our lives were also probably connected: The earlier death of Rob's father, his mother's situation, and the simple process of continued living in which death plays more of a part as parents die.

The psyche's truth, as I'm now learning, deals with a different order of events, yet one that is connected to the ordinary episodes of our lives. These truths are so richly woven that they often appear dramatically, clothed in symbols, transformed into art. Our cultural beliefs, unfortunately, make us suspect the psyche's deep knowledge, and we often try to hold down its manifestations to our own limited concepts.

The Sumari development is important if only because it shows so clearly the rise of additional potent energy into organized form, a form that then enriches normal life. The same kind of process happens, I'm convinced, in each of us at various times in our lives, even though the end product may be far different.

I don't recall my state of mind that evening of November 23. I was sorry about my father's death, but not grieving. ESP class had barely begun. People were laughing and talking, when I felt my attention drawn outside the bay windows again, to the spot where the hole had opened up in Dr. Sam's house.

Suddenly I had the impression that a group of people were coming out of that "other universe" into the room, and that their teacher stood just inside, facing me. We seemed to be communicating telepathically, though consciously I couldn't pick up what was being said. The group moved around the room and stood there, silently watching.

I was quite aware that physically, in our terms, no people stood there but I granted the validity of my own experience: It was true that I felt their presence and "saw" them with a different kind of vision.

Then I "heard" a babble of voices in strange languages. These seemed to come from far above me. This wasn't physical hearing. Instead, I had the impression of multitudinous sounds stacked in layers. I saw the sounds, in other words, as shapes: Some formed triangles, and some long rectangles. I sensed them as forms *and* sounds. They were all alien. I didn't know what I was supposed to do with them, but I knew that something was expected of me.

It would be impossible, I thought, for anyone to give voice to all that. I didn't think my tongue could make the sounds required. In fact, my tongue felt uneasy. Its muscles wiggled. It seemed incapable, clumsy. The sounds formed words, and all the other "languages" faded, so that one of them grew more prominent and became louder. The words came so swiftly, though, that it was hard to tell where they started or how to distinguish one from the other. Yet I felt that I was supposed to give voice to them somehow; to just open up and let them come through.

I'd be damned if I would, I thought. This kind of experience was completely new to me, and even while it was happening I was trying to fit it into some kind of context. Unfortunately, the first thing that came to mind was the "speaking in tongues" associated with fundamental religions. Granted, some valid psychic events may happen under those conditions, but still they aren't *my* kind of conditions; and if any yelling, contortions, or tremors—holy or otherwise—were going to be involved, then I was drawing the line.

While all of that went through my mind, the sounds seemed to disappear in the background to dim static, while one particular word, *Sumari,* grew louder and louder. It was sung rather than spoken. I realized that I was supposed to give it voice. I was intrigued; I hesitated; then decided to write the word down, rather than speak or sing it. I grabbed my pen and paper and scribbled what I got as fast as I could.

Other words followed; these, too, seemed to come to the foreground or come out of the other sounds, which correspondingly dimmed.

Then I turned my conscious focus back to the room,

and told my students what had happened. I started to read aloud what I'd written. Instead, according to class members, I chanted the words in a loud, ringing voice, flinging the paper to the floor.

Sumari
Ispania
Wena nefarie
Dena dena nefarie
Lona
Lona
Lona
Sumari

Then, in a whisper, "someone else" said in my voice, "I am Sumari. You are Sumari. It is your family name. Throughout the ages you have been Sumari. I am acquainting you with your heritage."

At the same time, a delicious warmth filled my body. It came like a glow, from inside, radiating outward. I felt what I can only explain as an astonishing graciousness, a delightful ancient-yet-young joy that was directed toward everyone in the room. According to my students, this was reflected in my bearing and manner as I sat forward in my chair, inclined toward them and addressing them with gentle eagerness.

Then the style of delivery changed. I spoke in a different voice, saying again, "I am Sumari. You are Sumari. We are Sumari. I am the same Sumari in different guise."

The first personality had seemed feminine. As the second one spoke, I felt as if large horizontal ridges crossed my forehead. This personality reminded me of an old man and a young boy at the same time—an ancient boy.

As "I" was speaking, Sue Watkins had a vision. She saw a three-dimensional figure behind me. It was dressed in gold-yellow and nearly reached the ceiling. Though she saw the figure in bulk, no features or other details showed.

I'd often told students to go to the Alpha One or Two state of consciousness whenever anything unusual was happening in class. Again, the idea behind this is that events exist at different levels of reality. So to *really* understand an event, theoretically you'd turn your focus in many directions, just as—physically —you might walk completely around an object to see it from all sides.

When I began to do the chant, then, many students switched over to Alpha. One woman had an excellent out-of-body experience, and slipped easily back into her body again. Another student saw groups of figures, and while he thought that distortions probably were involved, he had the impression of seeing three-part eyes. This was so clear that he drew a sketch of his vision. On seeing this drawing, a girl called out, claiming to have seen the same image.

Everyone was filled with exuberance and energy. And questions! Sumari "came through" several other times that night. On each occasion, a kind of smoothness and warmth swept over my body. My arms felt light enough to float. Mostly I was aware of that odd, exquisite graciousness. Through that focus, I kept observing the room.

At one point, "I" looked at one young man, Phil, and saw stretched behind him the images of his "reincarnational" selves. The closest one was a lovely dancer, a girl with dark skin and Oriental or East Indian dress. Sumari recognized Phil and cherished him as himself, and as all of his other reincarnational personalities also. She saw them in him and him in them.

The same applied to everyone in the room. When I looked at Bette, I saw the pioneer woman right behind her. The emotions felt by Sumari were so rich and multidimensional that my own usual feelings seemed shallow by contrast. Emotion in stereo! But these feelings were also steady, rich, sure, and beautifully coordinated. There was an excellent blend of intellectual and emotional experience. I felt as if I were becoming aware of a new kind of all-inclusive personhood that was my rightful heritage, and everyone else's.

Yet when class was over, I wondered again about the

"language." One of the students mentioned the ancient Sumerians whose historical existence is documented. But I was sure that I wasn't speaking any language from another civilization, not in usual terms. And what was meant by the phrase, "We are acquainting you with your heritage" or "You are Sumari"?

I went over to discuss the whole thing with Rob, only to find that he'd had an experience of his own. He'd been typing up the last Seth session in the small second kitchen off my studio. Suddenly his vision seemed to dim. It was hard for him to see the paper or his own hand. Then he saw a head shape, bathed in beautiful colorful jagged outline. It was brilliant, almost like fire, with shoots of light on the sides. Rob felt at the time that it had something to do with my father. Later he sketched the vision, and it is reproduced here.

Was it really related to Sumari? I wanted to know what was going on, so the next night we held a long Seth session. Our friend, Sue Watkins, even came over and recorded it so that Rob would be free of his usual note-taking chores and better able to ask questions.

The session lasted two hours. Sue, who typed it up this time, ended up with thirteen pages of double-spaced script.

First, Seth talked about Rob's vision. He said that Rob, in his own way, was picking up the energy connected with the Sumari development.

> *You were perceiving a core of energy that radiated outward and infringed upon this reality, hence the fragmented area about it, you see, and the seemingly jagged effect [of the vision] . . . .*
> *You were concentrating your perceptive abilities and energy almost in the same fashion . . . as a laser beam, for example, concentrates' energy. So the vision that you received, while it was microscopic, was still brilliant and radiated strong energy. Now such a vision is not only something that you see, and that intrudes upon this reality, but it has its effects upon your reality as well. You perceive the appearance of the vision, but its other effects escape you. The concentration of energy itself is highly important,*

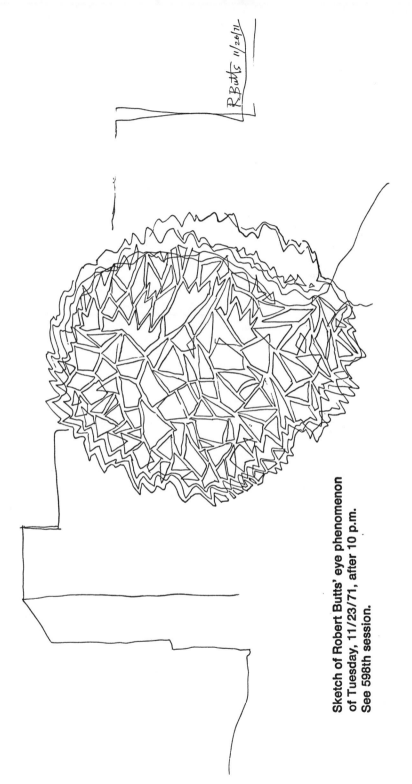

R Butts 11/26/71

Sketch of Robert Butts' eye phenomenon of Tuesday, 11/23/71, after 10 p.m. See 598th session.

you see, and changes the behavior even of the atoms and molecules within the neighborhood of its appearance.

Now, remember what I told you about black holes and the concentration of energy. Such occurrences allow you unusual exchanges of energy from one system to another. They are fountains, therefore, of new energy; and their very intrusion into your world activates that reality in a different fashion—usually in a quickening, stirring, transforming fashion—an activation, therefore, rather than a slowing down.

There are, incidentally, levels of motion so fast that they attain what seems to be a level of complete peace, where motion is not perceived. Beyond such levels, the motion is perceived again, and the period of peace seems over. Now in the case of your vision experience last evening, the image itself activated the air in the atmosphere. In that activation, however, it achieved finally a level of seeming peace where you do not perceive it, but in which it still exists . . .

Then Seth said that the Sumari could be compared to a psychic family, or to a guild of consciousnesses who worked together through the centuries. He made a joking reference to my "dislike of brotherhoods, alive or dead," but added that Sumari could be called a brotherhood in which we were now ready to take up conscious membership. Seth himself was in great form, addressing himself jovially to Rob who had time to ask as many questions as he wanted, for a change.

Seth emphasized that the Sumari were only one group or guild of consciousnesses. After a rather serious discussion of their purposes and characteristics, in which he stressed Sumari initiative and creativity, Seth grinned broadly and said that "they don't hang around to cut the grass, though." The main point seemed to be that the Sumari were primarily creators, nonconformists with superb use of energy who "initiated systems of reality," but weren't temperamentally suited to seeing a long project through, perhaps. They'd leave that to other groups who were gifted with different kinds of abilities and tendencies.

In a burst of husbandly intuitive insight, Rob asked Seth about my strange experience at the hospital with Dr. W.

(Actually, Rob wanted to know why I hadn't asked about this myself!) Seth said that he thought I should answer *that* question, but then he confirmed the suspicion behind Rob's query. Dr. W. was a Sumari. He had been involved with me in past lives, when we had a highly personal work relationship. We'd been "beloved colleagues." In answer to other questions, Seth said that the Sumari development had been latent since the beginning of our sessions, and that my ability to translate some ancient "Speaker" manuscripts had been dependent on my acceptance of this new aspect.

The Speakers are mentioned in *Seth Speaks* where they're described as teachers, physical and nonphysical, who help our race through the centuries. Rob wanted to know if all Speakers were Sumari, and Seth said that each guild had Speakers.

Seth's session intrigued me, yet its implications made me think twice: Did I want to go ahead with this new development or didn't I? He'd mentioned that the Sumari experience would expand in quite unexpected ways—and to my benefit. But speaking for Seth was one thing, an accepted part of my life and work. As usual, I decided to go ahead—while allowing myself full right to criticize whatever happened or to stop whenever I chose.

As for Dr. W., I felt that our meeting might have been one of the triggers for Sumari, and I could hardly deny what I'd felt when we met. But that was that. I had no curiosity about his present situation. In fact I knew that our past relationship, whatever it was, deserved its own privacy. It didn't belong in our current lives.

And Sumari *did* develop, almost in the same way the first Seth sessions did, so that within a month a variety of phenomena emerged more or less full-blown. In the following class, for example, I began talking and singing in Sumari. We had what we called a Sumari Circle, when one by one students spontaneously stood up, walked in a circle about me and began chanting with me in Sumari. This was supposed to *represent* ancient initiation ceremonies.

As Sumari, I drew diagrams which I explained carefully—in the Sumari "language." At the time, students nodded their heads. Yes, they understood; it was perfectly plain. But when I came out of trance, no one remembered what it was they had understood, or what the diagrams meant.

The uprush of class energy was obvious. Students reported many more out-of-body episodes and class dreams. But so far, Rob hadn't heard Sumari. I decided that I wasn't going to go ahead with it until Rob had a chance to observe Sumari and give me his opinion.

So one night we set up the recorder. I was Sumari almost instantly. She began by pointing to objects in the room, and giving Rob their Sumari names. Then Rob was expected to repeat the word. Before long, Rob found himself speaking Sumari spontaneously. Then, haltingly, he began to sing, with "me" correcting him as he went along. When the session was over, we were both astonished.

The next day I played back the tape and wrote the words of the song down phonetically. This took a good deal of time. As I was doing this, however, I began to get the English translation. The placement of the lines or sentences seemed to come naturally, but sometimes I'd get the translation of an entire phrase, or just one word.

The song was called *Song for Beginners*, and as you'll see later, it showed up in a different context in my novel, *The Education of Oversoul Seven*.

At least as far as I'm concerned, however, one of the most surprising elements of Sumari involved the vocal effects. I've had no musical training of any kind outside of singing in a church choir for a while as a child. That particular choir didn't involve any training, either; you just yelled out the words as loudly as you could, and that was that.

As Sumari, though, I quickly began to sing in a lovely musically-true voice of considerable range. The songs or scores show far greater musical sophistication than I have on a normal level. Two of my students who are musicians have put some of these songs to music. I can't even read notes, so I can't understand the scores, but one is reproduced in Chapter fifteen for those who do.

In class, the songs aren't just sung. My whole body is used as a vehicle of expression, and often some pantomime is involved. Almost at once, for example, Sumari dramas were established, where song and motion were used to act out a reincarnational episode. The characterization and the emotional meaning of the drama are absolutely clear despite the fact that English isn't being used. In this regard, the songs express emotional realities that are often very meaningful to students. These are also structured; that is, although the performance is completely spontaneous, the result is organized, poised, true to the requirements of meaningful discourse or communication.

I had a "trance language," then. Was it the language of the unconscious? Was I involved in a process that somehow paralleled the birth of language in any culture? Was my experience a private but perfect replica of what happens when a species begins verbal communication? What could the "language" really be used for? If I was going to be able to translate it, then what did I need it for in the first place?

I asked the questions, all right, and as winter came upon us, one by one some of the answers began to arrive.

8

Songs of the Silver Brothers

Successful living may result from a series of psychological births over a period of a lifetime, in which the psyche infuses the personality with new energy, insight, and direction in response to the physical situation and the personality's needs. In mundane terms, the result might be a sudden burst of health, the development of latent abilities, or the resolution of problems that before seemed insoluble.

Dreams, inspirations, and visions of one kind or another are, I believe, an important part of this process. Through them, the unconscious makes its material consciously available. Unfortunately, these experiences have been so structured by our institutions, that the individual impetus and meaning often become lost. We're taught to interpret revelations, dreams, and insights according to prescribed dogma—religious, scientific or psychological. But we're not encouraged to encounter such material directly.

It's at least possible that schizophrenia is a condition resulting when an individual is in the middle of such psychological birth, but unable to interpret his or her experiences within current frameworks. What we might need is a psychological midwife; someone to help us decode visions or revelations and then apply them to our daily lives.

My own experience leads me to such considerations, for there is no doubt that my own life has involved a series of revelations, each like a new birth emerging outward from an inner order of events, so that my exterior life was enriched and renewed. The "other-universe" experience mentioned earlier certainly stated its case symbolically. Even the long chute through which I travelled could be interpreted as a journey through the womb; although I made no such connection at the time, and I don't believe that experience to be *just* symbolic.

In that "other universe," I found myself learning to walk, as a young child; and several weeks later I was learning to talk a new "language." The language came from within, and not from the outside world. In fact, I had to learn to translate it. In my case, this trance language or language of the unconscious resulted in a new burst of creative activity.

All of this involved highly specific modes of communication and objectification. My unconscious was given clear voice. The birth of new material was relatively unimpeded, and my ego was replenished as a result. The Sumari language also presented a method of emotional expression. It is free of verbal stereotypes and hits home often because its emotional power, like music, lies in its sounds and rhythm.

It's almost as if I were born into a different civilization of myself; found a new self-land. But how many people are tormented instead of delighted by the same kind of experiences, unable to appreciate their meaning or creativity because of the religious or psychological implications they might be given? A man thinks he's speaking for Christ, for example, or receives automatic writing from a being on another planet—in the recognized true-or-false world, such experiences just don't fit. No one helps such a person work with his or her unconscious materials. What does Christ mean to such a man, and what is the message? Is the automatic writing a method of bringing valuable insights from another planet of the psyche? What creative and unique transformations of self are trying to be born, that only need interpretations in other terms?

The point is that such experiences *are* real, but as I hope to make clear later, their reality exists in a different order of events that must be correlated into normal living if their true creativity is to be utilized. I'm not saying that such events are *only* imaginatively valid either; I'm implying that their reality may be the fountainhead for the recognized world of experience.

What are the metaphysics of the unconscious? More, what *is* the unconscious? For certainly I don't accept the psychologists', or the priests', definitions or interpretations. For my own answers, at least, I look to my own experience. Though my symbolism may differ from any other individual's, I'm convinced that the journey into the psyche, the new birth from within it, and its emergence into our world will generally follow the same kind of path. As it does, it expands normal consciousness.

In a matter of weeks, for example, Sumari gave me an entirely different kind of poetry. For about three years I'd been working on nonfiction and my potery had suffered. I seemed to have reached a plateau. As I sat watching the oak tree, I could feel my awareness expand into ever widening and deepening levels. In that state one day, Sumari words suddenly came into my head in a different way. I "knew" that these were Sumari verses, ancient poetry that carried truths long forgotten by our race. Two levels of consciousness were involved; one, in which I picked up the Sumari, and the other in which the translations came. As a rule I couldn't get the English translation without the Sumari, even though I tried.

In poetry the Sumari songs, sung or written, delineate the metaphysics of the inner self. And that metaphysics is, I believe, truer to reality than the exterior dogmas and sciences that we accept as "truth."

Some of the songs were published in my novel *Oversoul Seven*. Here I'm including some previously unpublished ones, with the original Sumari. The Sumari words themselves are actually translations of Sumari signs, but these rarely concern me. The written words certainly look like a combination of bastard French and Latin—Romance languages, of course; yet as carriers of unconscious knowledge and creative expression, they could hardly be more apt. I'll have a little bit more to say about the language later, and I still have to study it thoroughly myself. But here is how it translates into poetry.

Thought-Bird Song

Enaji o J tumba
Reset-il a baragey
So tem responde
Sol tu detum
Som ambto site
Curiabus ta
Nimbo.

The birds outside my window
Are your thoughts sent to me.
They come flying; fledglings.
I feed them bread crumbs
So they do not go hungry,
Then they perch on the tree branch
With beaks open, singing:

Fra maronde taba
Usa filnoberi
Java sumbarabi
Lito tu sumba.
Gravi tumari
Silvo un domartum
Ilna sevento marro
Il no barijeti. Tu a
Me atum.

We come from the nest
Of yesterday and tomorrow.
God bless our journey.
We have flown from the inside
To the outside
World of your knowledge.
The cage door is wide open.
We burst out singing.
We fill all the treetops.

Sal Fra tambo
Til sa framago
Ta to tum.
Ilna illita. Reumbra
Framago. Tiombreago
Te mon de.
Allita.
Tomage.
Ilno tomage.

Splendid and glowing,
Tiny as tree bells
We dance on the tree branches
Night and day always.
Listen to us. Feed us.
We are your thoughts winging
Out of the nest of the birth-cage
Into summer and winter.
We perch on the branches
Of the minutes and seconds.

Ra bing tomage zee.   Our song is your heartbeat.
Lin deova   We move with your pulses.
Lin framadeo   You send us out perfect and shining,
Te olage. Framage   Each living and different
Tu amba.   To populate your kingdom.
          We sing outside your window
          And line up on the rooftops.

Jo solaris nefti   Separate and knowing
Enaande   We peer through the branches,
E O responde heri.   Surveying the inner
Fromage. Tu um tomorro Land of enchantment,
De a linagu frimba   The skyless and timeless
Tal toss severage ne   World of our birth.
Ne ray o marro
Ti a bra.

So jari ne remarro   We fly from our perches
Severandi newmarro Back and forth to our first nest,
Fra to tiara. Umbarge Vanishing inside
Desta. Nea desta.   The cage of your head,
Nea tumbo.   Then we fly out again
Tel to neambo   And sing at your window
Desta mora.   While you feed us bread crumbs
          From your hand.

   You might have noticed how much longer the third verse of *Thought-Bird Song* is than the original Sumari. I don't know how such a long stanza came out of a shorter one, but I do know that the Sumari did contain the "extra" meanings. Each verse is actually like a Rosetta Stone, though, because each Sumari stanza has meanings on various levels. Several layers of meaning are nested one within the other, so that actually the same Sumari words would have to be translated two or three times, to get one "full" song or poem. I think that more ancient songs still lie buried in *Thought-Bird Song* and many others, waiting till I translate them.

   As it is, I have to be in a very particular state of consciousness to get these verses; acutely focused, a part of me very passive and receptive while another part listens intensely to messages that seem to come beneath sound—from rhythm and inaudible sound patterns. As mentioned, sometimes these come too fast or slow for me to follow, but they usually emerge into the verses in a certain poised fashion. Often I may have the radio on, turned way down low, playing rock music. I think that unconsciously I use the music as a signal from the usual level of consciousness, and work my way "down" so many layers beneath it.

Someday I hope to do a whole book of Sumari poetry and other material and study the realms of Sumari words and diagrams that I already have. Certain things are already clear. Words or names change according to their relationships. The word for, say, pear tree, is different according to the aspects of the tree being considered, its relationships as a word in the sentence and as an object in space. In Sumari, object words—nouns—often disappear into verbs.

Here is *Song of the Pear Tree:*

Tul a frumage	*The pear tree grows*
Splendor a traum	*From the sweet pits*
Deliniage betum.	*Of your feeling,*
Ignor te a deus	*Sunken in the secret ground*
Grim a frundi	*Of your being.*
Glow in a tua	*It grows in the silence*
Sev er indo.	*Of atom and evening.*
Tel r	*It grows in the knowledge*
Tel e o	*Of your unknowing*
E nater um.	*And blossoms in the clear*
	Air of earth morning.
Le lo terume	*The pear tree stands*
La lay terum a	*Dazzling and glowing,*
Silva en a durum	*The fruit of your love*
Mag dur in e a	*Made living,*
Long de j de	*A gift to the seasons*
Marro.	*From the orchard of feeling,*
Gr pa deja nor.	*The atom's love,*
La ne sev silnor	*Multiplied.*
De naje or day ney.	

Deja a bonde
Sevra nev andu
Ignor ra france
Le a ray vetum.
Taj ja na more
Splen de a moribus
Grundi. Mespania
O ne a fra bundi
Meo.

Each leaf sings your praises.
The air is your breath
Through which each leaf dances.
As your love climbs
The steps of your spine
And blossoms in syllables
And images,
So your love flows, invisible,
Outside the window,
And rushes up hollow paths
Of air.

Say ja dor remi
Vem erage soldi nesta
Gromage teri tom to a
Is panita tor teritum
Sta veri ende
O nana par ser en dra
Ilna tor resteri
Teratum is ner o onta.

Your love charms the trees
Into growing
And carves living plants
Out of unknowing.
The pear tree and all trees
Grow
From the trance of your love.

Song of the Pear Tree in its own way is saying the same thing about the nature of reality that the Seth Material does, but it comes in at a completely different angle and views our usual environment from the approach of still another level of awareness.

Even as I am typing this manuscript, some of the deeper meanings of the poem have come to me. "Tul a frumage" is translated as "The pear tree grows," for example. Here, "tul" means pear tree specifically, but also as a member of its class and refers to other fruit-bearing trees as well. The word has to be considered along with its relationship with "frumage" which literally means "harvesting earth-self."

In the first line of the second verse, "Le lo terume" translates into "The pear tree stands." Here the literal meaning is "earth grows itself into a tree and becomes standing-earth-with-pear-faces," and the word, pear, comes from "ter" of terume.

The same kind of thing happens beneath all the words of the song as translated. "Ignor te a deus," in the first verse translates as "Sunken in the secret ground of your being" but that meaning springs from the deeper translation of the phrase. Literally it means "Gods closing their eyes" and the meaning or assumption underneath is this: When we, as gods, close our eyes in resting, we dream "our" lives, which live, and forget our god-selves. Our being is then secret from ourselves.

In the following, *Song of the Silver Brothers,* I came closest to one of the ancient songs, I think, even though this one began in a normal state of consciousness. I started it as a poem to Rob, but by the time I'd finished the first verse, I lapsed into Sumari. From then on I got a Sumari verse, then its translation, then another Sumari verse, and so forth. Yet in the middle of the poem two verses of translation came, without the Sumari. So far, this is the only time that has happened.

As I read the poem now, I know it is a rich source of inner meanings. Each word as given opens up. It will take some time to uncover the song's hidden "messages," but here, at least, is the first translation. I'm giving this poem exactly as I received it. You can read the Sumari and translation, or just read the English. Both together form their own kind of song poem, though.

Shrum Avaganda Vandita

(On one level, referring to Rob and me, this means *Our History Together.* On the next level it means *Song of the Silver Brothers.*)

> You took me to hearth and bed
> And grabbed hold
> Of more than you bargained for,
> At least in terms we knew then.
> The magic grew around our years
> Like a silver fence,
> To close or open,
> But there, sensed, a shining
> Circle of silence
> That would soon speak
> Strange tongues.
>
> Shu umba da lor
> La umbi namuta

Maja ra mar
Del turanda. Wanda.

Springing up about us,
Tongues that speak like flowers.
Moonlight strikes the night earth
Like a tuning fork. Listen:

Avar unde
Norj alota nosbi
Grec torunda
Vre badeda
Lor de a nesta.

Never lost I quieted
My rustling,
Hiding in silver shaken places,
Listening; unruffled yet
Intense in silences.

Ster a lalita
Linga nor lorunda
Far inga tol laleta
Framunge telito.

You brought me here,
Knowing and unknowing,
Children in the wizards of ourselves
Wandering secret forests.

Stella unda
Muta ar araba
Aje manage marbimba
El varroom daje

Knowing magic words
From times when beasts
And flowers, birds and rocks
Each spoke aloud
An alphabet

Rebarka munde
Del ar stel norba
Sha lor.

And held dialogues with earth
Who answered back

With birth.
Dear love,

We left living
Squiggles in the rock,
Small parts of tiny tissues,
Sliding through sunlit crevices,
Turning finally
Into fossil symbols; alphabets
That died
So languages could live.

All this history before
Our city craniums
Grew rich
With memory's ores;
Centuries overlaid
With births and deaths;
Miniature existences.
Nameless our tissues
Blinked on and off.

Sha ma a leta
Lor manda torinda
Tel jar unde
Res nes patita
Tol inda.

The sun
Stirs us now, as then.
Inching along sunlit cliffs
Of bone, we roused,
Wondering
At the light that now
Parts our bowels.

For darambi
Tol arado fromabe
Marjor astare
Fromage
O borare
Gravunde.

I speak
And syllables rearrange

My worlds;
Fossilings
Rise wiggling like seeds
To growth in words.

Gor shunda
Balika
Granunde
Gortalveri.

Unseen creatures
That we were—
Silver brothers—
Speak.

From a j stilla
Tor ande
T ej ande
De a no lel arg
Griming delmateo.
Sha veri
Silva tel a matita
Tur la vi de.

Climbing up the cliffs
Between the skull's
Bright flowers,
I sense a self
In which I, too, move
And am embedded,
Creeping through a history
As yet unspoken,
Yet with you still beside me,
And we are silver brothers.

I think that the Sumari songs tell of the birth of the
psyche as seen or experienced at various levels of awareness: some
cellular, but each further away from normal states of consciousness. More and more I'm convinced that the soul or psyche, going
into itself, finds the source of itself, uncovers its meanings and
translates these into art forms, religious and scientific frameworks

from which the self makes its own life—or in exceptional cases, from which whole civilizations are formed.

I think that in my own or any other comparable experience, we can retrace the steps from which the self is born as it rises from unconscious to conscious expression to form its alliances, civilizations, religions, arts, and sciences. I believe that this applies to each individual's development, and reflects the species' experience as well. In historic terms, we choose which set of metaphysics we want to follow, and certainly other very valid and perhaps superior roads could have been taken than our present western Christian one.

But any cultural way of looking at reality comes originally from a psychic birth, and according to its impetus, power and persuasion flourishes in our world or remains latent. I believe that when the exterior conceptual framework no longer reflects the inner psychic realizations and knowledge, it will be thrown off. Man returns to his visions and revelations, knowing instinctively that only the psyche's rich creativity can bring about new insights that will in their time coalesce into more meaningful organization.

The living psyche *is* alive. It must throw off old outworn garments and make new ones. Old gods don't die. They just fade away and others take their places. But the gods are also mirrors of the psyche. Only what *is* the psyche, and how vast is its private and mass experience, knowledge, and comprehension?

The answers lie within the psyche itself, and in our experiences with it. Belief systems are reflections of the psyche's knowledge, translated into cultural organization. Any such systems will seem self-evident to the civilization that holds them.

Briefly, I suspect that I turned aside from generally accepted systems of knowledge when they couldn't explain my private experience. In other terms, societies do the same thing. I think that the Seth Material and Sumari are also corrective, for example, in that they try to change trends now held as current beliefs.

Both, in stereo, represent elements of my psyche and

rise from it—Seth, the teacher of great presence, intellectually freer than I am, brilliantly expounding theories that I needed as an individual, and that are equally needed by the society of which I am part—and Sumari with the feminine qualities, as we think of them, bringing to the forefront the ancient priestess allegories. Seth is practical. He constantly applies revelationary material to daily life and uses it to illuminate and reorganize normal living patterns.

As you'll see later, I believe that much more is involved, but here I'm merely talking about the unconscious psyche and its powers of transformation and creativity.

Sumari metaphysics appear in the poetry and songs, then, in the guise of old manuscripts translated into modern terms. Beyond that, a system of higher mathematics is in the making—or rather, I'm in the process of receiving it. This material, incidentally, came to Rob in Sumari, but he couldn't translate it.

Other elements are still developing. As mentioned, sometimes I'll hear sounds too fast or slow to translate. My nervous system seems to be making certain adjustments, and these experiences are exhilarating and frustrating at the same time. Either it feels as if I'm trying to pick up a dialogue spoken at an incredible rate of speed, or at a rate so slow that it would take a century for a sentence to end. I've tried to translate such material, sometimes in Seth sessions, with varying degrees of success.

All of these developments appeared nearly full-blown within a month. I began speaking Sumari in my sleep. So did some of my students. Sometimes I'd feel the Sumari level of consciousness early in the day, tune into it, and receive and translate three or four songs. There were many Sumari dramas in class, with two voices predominant; the lilting female one and the much deeper male-sounding one.

I'm writing about the beginning of Sumari with the benefit of hindsight. At the time I was wondering about the purpose of the language and the implications of the phenomenon itself. We had several Seth sessions on the subject (asking one level of consciousness what was happening at another level). Consciously, I was more than pleased with the increase in creativity, and as always, I took this enrichment of normal life to mean that the inner events were beneficial.

And Seth began to organize and explain Sumari. I trusted Seth, so I also trusted his interpretation. In one session, the 599th, on December 8, 1971, he compared the Sumari language to a bridge. In that session he said:

> *In your work with me, various kinds of teaching methods will be provided. Steps and bridges will be used.*
>
> *It is senseless to ask whether or not a bridge is true. It exists. It gets you somewhere. A bridge is a valid reality, regardless of its architecture or the type of symbols that may be written upon it, or its color, or the material from which it is made. The Sumari language is a bridge and valid in those terms. It will lead you into the use of the inner senses, away from the confining nature of pet phrases and familiar language that is already loaded with its own connotations.*
>
> *The Sumari language is a bridge, then, in those terms; a method of communication. It is the beginning of a logically unstructured vehicle that will carry you, hopefully, into the inner heart of perception. I hope that eventually it will allow you to experience more fully the inner cognizance that is beneath physical perception and physical translation.*
>
> *A bridge serves both coming and going, and carries goods in both directions. The Sumari language in those terms will be used as a method of carrying you further into the nature of inner cognizance, and then allowing you to return again, retranslating what you have learned, but not automatically, into stereotyped verbal patterns. The language will effectively block the automatic translation of inner experience into stereotypes, therefore.*

Seth went on to give some evocative material on the nature of alphabets in general and the birth of languages. I'll be studying that material when I start trying to decipher all the Sumari that is accumulating, both tapes and manuscripts. Rather characteristically, Seth added, "Sumari will be used as a method of expanding your concepts, not of teaching you to translate experience into just another but different stereotyped form that happens to be more exclusive."

In the next, 600th session, he spoke about the *sounds* of Sumari as being important apart from the meanings given any particular words.

> *The sounds used in the language have their own importance and will be in their own way representative or suggestive of feelings that have been largely unconscious. The feelings, however, are the tail end of inner cognizance, and we will use the sounds to carry us further into inner landscapes where both objects and their representatives must finally desert us. We will be using the language so that we can finally cease using it, in other words. These will be the beginnings of somewhat more profound methods of working through the inner senses.*

In this session, too, Seth discussed alphabets, and gave some Sumari words with their equivalents: " 'shambaline" connotes the changing faces that the inner self adopts through its various experiences. This is a word that hints of relationships for which you have no word in *your* language; 'shambalina garapharti,' then, becomes 'the changing faces of the soul smile and laugh at each other'—all that is in the one phrase."

Returning to the sound values, Seth said again that there was a structure to the Sumari language, but it wasn't the kind we were used to. "Some of its effectiveness has to do with the synchronization of its rhythms with bodily rhythm. The sounds themselves activate portions of the brain not usually used in any conscious manner. It is a disciplined language in that spontaneity has a far greater order than any [order] you recognize."

Seth had used the Sumari word "cordella" frequently, as a kind of master alphabet. Here he elaborated:

> *Cordellas are invisible symbols that surface. As they do, they show the universe in a new light by the very nature of their relationships. In a very limited fashion, alphabets do the same thing, for once you have accepted certain basic verbal symbols they impose their discipline even upon your thoughts . . . and throw their particular light upon the reality you perceive.*

*Alphabets are nevertheless tools that shape and direct per-
ception. They are groups of relationships that you transpose upon
"reality." To this extent they shape your conceptions of the world
that you know. Their discipline and rigidity is considerable. Once
you think of a "tree" as a tree, it takes great effort before you can
see it freshly again, as a living individual entity.*

*Cordellas do not have the same rigidity. Inner invisible rela-
tionships are allowed to rise, [with] the acknowledged recognized
reality viewed through the lenses of these emerging relationships.*

Seth went considerably further here, saying that there
were cordellas of the senses: "It is as if you had alphabets that
worked for the senses, for touch and smell. Meanings are allowed
to rise and fall where, using your established ideas of language,
meanings are rigidly attached to given experiences, so that perception must be held within well-defined limits."

At the time we didn't quite understand Seth's reference
to cordellas and the senses (though later, as you'll see, we did make
some important correlations). But *was* Sumari a language, and if
so, in what terms? "In your terms," Seth said, "the Sumari language is not a language, since it was not spoken verbally by any
group of people in your history. In quite different terms, it *is* a
language that is at the base of all languages, and from which all
languages spring.

*In your terms, alphabets do not change, or you would con-
sider them relatively useless. Cordellas do change. Alphabets are
the physical aspect of cordellas. One small aspect of a cordella is
seized upon and frozen, so to speak, its ordinary motion and the
rhythm of its changes therefore become unrecognized.*

*The living vitality of the cordella rises out of the universe's
need to express and understand itself, to form in ever-changing
patterns and take itself by surprise. Patterned language allows for
no such surprises. The Sumari language is used in the dream state.
The language itself seeks out meanings. It is hidden within all
langvages, whether or not they sound at all similar . . . .*

*It builds up from feelings that are by their nature denied
clear expression through the specific but therefore limiting alphabet systems. It allos the perceiver to face experience more closely,
and having done this to some extent, he is free in other areas also.*

The last paragraph in that session really hit home to me, though, and helped me understand what Seth meant by the cordella and its application to the Sumari language. He said,

> *If you were an accomplished artist in many fields, you could translate a given feeling into a painting, a poem, a musical master-piece, a sculpture, a novel, an opera, and into a great work of architecture. You would be able to perceive and feel the experience with greater dimension, for your expression would not be limited to translating it automatically, without choice, into one specific area. So a cordella, as opposed to an alphabet, opens up greater varieties of experience and expression.*
>
> *Cordellas represent the ever-changing unfinished relationships that can never be fully expressed, yet constantly seek expression.*

Certainly such multi-expression is used often now in class, and I think it began just about the time Seth gave this session. He'll make a certain statement. Then I'll "go into Sumari," and through a Sumari song express the same statement in a different way. Often Seth will comment, and each expression brings out different aspects of the same point.

The Sumari development and these sessions took us through that winter of 1971 and into 1972. I was working on my autobiography and the book about class experiences at the same time, and we were spending Sundays with Rob's mother. By the end of January, we decided that we just had to take some time out, and we went to Florida during February.

I thought that enough new developments had taken place to last me a lifetime. Yet on our return, I could feel that odd stirring, and disconnected but definite inner series of events that I've learned to recognize. More was on its way. But more of *what?*

9

Oversoul Seven and the Birth of "Aspects"

It was unusually cold in Florida that winter. Our cabin was one of perhaps twenty in an area about equally divided between trailers and cabins; an unfashionable place but quite utilitarian, inhabited mostly by local fishermen and some construction crews who were working on a nearby bridge. I took my manuscripts with me. Though we were in the Florida Keys, we needed a heater, and it wasn't warm enough to swim.

When we drove back home, we found the remnants of an eighteen-inch snowfall. Two of my students had lived in our apartments and taken care of our cats and plants when we were gone. So the first thing I did was reorganize everything, making the place ours again. Only a few days later, the galley proofs came for *Seth Speaks,* and Rob and I settled down to correct them.

The night of March 13 was cold and windy. We were proofreading. I looked over at Rob, struck by the intimacy of the domestic scene; the both of us, working; the cats asleep on the blue rug; the evening shadows just descending. I went over and kissed Rob's forehead. As I did, the oddest sensation caught my attention. Something different was happening in my consciousness, but what was it? I was tempted to ignore it—we had so much work to do—but I've trained myself to be alert to my subjective states. So I waited for a few minutes, then mentioned my feeling to Rob.

In the meantime the cats woke up. They wandered over, looking for attention. Rob suggested that we take them in the other room so they wouldn't distract me, so we went into the large living room, with the cats behind us. I was going to trick them; go just inside then close the door quickly. Instead, I went to the window and nonchalantly glanced outside. Instantly I became transfixed. I saw the corner intersection below with a clarity literally astounding to me at the time; as if I'd never seen it or any other corner before in my whole life. The entire scene was endowed with a rushing vitality impossible to describe.

I couldn't take my eyes off the sight, and I could hardly speak. Rob realized that something was happening. He went to get the recorder and set it up beside me. I hardly knew it. For four hours such an ecstasy filled me that I was lost in the scene below: the few inches of snow; the car lights swooping through the darkness; the exquisite private shadows all endowed with a superlife that evades all words.

My stomach swooped as each car went over the very small rise in the road just beneath the traffic light; I never even realized there was a rise there before. I cried out with unabashed joy many times, caught in surprise by a new shadow or the sudden motion of a telephone wire. I'd never seen such brilliant colors, except twice in out-of-body states. It seemed as if the world had been flat before. Now colors had hills and valleys and depths and distances inside themselves. The field across the street bristled; the snow was like a live sponge, responsive to everything. When headlights swept across this living snow, I could hardly bear it.

As cars passed, I was aware of some positive relationship between each of them—elastic, I think—and I felt the air changes that happened between one car and another; the abrupt yet perfect alterations in all this as one car turned; and the oneness of this motion with all the other motion simultaneously occurring.

Yet the highlight of the experience involved a piece of crumpled newspaper that kept blowing in the wind. I was kinetically a part of its flights, and while it was impossible for me to describe my feelings at the time, later the event became part of a poem. While I was actually watching the paper move, all I could say was, "Wow . . . oh, incredible." One day a year later, though, while I was writing, the episode came back to me, only I was separated enough from it to descirbe it. These three verses from *Dialogues of the Soul and Mortal Self in Time* explain what I mean.

The Paper

But wait—
I see a piece of paper
outside the window
in the street.
Oh watch it move,
surfing in the waves of air,
just waiting for the highest surge
and jumping in
or leaping up the shining hills of space
and flying down
the valley side.

It lands by a blue dark shadow
that isn't flat at all,
but a smooth, cool and secret
creature brought to life
by the moment's
wind and light.
Oh, shadow, brilliant
and dark at once,
how dear you are in this
bright instant
of the universe.
Now, oh now the paper moves,
I swear by its own accord.

It wants
to feel the breeze beneath it push
and thrills to give its own response.

Oh watch it go,
skimming like a floppy butterfly,
wings flapping,
touching, but not quite touching
the walk
and lifted up again,
dizzy, delirious,
its own sounds crackling
against its undersides
and the air rubbing
upon its edges
with a muted twang.
If that paper moves again,
I think I'll die.
I swear I can't look
any longer
or I'll take leave
of all my sense.

I was in a heightened state of consciousness, for that matter, when I wrote the poem, but then inspiration and words were wedded. In the original experience, words were so inadequate that I should have been terribly frustrated. Instead, I felt myself in a world where words had no application. Rob kept trying to get something definite down on tape, for example, so he asked questions now and then.

His questions made no sense to me; that is, in my state of consciousness they were basically meaningless. I understood them, the words and what they meant, but they just didn't apply to where I was. All Rob got on tape is four hours of "oh's," "ah's," wow's," and excited breathing.

For about a week afterward, I'd suddenly see the world in this super-real fashion, and feel a part of everything I saw. I felt regenerated, and wondered if the experience would splash over to other aspects of my life in any way. A few nights later, on March 19, I woke up with the feeling that I'd had a terrific dream, filled with some kind of new creativity, but I couldn't recall anything else about it. Two nights later the same thing happened. I recorded both instances in my dream notebook and forgot about them.

For one thing, Tam Mossman, my editor, was driving up to discuss the publication of the book about our class experiences. My mind was on that manuscript, which was partially completed. I was trying to get it into shape, and it was stacked on my desk. At the same time I was planning a dinner for company, and straightening the house up. On March 23, the day Tam was to arrive, I was bustling about and paused to dust my desk when a few lines popped into my mind. I shrugged, and wrote them down:

> *Oversoul Seven grimaced at Cyprus and began the examination. "Let's see," he said. "In Earth terms, using an analogy, I'm a man on Wednesday and Friday, a woman on Sunday and Thursday, and have the rest of the time off for independent study."*

Now, what was that supposed to mean? I wondered. I shoved the note aside and went about my housework. About an hour later I felt an impluse to go to my desk. Somewhat confused, I stood there for a moment. What had I wanted to do? My book manuscript was stacked and ready; Tam would arrive shortly; it was time to fix dinner. Still I stood there, growing more puzzled. Then a few more sentences came into my mind that obviously belonged with what I'd written before. I scribbled these down, and two more pages.

The lines "just came," seemingly from nowhere. They read like the beginning of a novel, I thought, which was odd: A novel was furthest from my mind just then, and all my attention was devoted to the book about class. Tam was coming particularly to discuss it. The passages were terrific in their way, though, so I showed them to Rob and then forgot about them.

Tam arrived. As our business discussion began, he said that he didn't think the time was right for the class book. *Seth*

Speaks hadn't come out yet, and sales of *The Seth Material* were all we had to go by. More than that, as we talked I realized that I didn't feel happy with the manuscript at all. I still couldn't explain some of the class events to my satisfaction. (In fact, not until the beginning of Aspects and this book was I able to handle that material.) The autobiography I'd begun wasn't nearly ready to show. It seemed that I'd hit a momentary impasse.

Something Tam said reminded me of the two scribbled pages I'd done earlier. It was Rob who suggested that I show the material to Tam, so laughing, I told him about the idea and instead of a neatly typed manuscript, I handed him two messy sheets of paper, entitled *The Education of Oversoul Seven*.

Tam was intrigued. As we talked, excitedly, I realized that I'd wanted to get back to fiction for a change. I hadn't wanted to do the class book—not then, at least. Yet I *did* want a contract. Those scribbled pages solved a dilemma that consciously I'd tried to ignore.

In the next four days I had three chapters done. I just sat down, and the words came into my head as quickly as I could write them down. The book was definitely coming from a different level of consciousness than usual, though I took it down in my normal state. Any attempt to tamper with it from another level loused it up. For instance, whenever I tried to "improve" a passage by re-writing, to add "depth," it lost its original force. Or sometimes I thought a chapter would end one way, but it ended another way. I learned to go on faith with it, write down what I got, and leave it alone otherwise.

The vocabulary was very simple, yet lucid. In the beginning I worried about the childlike aspects of some of the scenes, but as the book continued, I saw that these had their own sparkling seamless quality.

The book spilled over into my dreams. Whole chapters came in the dream state. I only had to write them down in the morning. Oversoul Seven, the main character, attained his own kind of reality for me. When I sat down to write, I'd ask him, mentally, for the next chapter—and there it was, the words as polished and brilliant as river pebbles, slipping into my mind. I never "saw" Seven, yet he seemed beautifully immediate, and accessible. I ended up asking his advice on various personal matters, and his answers came as the book did, through writing. I was easy with him, and for a while anyway, I didn't worry about the nature of his reality.

Seven was free! No one was going to write him as they did Seth, asking for help with personal problems. Because . . . , well because Seven was just a fictional character. Wasn't he? He sure as the devil was, and I was going to keep him that way. But Cyprus, Seven's teacher in the book, was something else again.

I recognized her the first time she appeared in the book: She was the personality that I felt I was when I sang Sumari. In fact, as the book wrote itself, it described an ancient civilization which used a system of mathematics already familiar to me—the same system I was getting in Sumari and trying to translate. In some places, Sumari poems were to be inserted. Others, used in the book, came to me on the spot. Seth's "Speakers" also turned up in *Oversoul Seven.*

While all this was going on, I enjoyed the fullest creative and psychic freedom. Seth had already begun dictating *his* next book, *The Nature of Personal Reality,* in our regular sessions. But I couldn't wait to get to *Seven* each day. The book was certainly pointing out the concept of simultaneous time, and in the funniest fashion. One day I might get Chapter Ten, and the next day, Chapter Five. I never knew what was going to happen to the characters. If I knew where they were in, say, Chapter Nineteen, I didn't know how they got there, because I didn't have Seventeen or Eighteen yet.

Yet in *our* time, other events intruded. My mother was very ill. She lived in another part of the state, and I hadn't seen *her* in years either. My aunt notified me of her illness about two days before I was to speak at a nearby college. It was the first speaking engagement I'd accepted in ages. I'd also accepted a second one, set for the week after the first. Both had been set up months in advance.

The first engagement gave me my largest face-to-face audience to date. I'd been asked to speak by the head of the philosophy department. Five hundred college students crowded together in a garishly lit arena. I'd made it clear, as always, that I would lecture or answer questions but not have a Seth session. This gives me freedom. If Seth wants to "come through" and the time seems right, then it's an extra. Actually, this has only happened twice, and when Seth did speak (both times on television) he did so with great effectiveness. But I'm a writer, not a performer, so I'd made all this quite clear.

But as I discovered later, this fine open-minded academician had set me up.

While pretending to agree and understand, the professor stacked the audience with students prepared with prearranged, numbered questions. Each question was "stiffer and more critical" than the last. As he explained to his students ahead of time, I was to be driven up the wall so that I would *need* Seth—whoever or whatever he was—to bail me out.

The professor took it for granted that these witty questions would just be so devastating that I'd have no other recourse. He had a lot to learn. Besides this, in an amusing turnabout, he had half of the students concentrating as hard as they could, saying, "There is no Seth," while the other half sent mental messages telling me to let Seth come through and prove the first group wrong.

During dinner with this gallant gentleman of intrigue, and another professor, I started to grow uneasy. So did Rob. Our hosts chatted, all collegiate gentility, and it was hard to pay attention to the topside of events where everything seemed hunky-dory, and to the sensed underside, where it all felt wrong. As soon as I began to speak though, and was faced with all those students and the contradictory mental messages, I was furious. The atmosphere would have been obvious even to a psychic idiot.

I wasn't consciously aware of the specific messages being sent, only of the charged emotions and the basic setup. I felt Seth around, too, and knew he'd go along with whatever I decided. I decided no. Instead, I dipped into another level of awareness. A sort of Sumari smoothness slipped over me. Speaking, I'd never been so gracious. The questions were answered with unperturbed ease. There were also people there not in on the professor's game, of course, and I more or less addressed myself to them. Later, at a party, some of the students sheepishly told me what had been involved.

Certainly such an attitude isn't prevalent at most colleges; far from it. Yet it was indicative of what is loosely thought of as the intellectual-critical framework—at its worst. The true intellectual or scientist is open-minded. I was upset, though, because I'd expected a philosophy professor to be curious about philosophies and ideas and intellectually and creatively vigorous.

As a young writer in college, at least my abilities had been respected. "You've come a long way, Baby," I thought. "Look what the colleges think of you now." And when I got through being angry I saw for the first time how limiting established education *can* be; not that it has to be that way; or that it always is.

The second engagement came about a week later. The day before, my mother died, rather unexpectedly. We were just beginning creative writing class when the phone call came.

There was nothing I could do, so I held the class anyway. The lecture had been scheduled months in advance, too, and I hated to disappoint all those people. The meeting was in a city several hours away, so Rob and I left early the next morning.

I had no conscious foreknowledge of my mother's death, incidentally. Yet two nights earlier I had a dream experience, rather frightening, in which I was falling and calling out for help, and awoke knowing that this was the reflection of someone else's experience. That morning, the entire dream appeared in the *Oversoul Seven* manuscript, in the chapter in which Lydia, one of the main characters, dies. The dream in the book is Seven's. The entire chapter involving that character's death, was written the day before my mother died.

It was early May, and I actually enjoyed the ride across state. Everything seemed brilliant and alive from our side of creaturehood, as I wondered what my mother was experiencing on that other side that seems so effectively closed to our vision.

Then: the lecture. This was a religiously oriented organization. I was greeted by people who really wanted to hear me speak. I was struck by their desire to help themselves and others. These were well-meaning, serious men and women. They believed in the survival of personality after death, and I was their latest evidence. Seth was a spirit guide in their most conventional of terms; a "good" spirit who also protected me from the "bad" ones; someone who was spiritually evolved, yet available to solve personal problems; a combination guardian angel, father figure, and bodiless knight-in-spiritual-armor all at once.

In the meantime, my own experiences with Sumari and Oversoul Seven were intensifying my own questions. Many of these people didn't want me to question, though; and to that extent I made them uneasy. Fraud or saint? Knowing I was exaggerating to some degree, it still seemed that my experiences put me in one category or the other, according to peoples' beliefs. For me, these two speaking engagements represented the two opposing belief systems in which psychic events are usually considered. I didn't know what I *was* going to do, but I knew I wouldn't operate within either of those two frameworks.

No matter how often I said, "Look, we don't know enough about the nature of consciousness or reality yet to understand our own personalities, much less a Seth," some people would consider him almost omnipotent. That reaction bothered me deeply. Others would bring up unconscious fraud. Good God, I thought, people forsake all sense when confronted with anything they don't understand. But—I myself was still caught in the same framework, or the lectures wouldn't have impressed me in just that way.

In the meantime, I was finishing *Oversoul Seven*. Now I was concerned not only with the nature of the reality of Seth and Seth Two: How real—in our terms—were Sumari, Cyprus, and Seven? Where did all these experiences fit into *any* concepts about human personality? They just didn't; at least not to me. Not only was I speaking for Seth and delivering his books in the trance state, but I was speaking and singing in Sumari, writing poetry in Sumari and translating it, and writing *Oversoul Seven*. I was using at least seven separate levels of consciousness and juggling them, really, with relative ease. My sphere of operation was certainly expanding. But something had to expand in my world of concepts.

I don't know how many hours I spent trying to find answers that were acceptable to me. By the end of June I'd finished *Seven*, and was ready to type the final manuscript. The book had only taken me three months to write. My mind was on that, not on any questions, when one night I was suddenly presented with just what I needed—a new framework, or at least the beginning of one.

I was looking at the *Seven* manuscript. Writing it had been such fun that I was almost sorry it was finished. The next minute I recognized a certain acceleration of consciousness with which I'm familiar, and I knew that there would be six more Oversoul books if I wanted them. A rough outline for the entire series rushed into my mind. "In a flash" I saw the separate books, what they involved, and how each would fit into the overall pattern.

I was still surprised and astonished at this new creative material. I was writing notes as fast as I could when I felt my consciousness accelerate still further. Within a few moments, Aspects was "born."

Everything clicked and fell into place. I saw Seth,

Seth Two, the Sumari, Cyprus and Seven—and myself—as Aspects of a single but multidimensional entity or consciousness. I wrote down what was coming to me in big excited scribbles, abbreviating words wherever I could, as insight followed insight for some three hours. What I learned is actually just now emerging in our time because the initial experience contained the germs of this present book.

Here are a few excerpts of those original unedited notes:

"All of these personalities have to be considered as Aspects of the entity, and this includes my personality which is the present physical one . . . from which I am viewing these other Aspects of myself, through a kind of psychological window."

"I travel through my psyche, using it as a window, postulating, of course, the extra I who disconnects itself from the usual I to do the traveling."

"Traveling through the psyche this way automatically means moving through time, which is a different kind of 'Structure.' "

"Seth, Seth Two, Cyprus and even Seven are all Aspects, then, of one multidimensional entity. Because of my own abilities, I'm able to tune into these Aspects better than most people, but they represent the 'components' of personality and the portions of our being that exist outside of our three-dimensional framework."

"Signs of these Aspects appear sometimes in 'normal' behavior as uncharacteristic or odd moods or emotions; creative productions, daydreams, and so forth. (They may sometimes be picked up through use of a Ouija board where they will often be interpreted as guides, etc.)"

"As I bring these Aspects back through my psychological window, are they automatically personified by the rich stuff of the psyche? What relationship does such a personification have to the original Aspect it represents?"

"Our current concepts so limit our understanding of ourselves that we, in turn, limit our own experience to fit. Any communications or hints from Aspects then seem unnatural, supernatural, or signs of mental disorder."

"Would a Seth, experiencing a Jane, think of her as a lesser developed personality? Maybe. But just maybe, he'd think of her as one with great potential, to be encouraged so that in time terms he could emerge. He would be me in my present time, developing abilities that would later let him be him. He would be communicating with me in my time from my future—his present."

"Our greater consciousness or "source self" dips in and out of time and has existences in other dimensions, showering Aspects of itself out in all directions. These Aspects are alive, active, but latent in each of us, where their abilities help form the stuff of our own personalities. They aren't dominant here but they are in their own realities, though perhaps in ways difficult for us to understand."

I ended up with over twenty pages of notes that night, but here I've just included a few basic ideas. I was dazed by some of the implications I sensed, and already filled with questions. Still, when the evening was over, I felt triumphant. At least I was on my way to some kind of theory that would make sense of my own experience.

If I was caught up in a flood of creative activity, Rob and I were about to become involved in a flood of a different kind. The night after the origin of Aspects, we were hit by the Agnes Flood of 1972. I finished typing *Seven* while the whole place was in turmoil. Ten feet of water filled the downstairs while Rob and I watched from our second floor. There was no drinkable water without boiling, no heat, no hot baths, and mud all over. Our flooded car looked like a prehistoric monster, its hulk buried in piles of mud.

We turned over one of our apartments to a couple who had been flooded out of their home. Seth had just begun his second book, *The Nature Of Personal Reality: A Seth Book,* but even that had to wait till we regained our privacy. As our lives returned to normal, we resumed the Seth sessions, and every once in a while I'd feel my "Aspects" channel open and I'd take down a raft of notes that seemed to just come out of thin air.

In the meantime I began to have a series of "psychic" experiences that followed one after the other. Some came as I followed the instructions Seth was giving in *Personal Reality.* The affair started one night when I suddenly began writing what I thought was a short group of poems called *Dialogues of the Soul and Mortal Self in Time.* Instead, the poems evolved into an entire book and often the questions asked by the mortal self (which were mine, of course) were answered through a "psyche-delic" experience which was then explained by the Soul.

No sooner was that book finished than my "Aspects" channel opened again, and in the summer of 1973 the body of the theory came to me in various altered states of consciousness. The rest of this book, then, will serve as an introduction to Aspect Psychology. I present it as a conceptual framework in which our experiences, intuitions, psychic abilities, and most deeply creative endeavors can be considered and explored.

I see Aspect Psychology as a way of looking at life and of viewing personality in its physical and nonphysical aspects. Obviously then, this is my version of reality, as experienced through several layers of the psyche. I am not offering it as The Truth, but as a means of discovering what the truths of ourselves are.

I don't present Aspects as a dogma, but as a means of cutting through dogmas. At the same time, I'm going to refrain as much as possible from using phrases like "It seems to me," or "perhaps this is so," or other qualifying statements. Obviously Aspects *is* the way reality appears to me.

There are some new terms, not too many, and I am including them in a glossary at the end of the book for handy reference.

PART TWO

AN INTRODUCTION TO ASPECT PSYCHOLOGY

10

The Source Self. The Focus (or Particle) Personality, Aspects and Personagrams

From beyond the boundaries of the known self, intuitions, creativity, precognitive information and revelatory knowledge spring into our experience. Our nightly dreams also provide dramas of multidimensional nature, in which the known and unknown selves meet.

The known self perceives its reality in creaturehood. It focuses its attention upon the physical world which is the three-dimensional reflection of its own kind of consciousness; a consciousness deflected and sifted through a molecular lens.

This conscious self is only one aspect of our greater reality, however; the part that springs into earthknowing. It can be called the "focus personality," because through it we perceive our three-dimensional life. It contains within it, however, traces of the unknown or "source self" out of which it constantly emerges.

The source self is the fountainhead of our present physical being, but it exists outside of that frame of reference. We are earth versions of ourselves, beautifully tuned into corporal experience. Our known consciousness is filtered through perceptive mechanisms that are a part of what they perceive. We are the instruments through which we know the earth.

In other terms, we are particles of energy, flowing from the source self into physical materialization. Each source self forms many such particles or "Aspect selves" that impinge upon three-dimensional reality, striking our space-time continuum. Others are not physical at all, but have their existence in completely different systems of reality. Each Aspect self is connected to the other, however, through the common experience of the source self, and can to some degree draw on the knowledge, abilities, and perceptions of the other Aspects.

Psychologically, these other Aspects appear within the known self as personality traits, characteristics, and talents that are uniquely ours. The individual is the particle or focus personality, formed by the intersection of the unknown self with space and time. We can follow any of our traits or emotions back to this source self, or at least to a recognition of its existence. I believe that we can also use the Aspects of this source self within us to expand our conscious knowledge and experience.

Human personality is not dead-ended and static. It is, instead, ever-changing, psychically charged individualized energy, personified in creaturehood. Inherently it also possesses the perceptive freedom of the source self, which means that to some extent, it is free of space and time.

The unknown or source self can be thought of as an entity, a personified energy gestalt—energy that knows itself—that creates and then perceives itself through experience, as it constantly sends "waves" of itself into dimensional activity. These energy waves, striking our system, form the individual "particle" with its focus (of particle) personality. The energy waves bounce back and forth, to and from the source self, so that there is constant interaction.

The individual focus personalities—you and I—also replenish the energy source by our experiencing. Our activities create fresh energy waves that keep making a pathway between it and us; habitual and maybe mathematically predictable exchanges that are active during our lifetimes, but latent; not apparent but present, both before and after.

This inflow and influx happens all the time, but we can consciously accelerate, direct it, and deliberately actualize more of the unknown self and its Aspects, not only opening up our own consciousness, but also expanding the possibilities of creature consciousness in general.

Only by recognizing our multidimensional origin can we begin to understand our life in time and space. Only in this way can we begin to understand our own psychic experiences, those for which religion and science so far have no adequate answers.

Those events with their unknown quality are precisely those that give us the greatest clues to the existence of the source self, yet they are the same ones that can also illuminate our creaturehood, and make sense of it as the brilliant focus of consciousness, impinging upon and giving life to fields of energy. These fields lie latent, unused, unknown, and fallow until they are fertilized by our kind of consciousness, which brings them into perceived reality.

There is a certain maximum focus where the source energy hits the three-dimensional field, spreading out into a pool of now, which in earth terms is, our "living area" (see Diagram 1).

This "now" happens at a certain "point" from which our experience actually spreads out in all directions. As creatures, however, we're only aware of the horizontal spread from "here to there" that appears as time.

But at either end, toward birth or death, the focus is somewhat blurred because of the angle of intersection; and in an odd way, I believe that our present causes our future and our past as well; that our experience always spreads out from the now point of intersection, forming our perception of past and future,

Diagram 1. Source self, focus personality, and Aspects

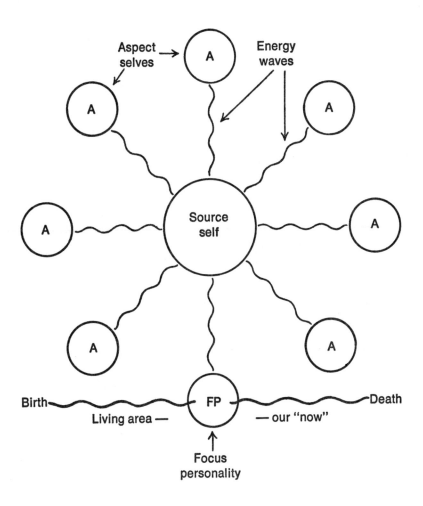

The point of intersection of the Aspect self with the living area forms the focus personality, the earth aspect of the source self in our time.

(at either end of the now intersection point). Because of our corporal reality, we experience birth first and death last, but this may have little to do with the basic phenomenon involved.

By realizing this and imaginatively placing ourselves at that intersection point, we can sense our immediate energy, unkink ourselves, and perceive our living reality as freshly emerging into us now. Instead, we usually think of ourselves as having been given a certain amount of energy at birth, which is used up by death, and not replenished in between.

In a way, the Aspects may orbit the source self while still being a part of it. Imagine a multidimensional ferris wheel, each separate section being an Aspect self. As our "seat" approaches the ground level, we're the Aspect who intersects with the space-time continuum, and life starts. But this ferris wheel moves in every possible direction, and its spokes are ever-moving waves of energy, connecting the Aspects with the center source. Each other position intersects with a different kind of reality in which it is, in turn, immersed. The spokes bud at the ends into Aspect selves, through whose experiencing the entity perceives various kinds of existence (which it creates by the intersections). Each Aspect self is connected to its source and to all other Aspect selves.

The experiencing of these separate lives enriches and changes the source self, which in turn generates new energy. Each Aspect self is an entity in miniature (or, a source self in miniature), and sends out its own spokes—Aspects of itself—into "lesser" dimensions than its own.

The Aspects, however, have complete freedom within the given dimensions of their existence. Their experience is not predestined or predetermined. Their particle nature defines both their freedom and limitations, for it is this pooling of source energy into particles (and thus boundaries) that forms the individual identity, and yet closes it off to some extent from using the entity's full abilities, which can't be actualized completely in any one system.

From our standpoint, the particle is the physical body with its focus personality immersed in three-dimensional life. The particle is formed of waves, however; the particle formation being the result of the energy waves' intersection with this field. At death, the particle breaks down, no longer illuminated or given life by the wave patterns which contain our memories and the potentiality for earth experiencing.

Again: Each individual Aspect self contains traces of the others that are a part of the same source self. Our personalities are composed psychically from trace elements of the source self, which appear "at our end" as our own unique characteristics. We may concentrate on only a few of these, so that they are our official interests and abilities. Others, however, unknown and unrecognized by us, are stressed by Aspect selves, in whom our primary concerns lie latent or in a probable state.

Since the other Aspects have a different kind of reality, however, these trace abilities or characteristics will be "earthized" in us, or appear as earth versions of tendencies that may actually be quite dissimilar in their natural state.

In the entire play of the personality, all of these Aspects or traces of the unknown self act as basic components. In most circumstances, they blend so smoothly into the formation of the personality that they are invisible and unsuspected. In our society, at least, only when some unusual psychic activity erupts do we even begin to glimpse these basic portions of the self we know.

A part of the unknown self, even if only a trace, rises to confront us. In many psychic experiences, the personality also shows some manifestation of an Aspect self, and not just traces—if not in isolated form, as with Seth—then at least illuminated and highlighted. Often such Aspects act as initiators of expansions of consciousness, so that previously inhibited psychic or creative abilities can be activated.

I think that these Aspect selves correlate with Jung's archetypes to some degree, as well as with the Greek ideas of muses and daemons. Together, they help form the personality as we understand it. Again, these basic components represent other Aspect selves, operating in different realities than ours, and each can be isolated, tuned into, magnified; its particular abilities used to enrich the personality and throw light on the source of its being.

Our interpretation of the ego and intellect has served to limit the clear function of the intellect and immobilize the ego, which I believe is far more flexible by nature, and acts as the director of these Aspects as they interact within personality.

Instead, we've allowed the ego one function only, that of directing physical focus. We believe that it must and should be left behind if we want to explore alternate states of consciousness, rather than thinking of it as a springboard for such activity. In drug or drugless manipulations of consciousness, we often imagine that we must die to ourselves in order to find ourselves.

Instead, the ego has a two fold function. Besides directing physical focus, it also receives inner perceptions—when it is allowed to; when our religious and cultural fears don't inhibit us. When the ego *does* perform this function, we usually think that it is impaired instead. Therefore, it is seldom allowed to assimilate or organize the inner material or relate it to ordinary experience. We don't give it the chance.

In other words, the ego can also use its abilities to look inward, correlate psychic experiences and psychedelic activity that might otherwise remain untranslatable. Rather than encourage such tendencies, however, we regard the ego as rigid and unyielding. Seth's material stresses this resiliency, particularly in *The Nature Of Personal Reality,* and my own experience confirms it. The ego as the known "I" can meet other Aspects of the source self.

Granted, this meeting is an opaque one. Yet whole portions of Aspect Psychology were written in altered states of consciousness, and my ego was not experienced as less. It was just acting in a different way. In fact, almost the entire Part Two of this book was produced in just such a fashion. As I wrote, I had no conscious idea which word would follow another. I wasn't pondering or even thinking in generally accepted terms. I was just taking down what came from other levels of consciousness. I sat down, felt within myself for what I call "my Aspects channel" and wrote down the words that sprang into my usual conscious awareness. I was drinking coffee, smoking, and often, listening to rock music on the radio. Egotistically I was fully aware, yet one part of my awareness was tuned to one particular station, and to some extent merged with it. It's like sitting at the threshold of yourself.

On the other hand, Chapters One through Eight were written in a more usual manner, as I related events that had already happened. Most of the material on Aspects itself came from other levels. Yet while it was coming to me, my intellect operated beautifully, automatically, going along with the intuitions rather than hampering them. At times my body was extremely relaxed, my mind passive yet poised. Now and then I'd become drowsy. Then I'd readjust my focus again, to hold the delicate balance necessary. The ego was not shunted aside, however. On the contrary, it was an active participant, though it was in a "holding position."

To some extent the ego does displace itself, but voluntarily, as a method of increasing its own knowledge.

But the ego is not a possession that we must protect at all costs. It is simply one focus of consciousness, the most familiar, accepted one. Let's see what happens to it when it comes into the field of an Aspect self. The following is simply one way of considering what may happen in a mediumistic trance of a certain kind, and is not meant to be a blanket explanation. Later we'll also explore the same subject from a different viewpoint.

Again, we'll refer to the focus personality as the entity's Aspect in our time, the one corner of it perceived in our dimensions; its three-dimensional face. A multidimensional object could not appear fully to us in our world. Certain portions of it would be invisible to us. The same applies to the entity or source self.

In say, a Seth trance, my focus personality goes out of focus on purpose, blurs through some kind of acceleration, and to varying extents takes on the characteristics of another Aspect of the entity; draws them into range where they show themselves through their effect on the physical medium. They appear on the off-focus personality, transposed on its rich psychological bed instead of on a flat screen.

The appearing Aspect is also blurred to some extent. It had to unscramble itself and rise from its own field at "the other end." It could be called the "donor Aspect," and the receiving off-focus field of the usual personality could be called the "receiving Aspect." There is at least a correlation between this and the "traps" that physicists speak of, in which the values of an electron are captured, or drawn into an unstable situation.

A like condition, a psychological trap or nest, is set up by the off-focus personality which then attracts other electromagnetic values not its own. In unfocusing, the personality disturbs its own field of activity and unbalances it enough so that perhaps it momentarily needs other values (which it is purposely withholding from itself). Therefore, it reaches out for others.

Like the electron trap, however, the personality field will only accept certain values and not others. Physicists try to "feed" such traps with various kinds of values, and don't know why they will accept some and not others.

I said that the personality, after displacing or unfocusing itself, draws or attracts other Aspects of its entity (the entity or source self and its Aspects all belonging to the same multidimensional field), but this doesn't imply that the "closest" Aspects are captured. Hidden values, electromagnetic as well as psychological, may determine the Aspects that will best fit into the displaced field.

The other-dimensional Aspect must appear superimposed on the receiving personality, which must be off center or unfocused enough to allow the juxtaposition.

Since anything more than a three-dimensional reality would be larger than life in our terms, then any glimpse we received of it, no matter how powerful it seemed to us, would be but a trace or symbol of its greater existence.

When such traces are perceived in terms of personality characteristics and are superimposed on the displaced field of the focus personality, they can be said to form "Aspect-prints"; messages written in the psyche, for example, as the wind sketches messages in sand.

The wind's scribbles in the sand are valid enough, though the wiggles and ridges may appear literally meaningless. Someone who knows how to decipher them, however, can tell the wind's direction, origin, and velocity from their arrangement. If the wind deposits alien granules of sand upon native ground, then a study of these can also tell us something about the nature of the land from which the wind blew.

In terms of the psyche, the alien personality characteristics that appear in some trances can be compared to the grains of sand carried from one location to another, or as multidimensional psychological apports that appear as strange traces transposed upon the usual personality. These Aspect-prints, taken together, form the trance personality which in this context can be called a "personagram."

Just as a telegram is composed of symbols called words, so the personagram is made of Aspect-prints that together combine to form the message. Only this message is written "on" a psychological structure by psychologically animate symbols. A telegram is inert itself; the information appears upon it, but it can't send a message or interpret its own. A personagram can.

To make this clearer: The appearance of the personagram (or trance personality) is the message, and the personality characteristics displayed are the Aspect-prints (comparable to the words in the telegram or the ridges in the sand). Only *these* Aspect-prints are charged by a psyche and formed into a living personality profile (instead of, say, a flat sketch of a face in the sand), and endowed with our kind of expression or its approximation. The personagram is a representation of certain Aspects of the entity that are "too large" to fit into our usual framework—transposed upon or within the displaced field of the receiving personality.

These psychically charged Aspect-prints form the trance personality. The more efficient the usual focus personality is at blurring its own field, the clearer our perception of the personagram will be.

The personagram, then, is an electromagnetic and psychological structure that exists potentially under certain conditions. It is a bridge personality, a unique psychological being equipped to operate between systems of reality, but its source may well be entirely outside of the three-dimensional system. It *is* a psychological apport, but dependent for its physical expression upon the receiving personality with which it merges to some extent.

When the usual personality unfocuses and scrambles its own field, reduces or minimizes its own electromagnetic values, it also takes its own charge or its "mark" away from that section of its identity field. That portion can then be impressed with the alien charges that are the Aspect-prints.

The personagram comes "to life" in our terms—or comes into our kind of life when it mixes with our type of living structure and is imprinted in our psychological field. Otherwise it remains latent. The personagram must be "read" or experienced as a highly individualized and sophisticated message, appearing through the auspices of the receiving personality.

Seth would be Seth as patterned through Jane, for example; not Jane's version of Seth, necessarily, but the Jane version of Seth. Such a personagram would have greater knowledge than we, or at least would possess a knowledge of different kinds of reality than the one we're familiar with, but it would have to be sifted through the pattern of the receiver.

The personagram then, is a multidimensional personification of another Aspect of the entity or source self, as expressed through the medium. (I am not speaking here of communications between the living and the dead, in usual terms, but of trance personalities like Seth.) I'm not implying that the usual personality just acts out psychically received information, personifying it, as an actor would. Instead, through its own displacement, the receiving personality allows these other effects to play upon its own psyche and form their Aspect-prints or personality patterns which compose the personagram, then lets these be transposed onto its own psychological field where they can be perceived and experienced.

The effects, or alien charged "particles," are assembled at this end as they fall into the receiver's field. I don't believe these Aspect-prints appear out of their own systems except when they are attracted by belief or intent on the receiver's end. The intent, psychologically and emotionally, sets up contact with electromagnetic pathways that exist whether we use them or not.

Basically these systems are open and interrelated, all Aspects of an entity or source self sharing an overall field of identity. The present personality takes in from other realities only the data it wants to handle, as it must be primarily focused here. This system is mainly concerned with the transformation of energy into physical form, according to intents set by ideas and beliefs.

As the entity or source self has many Aspects, so any one personagram could also be considered as only one larger Aspect-print in itself, of a still more extensive personagram. (The Aspect-prints, again, represent traces of another Aspect of the entity.) So one such personagram such as Seth would represent only one face of the entity; one multidimensional Aspect of many; one characteristic in the nature of a kind of entity we can hardly comprehend.

Many such personagrams, then, would be needed to show the facets of the entity or give any blueprint of its characteristics or purposes. Such a blueprint, theoretically, would provide a multidimensional psychological and psychic map or graph of the other kinds of reality in which the entity or source self has its existence.

Seth, Seth Two, Oversoul Seven, Sumari, and Helper may in my case represent first steps in forming that kind of living psychic graph or representation. Even then, certain limitations would be built-in, for any such personagrams would have to be sifted through my psyche—which would also be another Aspect, of course, of the same entity, alive in our world.

While I've used the term "displaced," my personality is not shunted aside in a Seth trance; it voluntarily steps to another position—*I* voluntarily step to another psychological position because *I* want to learn. "My" usual focus of awareness becomes peripheral while other psychological and psychic adjustments are made.

I believe that the most intimate dynamics of being are involved. Later I'll discuss the independence, origin and nature of these Aspects—as divorced from our perception of them. For now it's enough to say that I see them as mobile, ever-changing, and as contributing to our own identities and uniqueness by providing a living bank of characteristics and abilities from which each of us draw.

In my own case, I'm learning to isolate these Aspects to some degree, but I believe that Aspects are also firmly rooted in the body's integrity, expressing themselves quite naturally and constantly in the world of sense. At least a portion of this book will be concerned with the normal interaction of these Aspects in our lives, and with a few methods of utilizing them to increase the range of our own experience and consciousness.

Our present personalities, then, are Aspects of a far greater consciousness of which our individual awareness is but a part, though an inviolate one. Our personalities are composed of other Aspects, each dominant in other realities. I believe that these connect the physical and nonphysical portions of our being; the soul and the body; the known and unknown elements of our experience.

11

Basic Source Aspects

Basic source Aspects are huge power centers, main cores of the personality, containing relatively more source energy in easily accessible form. These are usually psychologically invisible, but represent one of the focus personality's greatest strengths, possessing strong organizational abilities and operating as a stabilizing factor. Such basic source Aspects represent the greatest concentrations of source energy, functionally serve as centers of the focus personality, and utilize multidimensional abilities, not having to focus themselves in corporal living. They can also accelerate energy flow.

But since these are basic source Aspects, they are the representatives in the psyche of vital Aspect selves, that do operate in other systems of reality while being held in solution or suspension here. In their own systems they are dominant focus personalities, and our characteristics lie "latent."

I believe that the source self creates a multiplicity of fields of actuality or systems that exist simultaneously, splashing or spreading out in all probable directions, so that the basic source Aspects in the psyche are reflections of Aspect selves with a greater dimensionality than our own.

If activated—like Seth—they would have to communicate through the psychic fabric of the focus personality. They would have to appear in line with our ideas of personhood, though their own reality might exist in quite different terms.

I think that I always sensed this about Seth. It wasn't that I mistrusted the Seth personality, but I felt it was a personification of something else—and that "something else" wasn't a person in our terms. It was, I felt, a consciousness different from mine, but to call Seth a spirit guide, meaning a nonphysical person in usual terms, just didn't fit to me.

Yet in an odd way I felt that he was more than that, or represented more; that his psychological reality straddled worlds in a way that I couldn't understand. I sensed a multidimensionality of personality that I couldn't define.

SETH AS A BASIC SOURCE ASPECT

As a basic source Aspect, Seth represents a multidimensional consciousness reflected through my experience; a deep part of the structure of my psyche, but also a definite personification of a multi-world or multi-reality consciousness that may well be beyond our persent ideas of personhood.

Through the focus personality's experiences these basic source Aspects perceive physical reality. In Seth's case, he's able to comment on it from his relatively freer standpoint, and can use his greater knowledge to explain it to us.

The basic source Aspect can't be actualized in this system because its reality is too big to fit. It *is* dominant at another level. But it has a living quality, patterned on our ideas of wisdom, super-existence and so forth, and is earthized in a personification that makes some kind of sense to us. Behind or within this personification is the being or consciousness that is so represented. On the one hand, it is independent in its own system; on the other, it is a basic source Aspect in the present psyche; in suspension within the focus personality, and a personification of its own greater reality.

The focus personality is like a living frame for the psyche and rises out of it. The furthest "edges" of the frame define the boundaries of the particle from an energy standpoint, and form the perspective through which we experience three-dimensional reality.

The focus personality is not static, but constantly changes the relationship of its components, with different Aspects merging or surfacing to meet physical circumstances. The multitudinous psychological and psychic components provide a basic non-predictability that is the opposite of predetermination, whether by heredity or environment.

The basic source Aspects can act as teachers, whether personified or not, appearing in the psyche as the voice of the inner self, and infusing the focus personality with additional strength and vitality in times of stress.

But what happens when one of the basic source Aspects steps out of psychological invisibility and addresses itself to the usual self? The answer depends on the beliefs of the focus personality. Sometimes only a caricature would come through, as I'll explain later.

If left alone in such circumstances, will the basic source Aspect change its characteristics? Each case would be different, but if the personification was fairly complete and living, then it would show flexibility and motion and be receptive rather than rigid. Most likely though, as with Seth, the stable characteristics provided as the basis of the personification would be retained.

One such Aspect might, however, indicate the reality of other "higher" ones that wouldn't fit into the original pattern provided by the focus personality's idealizations. In fact, the first prime Aspect might in turn act as a bridge to another "more distant" Aspect, functioning as a receiving station. In this case, it would act as a psychic or psychological base, just that much further away from the focus personality's three-dimensional home.

Seth Two could be looked at in this fashion. You could say that the focus personality activates its own components, senses the Aspects within its own psyche, and isolates them, bringing them alive to itself through personification. This establishes a base of understanding and information that the focus personality then uses to see beyond its own atmospheric conditions—the imposed time-space orientation of corporal life.

BASIC ASPECTS AS RECEIVING STATIONS

When one such "base" is established and endowed with living-like characteristics, as with Seth, then other bases can be sent out from that further point. In each case, the focus personality is sending out psychic constructs, each freer from its own physical limitations, each acting as a receiving station in turn, pulling in more information about other dimensional existence—and, something usually missed—also providing invaluable data about the structure and reaches of the human psyche itself.

Each of these basic Aspects would be personified according to the ideas of the focus personality, in line with the dimensional level being contacted. The kind of personification would tell us something, then, about that particular level of the psyche, and also about the other dimensional area of activity in which it was operating.

Since I believe at this point that these prime Aspects have their own reality outside of us, while acting here as components in the psyche, then hopefully their personifications would bear at least some resemblance to their own separate existences. It might take several such personifications, however, to contain the characteristics of a multi-person kind of being. It's very possible, for example, that Seth and Seth Two are parts of one prime Aspect, that can only be hinted at here as separate constructs.

In other cases only caricatures may come through, with the focus personality playacting at its end too much, not letting the natural creative abilities follow the inner representation, but taking the lead. Here, you would get a two-dimensional effect rather than a multidimensional one; a grotesqueness, as if a puppet were trying to be human; a lesser rather than a fuller personality.

In such instances the basic Aspect isn't allowed much freedom at all, but is worn or put on like a mask, without the flexibility to develop its own characteristics. I think that this happens in many dramatizations of "trance personalities." The vital psychic elements are clothed in all too familiar garments—the Indian guide, the monk, or the ancient soul—thus effectively blocking fuller developments.

When this happens, the prime Aspect can return to psychological invisibility again, to operate as before as a part of the whole psyche in solution or suspension, guiding indirectly rather than directly. Or it can be kept as an immature personification, undeveloped, a handy enough mechanism but one that spouts primarily the "higher" ideas of the focus personality—its best perhaps—but without the breakthrough into true psychic wisdom or knowledge.

INTERACTION OF ASPECTS IN THE PSYCHE

Whatever the circumstances, Aspects interact. They inhabit the same psychic space (the psyche), and are ever-shifting focuses or concentrations of abilities—all attributes of the source self. These Aspects or "faces" of the multidimensional self revolve, symbolically speaking, surfacing just beneath conscious awareness at various times.

Usually the Aspects slide transparently through the focus personality, merely coloring or tinting its experience with their own particular vision. The focus personality often looks through an Aspect without realizing it, aware only that its days seem different, altered in some subtle way. At such times we may feel as if we're looking at experience through someone else's eyes, someone like ourself, yet almost nostalgically different.

Occasionally we are suddenly aware of this sense of strangeness in our perception of the world, or sometimes we gradually realize that the world has seemed other or different for some time; until the "new" vision becomes so familiar that we have trouble remembering what the old one was like.

But Aspects constantly interact, and the experiences of the focus personality, through association and attraction, constantly call up various Aspects to meet changing conditions. At other levels of reality, the physical Aspect is activated in the same manner.

The Aspects orbit or revolve out of the entity or source self, which is pure energy, constantly being replenished, infinitely creative, and always forming new dimensions for experience and fulfillment. Each "face" looks out into its own dimension, yet all faces glide past, so that the self moves through itself constantly.

Each focus personality contains traces of its own Aspects, then, and can to some extent glimpse its own multidimensional reality. Therefore any individual can follow his or her own characteristics and abilities inward to their source; at least theoretically. The multidimensional self is literally unlimited and contains within it many Aspect abilities that can be used to advantage. Some may be so slight in practical experience as to be relatively nonexistent, yet even these can be recognized and cultivated to some degree. Some will be more amenable than others to physical translation. These Aspects must be glimpsed through the structure of the individual psyche, which must deflect and distort them to some degree, and reflect them through its own nature.

The reflection of a tree in a river follows the nature of the medium—the river—and not its own, for example, and in the same way Aspects will follow the contours of the individual psyche rather than their own. The tree does not grow downward, though we perceive its reflection in water that way. A study of the distortions themselves may be of help. We understand the rules that govern the tree's reflection in the river. But when an Aspect is reflected through the rich medium of the human psyche, we are much more apt to take appearances at their face value.

The Aspects form loving personifications that usually remain unconscious as far as we're concerned. These also provide the source material from which our own personalities spring, and so literally the spirit becomes flesh. I believe that these inner personifications gave rise to our concepts of God, gods, goddesses and perhaps of demons and devils also; possibly in historic terms they were once more psychologically visible than they are now.

These inner personifications *are* us, and are not us at the same time. We're still caught up in ideas of one-personhood. Again in my case, Seth, Seth Two, Seven, Cyprus and Helper might all be personifications of various Aspects of my source self, for instance; each Aspect independent in its own level of reality, while operating here in another fashion. Only by considering them all together would we get any glimpse of multi-personhood (which would be a characteristic of the source self); and by considering their relationship with each other and with the usual self, uncover some of the components of personality.

At this end, the prime Aspects usually form psychologically invisible personifications of themselves, sifted through our ideas of personhood. In their own realities, they would be themselves, endowed with higher dimensional activity and knowledge; independent, yet united in ways still beyond our present comprehension.

At this end, again, their characteristics would be reflected in strong basic drives, or in trace abilities. Whether or not such Aspects are activated or isolated as in my case, however, they would still act as guides or teachers at unconscious levels and in dream states. They would still glide transparently through the focus personality, at its service, bringing to it a rich source of abilities and information.

12

Inspiration, Free Awareness, and Prejudiced Perception

Dimensions slide through each other and overlap, but each has its own inviolate nature, in which all actions within it share. Instrusions from an "alien" area will automatically take on the characteristics of any other dimension in which they overlap. If these intrusions are perceived at all, it will be opaquely, cast in the natural guise of the "native" area.

Alien dimensional events also ride transparently within all reality systems, rippling beneath the surface. Clear differentiation and focus occurs as the result of certain concentrations formed by energy field intersections, and the electromagnetic interrelationships thus established. These areas become the experienced and perceived reality of activity, and set up the possibilities and limitations of any such life field.

Inspiration is a sudden three-dimensional breakthrough of trans-dimensional information into conscious patterning. The feeling of energy and surprise has to do with the power of emergence; a sort of mental propulsion that literally thrusts the data into a three-dimensional focus. Then we attempt to capture the revelatory material with the "hands" of our ordinary minds and translate it by letting it work on our current ideas to form new patterns. If we have a relative scarcity of images and interior symbols to work with, then the inspiration will simply get frozen in them.

Quite valid revelatory information often results in shoddy manuscripts or inane descriptions because the person involved grabs a hold of it with rigid mental hands. While everyone is inspired at one time or another, artists in any field keep on hand certain definite ways of structuring revelatory material into form.

The highest levels of inspiration involve creativity at trans-dimensional levels, and communication between the known focus personality and unknown source self. Two steps are always involved, although with many variations: the initial contact with the other-dimensional information, and the high selectivity at this end, where all image and thought patterns available to the person are sifted, and the proper ones chosen to three-dimensionalize the event or concept.

Much of this sorting process takes place unconsciously. The creative personality, however, constantly works with conscious and unconscious material, mixing and matching it, and putting it together in new ways. If this isn't done, those image and idea patterns are limited and serve to straitjacket revelation and inspiration rather than provide them with a fluent form.

FLAT-SHEET-OF-WHITE-PAPER ANALOGY

Make a square on a white sheet of paper. The area within the square is still white, yet it seems significantly different from the rest of the white page because of the pattern. Once the pattern is formed, this significance arises and becomes a focus for consciousness; providing a tendency, then, to translate that portion of the page as squareness. The rest of the paper becomes a background out of which the square emerges, perceived only in relation to the square pattern, and largely overlooked otherwise.

The whiteness is actually a part of the entire surface, of course, no different intrinsically from the white inside the pattern.

The hand that drew the square came from outside its surface, and does not consciously know the mechanisms it used to perform the action. The conscious mind, giving the directions to draw the square, is equally unaware of the inner mechanisms involved. The hand and eyes, being physically focused, see the results but not the invisible work behind the performance.

But as the hand came from outside the paper's dimensions to draw the square, so the self who possesses the hand came into three-dimensional life from another level, becoming a "particle" or focus personality in the three-dimensional field in the same way that the square appeared on the paper.

The square can't move off the paper, and has no knowledge of its own existence *in our terms*. The atoms and molecules that compose the paper are aware of themselves, but, again, not of the square pattern. They may well "sense" the alterations and imprints made by the ink or pencil marks, but without perceiving their significance.

Yet the character of the paper has been impressed, and it is different from a piece of paper containing no pattern. The paper itself has capabilities and limitations. It can only be impressed in so many ways. It exists, and in a higher dimensional context than itself. It can be burned, but it cannot decide to burn itself. It can be written upon, but cannot write upon itself. Nor can it refuse to be written upon. It cannot understand the simplest words in our terms, though a great treatise may be impressed upon it for others to read. And it certainly can't read itself.

At the same time, the significance of the letters on the paper can alter our own three-dimensional experience, and even help propel our consciousness beyond it. The paper, however, *does not experience the imprints as intrusions* from another dimension, but as natural events, characteristic of its own reality. Yet these "natural" events are also intrusions from the writer's field of activity to the paper's.

This same kind of thing happens constantly in our own dimension, when events are written in the living parchment of space. Here the "squares," patterns and scribbles—the particles—become alive, are endowed with self-consciousness that can itself question its origin and wonder about the higher dimensional reality from which it came.

A very simple example, on another level, involves the writing of this entire passage dealing with the white paper analogy. As I began to write the passage, I was writing "blind." That is, on a normally conscious level I didn't know where the words themselves were coming from, or what the analogy was supposed to represent. Not until the point was made in the writing itself, did *I* get the point! I took it for granted that what I was writing was making sense, and that as I continued, I would see the line of thought and development. In a small way this is like an extension of what happens when we speak, not always knowing how we will say what we want to, or even how we form the words, but going on faith that our speaking makes sense. In the case of the passage in question, though, "I" took it for granted from my viewpoint that the first line (coming from outside my usual consciousness) would reveal its message clearly. Now I am commenting on the analogy delivered to me at that other level. In small terms, was that analogy, then, an "intrusion"? A "natural intrusion"?

Actually I think that we have a kind of "prejudiced perception," and that any data free of that prejudice to whatever degree seems like an intrusive event. In writing the paper analogy, which commented on the patterning of perception, my own consciousness became slightly unprejudiced. I was able to identify with a self beyond the self we usually deal with, and get as far outside that self as, say, my hand would be outside of the dimension of the paper upon which it was then writing.

I like the term "free awareness" to express the kind of perception we have potentially as apart from the three-dimensional orientation of usual sense data.

FREE AWARENESS OR PRE-PERCEPTION

Free awareness, or from our standpoint, "pre-perception," is the basis for our physically focused sense perceptions. Pre-perception is undifferentiated; it is an ability to, or potential for, organizing awareness along certain specific lines. Our regular perception brings the earth alive for us by structuring our basic awareness, sifting it through the differentiated senses and alternately blocking out other data that might otherwise also "come alive" to us.

What we think of as perception is dependent upon a highly organized not-perceiving, so that significant data is illuminated, sharpened, and focused. To achieve that clarity, we cut down the field of awareness otherwise available.

Without such prejudiced perception, three-dimensional life as we know it would be impossible. The senses, then, direct and focus our free awareness by blocking out as much information as they let in. Free awareness is a suspended potential field, out of which all specific sense impressions come; the raw material. Sense experience is the form that free awareness takes in physical life. But our biological mechanisms themselves are, I believe, far less prejudiced in their use of free awareness, which is the springboard for the organizational tendencies of the atoms and molecules that compose our cells.

Any of the atoms and molecules in the body could go into the formation of cells in any part of the body at basic levels. The tissue in my elbow could just as well have become part of the ear and developed as a sense organ. In certain terms, the body is an alive sensing be-ing, physically composed of the same source stuff as the phenomena it perceives. At physical levels it certainly is part and parcel of the world it inhabits.

This sensitive being-in-the-worldness is dependent upon the most delicate yet durable sense focus, and this rests firmly and biologically upon the unprejudiced free awareness out of which specific perceptions emerge. Our usual perception, then, is a package deal, pre-structured and organized from a much larger available area of probable perception.

In terms of the paper analogy given earlier, physical life is the square on the paper. We ignore the background.

I believe that our biological functioning has built-in potentials not yet recognized and that free awareness can be triggered, at least, on a conscious basis. Such triggering then turns on inner mechanisms that allow us to consciously pick up data from undifferentiated areas (against which we're usually prejudiced) and translate it into usable terms.

PERCEPTION AND EVENTS
INDIVIDUAL AND RACIAL LIVING AREAS OR
"NOWS"

Events seem inviolate, set and definite. Actually, of course, they're our prejudiced interpretation of action, and also the result of perceiving reality in a certain specialized fashion. In sifting data, our senses screen out other dimensions in which recognized events also exist. If time is not *basically* consecutive, then events aren't either. Our free awareness would be able to perceive events both before and after their physical happening. It would also be operating at cellular levels, where the body would be prepared "ahead of time" to maintain its equilibrium in the face of countless in-time encounters. Here free awareness would help insure survival.

As individuals seem to grow in time, emerging from the multidimensional source self into physical life, so the race may have a "racial living area" or many, when group source self energy intersects with our system and spreads out in time which would form our historic context. The racial living area would be vast in comparison to an individual one, and its spread would reach further at each end. Like the person, the race would seem to emerge first in a birth or creation and then die off or disappear.

Actually as with the individual, the point of intersection with three-dimensional life would always be the present, and the ripples at each end would be experienced as time and experience. The ripples would go out in all directions, but the "Particle" or focus personality, the person in individual terms, or the race in group terms, would only experience these ripples at the living area as they travelled outward from the point of intersection. Physical perception happens only in the living area (see Diagram 2).

Other levels besides the focus consciousness might register, experience and react to other events than those sensed at the living area. A single event in our terms may take, say, ten minutes on the living area, for instance, yet other portions of our consciousness might react ahead of time, or retroactively, as experience on the living area "progresses." Only the topmost surface portion of an event may appear at the living area level, while the body's molecular experience may be timeless, and other "higher" levels of our consciousness may also continually experience events out of our time context.

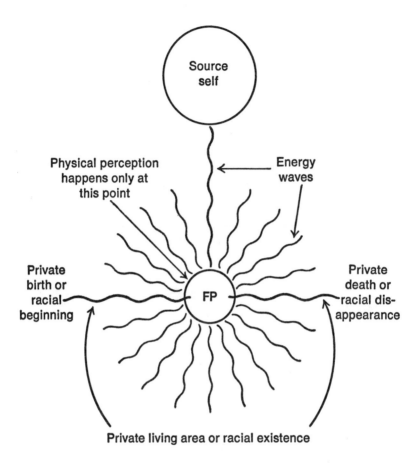

Diagram 2. Individual or racial living area

The source self's intersection with the three-dimensional field forms the particle focus personality in individual terms, or the racial focus personality in mass terms, and a living area of experienced time. This area is surrounded by an energy field of unperceived events.

13

The Source Self, The Focus Personality, Probabilities, and Reincarnation

The source self is an ever-aware stock of consciousness, sending individual selves or focus personalities into all systems of reality. Each focus personality is unique, independent, "born" into its particular dimensional area and becoming itself as fully as possible within that framework, where it takes part in the constant creation and maintenance of the system in which it has its existence. This is not a *descent* of soul, but a consciousness embarked in the creation of experienced realities, in which it then participates.

Yet we are like psycho-aware seeds of consciousness, sent out by our source selves, falling into different dimensions instead of back yards, carrying within us all the abilities of our parent selves, and free because of our nature to program our own journey, choose our dimensional spot—the time and place of our growth.

Yet we send out still other seeds of which we are usually unaware: dreams and thoughts that escape from us as easily as leaves from an autumn tree. These live in dimensions apart from our living, yet they are Aspects of us and carry our potentials within them. Perhaps they are future ghosts of ourselves; mental patterns that will some day be filled with form and walk this earth or a different one, in a space and time that will be theirs, not ours.

Yet the selves we know now, our focus personalities, exist in bodies that bloom only for a personal time, at least to our usual experience. And in the fullness of that season we live on an earth that is ours, closed to all other beings who came before or who will come after. We have the world, for a while, to ourselves. The gracious focus of our physical senses gives us that privacy and protects the personal space we've made in a world of moments.

Perhaps our senses alone keep us uniquely apart from other times and places, cozy in our own domesticized nest. Otherwise, with free awareness, we might see the dimensions merge and lose our one-line-of-time track; see our other Aspects in all stages of our own and their becoming.

We might experience the earth's centuries as one cosmic living tapestry, with each year we know only our official picture of a thousand other versions of the same January to December. What event happened when? To whom? How could we tell? Not until our own consciousness met its multidimensional nature could we hold memory of it, and acknowledge our experience apart from it in the face of such extensive awareness.

These same physical senses that cause us to experience all events *in* time, also endow them with a once-and-forever nature that highlights their significance. Our whole idea of memory is based on this: a past event, re-called.

So how we savor our memories, secret from all others; recall in old age, for example, the endless lost Mondays and Tuesdays when we tucked our children (now grown) into bed, or talked through a thousand separate suppers. Those events gain their meaning because of the way we experience them. And for all our talk about wanting to expand our consciousness, perhaps we fear losing that small but brilliant focus that makes events and memories so dear.

Yet still we yearn for that greater awareness that can perceive the countless daily events of our years clearly, yet with an overall vision that also sees what we do not see—the pattern of our lives the "shape" of our earthly inner being. To some extent we achieve this, of course, if only in imagination. The mother may envision the future man or woman in the child who sits in the highchair; and the old woman may see in the face of her grown son or daughter the child that was. In greater terms, each exist at once; young, old, born, dying—in an "at once" or spacious present that happens to be large enough to contain our lives.

Since time does not really exist as a series of moments, then basically what we are now is not the result of what we have been; any more than what we are now is the result of what we will be. Present, past and future exist in a now that our senses force us to perceive in segments. In a way we take ourselves out of context, experiencing only portions of ourselves at any given moment; reading our lives a page at a time *in* time, while at another level we write the entire book at once, constantly revising the pages "already" experienced.

Unknowingly, we are as affected now by our deaths as by our births.

The fact of death certainly casts its light over all the events of our lives. We're aware of the *fact-in-the-future,* though, and remain unaware of the specifics. For that matter, we can only handle so many events on a conscious level. We react to some others unconsciously.

Here again, terms can be misleading, for I believe that the "unconscious" *is* conscious. It represents the portion of ourselves from which the focus personality springs, with its "ego." The ego is the direct psychological confrontation point, rising out of the focus personality to deal with physical life. Since the focus personality can only handle so much data in its time system, it chooses from the field of the unconscious only those perceptions it wants to accept in line with its beliefs about the nature of its own reality (see Diagram 3).

Diagram 3. The personal unconscious field of perception

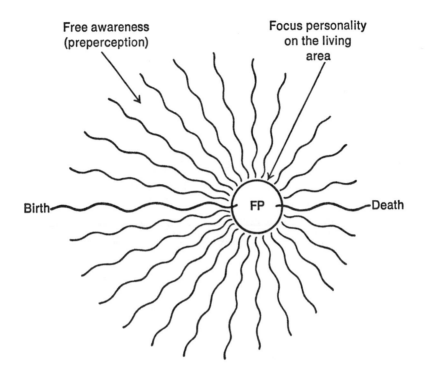

In the nonphysical field surrounding the focus personality, perception is free, not bound by space and time. The field consists of probable events. From these the focus personality materializes physical events as it moves along the living area.

At this level, perception is not time-bound. Events and probable events are equally "known" in a stage we could call pre-perception, because the data aren't physically actualized. We would "per-ceptualize" in our living area only certain events from all of the probable ones of which our unconscious is aware.

But let's look at these probable events more closely.

STATUS OF PROBABLE EVENTS

I was going to begin with the joking remark that probable events can only have a probable status—what else?—but in a way all events are probable. We just actualize some of these and call them physical. I think that we are creatures of incredible freedom, with immense resources from which we form our experience. We choose physical events, then, from all the pre-perceptions of which the unconscious is aware. And this choice never stops. We aren't locked into one series of happenings. At any time we can pick another line of development from all of the probabilities available to us. Recognition of this would relieve many people from feelings of powerlessness, and allow them to change their lives in a practical manner.

I believe that we do make such alterations often, even if we're not consciously aware of the mechanisms or reasons involved. In such a case, the new alternate probable actions happen on the living area, and the events that might have happened otherwise—the old ones—are discarded but still happening *off* the living area.

I think that this kind of process occurs often when we change direction in midstream, suddenly alter our circumstances, or seem to be so different from our usual self that this is noticeable to others. At first, such actions may amaze and confuse us. We may not understand what we have done, or even how we did it. Yet a careful examination of the facts will show us that our "new" course was always a probability in our experience, though we may not have regarded it as such.

The crossroads of our lives may involve quite real though invisible intersections, where probabilities meet at definite points in our time and space. They may act as escape hatches from conditions we may have chosen once but no longer accept, or now see as flawed. These probability points would be concentrations of energy formed unconsciously by us adjacent to our living areas. They would be created by intense desires and beliefs that we had entertained, but never chosen as physical events.

On the other hand, some may have been accepted (if not literally actualized) on a living area level at one time, and were then shunted aside, like a railroad car, off the main track. All desires and ideas are action. So these continue adjacent to our living, but form probable patterns all about us. Unconsciously, they will also be latent or inactive at the living area level.

To me, the richness of our experience can't be explained without accepting the existence of probable actions and events as a source for physical experience. The same applies to the experience of our species in general, and to the historic events of the centuries as we know them.

The probability points would represent exchanges between probability and living area actions. I've made two simple diagrams to show what would happen when we change our "line of probabilities" (see Diagrams 4 and 5).

Diagram 4 shows a focus personality at the midpoint of its living area. Behind it is a past of actualized events already chosen from probable ones bringing about its own probable future as per the choices that the focus personality has made this far in our terms of time. Following as it has gone, the focus personality would be continuing on with the main line development of the living area.

Instead, in Diagram 5, the focus personality chooses an alternate probability, and "brings it" into the living area, changing the living area at that point. The alternate probability, (2), drops down into the living area time spot and becomes "the future" instead of the one chosen earlier.

The part of the focus personality who had decided upon the living area probability as it existed *before* the decision follows through—but *not* on the living area. A new focus personality

Diagram 4. The focus personality at a point of decision

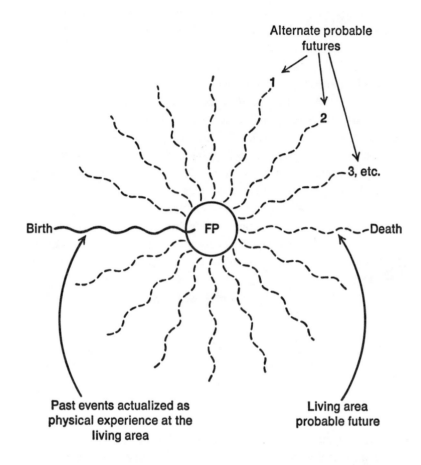

Alternate probable futures

1

2

3, etc.

Birth

FP

Death

Past events actualized as physical experience at the living area

Living area probable future

While the past as experienced suggests its own probable future, the focus personality is free at any time to choose from alternate probable futures instead.

Diagram 5. The focus personality after a point of decision

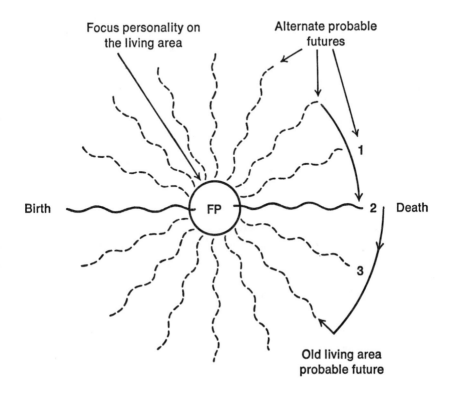

Focus personality on
the living area

Alternate probable
futures

Birth

FP

1

2   Death

3

Old living area
probable future

The "earlier" alternate future probability (2) drops into the living
area time slot.

is created, a "probable one," projected into a different kind of reality with the same abilities and previous experience as existed up to the point when the decision was made. In other words, the probable focus personality (or probable self) has a given heritage. It, too, begins to choose from probabilities. The initial focus personality (or physically tuned self) keeps its identity, yet having made the decision to change probabilities, it becomes different than it would have been had it not made the choice.

We talk about the genes and the miracle of unique creatures never duplicated within the framework of biological intricacy. Probabilities provide a psychic and psychological counterpart, but a far more flexible one in which our consciousness has greater freedom of choice, yet a unique quality that gives individuality its indestructible focus at the same time. For no two individuals would be presented with the same set of probabilities, or even make such choices from the same point.

For that matter, reincarnation most likely involves probable existences in alternate living areas. Our life as we know it may be just one time focus in space among others. To get into time we may have to leave space, returning at a new intersection point. Birth and death may indeed be doors into three-dimensional activity; and death the way out of what would otherwise be a dimensional dilemma in which further development would be impossible. Instead, we'd be locked into one time-and-space slot. Our present lifetime may be one of the dimensions of our being, like our weight and height, but one that can't appear to us fully in space.

Events, then, would also have other dimensions than the ones we usually perceive. What we think of as one event is instead only one Aspect of a multidimensional happening. When we experience an event, it seems as solid and definite in its way as an object is. The atoms and molecules within objects are invisible. Events, I believe, also have their own equivalent of atoms and molecules—the million unseen probable actions within, upon which they ride to surface as definite physical acts. Events are like psychological objects placed in the inner rooms of the mind. They are always there, always encountered, particularly memories of past events that indubitably happened it seems, and therefore can never be changed.

We can move furniture, get rid of it and start over. But aren't we more or less at the mercy of past events? I don't believe so. In fact, I think that we change the past, and in the only way that makes any practical sense. More, I think that we do this so effortlessly and efficiently that often the change is obvious to others but not to ourselves.

Seth's books have insisted on this freedom from past events, and Seth constantly asserts the individual's power in the present over the past. The idea has fascinated me from the beginning, but it was personal experience that showed me how cleverly and thoroughly the past can be changed by someone who really wants to blot out certain aspects of past experience and substitute alternate events; along with a "new memory" of the once probable events that now seem to have occurred.

My father-in-law died in 1971. When Father Butts became ill, his mental powers rapidly deteriorated and we had to put him in a home for the aged. He and Mother Butts had had a good share of misunderstandings through the years, but these, and all memory of them, vanished for Mother Butts shortly after she began living alone. Any events well known to the family that corroborated the misunderstandings were completely forgotten as far as my mother-in-law was concerned.

They did not leave any holes or vacancies, however. They were replaced by a new group of memories that made perfect sense to Mother and reinforced each other. The trouble was, that this new probable past was chosen by only one member of the family. The other members still clung to the old past events.

I'm quite aware that this sort of thing happens frequently with the very elderly, and that we usually explain it away by saying that a faulty memory is involved. We say that certain events happened in the past, and that's the end of it: A person can forget the events or pretend that they didn't happen, but this in no way alters the "fact" of the matter. I think, to the contrary, that events can't exist independently of the people who experienced them—the people are a part of the events—and as the people change, so do the events.

The so-called concrete event is diminished if energy is withdrawn from it. If we're supposed to react in the present because of what happened to us in the past, then Mother was reacting to a new past. This was highly important psychologically. No longer was she a woman who had argued constantly with her husband through the long years of marriage. She was a woman whose beloved husband was in his last illness, a husband who never deeply upset her or caused her any pain. She was not pretending, or being a hypocrite.

In other words, often the new past takes hold so beautifully that the old one becomes unreal, forgotten, and in practical psychological terms, unreal—for we no longer even react to it. Instead, all of our present actions and our attitudes toward them are based upon an entirely different hypothesis that is quite as valid to us as the old one. Sometimes this new past is so radically different from the old one that friends and relatives object.

Yet each present action changes the past, for those past events were only the mountaintops or three-dimensional tips of far greater happenings. Each act causes the surface crust of time and space to shift slightly. Probable events are the psychological pre-acts from which physical events emerge; the creative inner stuff from which actions take earth form.

Only when our awareness directly intersects with the three-dimensional field do events take on the same sharp reality as objects (which are, of course, events of a different kind). Only then do they seem solid psychologically. But once we've passed them in time, their true fluidity and plasticity returns. We don't ever meet them in time the same way again.

Because of their very plastic nature, we have a constant probable past to work with. Events as we remember them are far more important than those that may have "actually" happened. Our changing attitudes are a part of each event we remember. Extensions of it reach literally from any "now point" backward into the past and ahead into the future.

I believe that Aspects at birth provide a luxurious bank of characteristics and abilities to be activated as needed, according to specific environmental conditions, and from these hidden Aspects rises the resiliency that allows us to face so many global and personal situations. Our psychic and psychological makeup is at least as intricate as our physical composition.

Seth speaks of mental enzymes and mental genes. Surely these refer to psychic and psychological counterparts of the genes and chromosomes, to the inner organization from which our personal living springs and through whose auspices our experience constantly emerges.

TIME, REINCARNATION, AND PROBABILITIES

Once again, think of the amazing integrity, the pristine privacy of existence, in which experience rises up from undifferentiated probabilities into significance—all the more dear because each event is so highly personal, so ours, that not even a god could get inside it *in the same way,* or feel it from our own secret perspective.

Privileged interpreters and perceivers! Our physical perception *is* prejudiced, limited—yes, but only in the same way that a light is, when focused in one direction and not another. This in no way lessens the quality of the light of awareness, which on other levels *does* spread out into areas that now seem darkened.

But out of undifferentiated cosmic backgrounds, out of vast areas of "pre-being," spring these particular moments holding incredible significance—our individual experiences. Mornings and evenings, Tuseday night suppers, all of these are somehow held brilliantly focused, private, leaping apart from the rest of human and cosmic events. They are not folded away in the centuries, not crushed in a gigantic over-being in which they are indistinguishable, but held out inviolately separate, if only for the moment. But that moment is a triumph of consciousness and creativity and contains an emotional acceleration that is somehow eternal.

Yet that privacy rises through a cooperation that is equally staggering; it reflects such inner dimensions of activity. For what worlds merge within us, spiraling, before we can perceive the simplest event? And look at *us*, living psychological events who perceive ourselves, and from within those events we move through our own dimensions; order our experiences in sequence, and isolate from the immensity of our being all those separate episodes that compose our lives. For our lives are only the physical events of ourselves, and while we live we still continue our other-than-physical being upon which our corporal lives ride.

So perhaps we also have many lives on this planet, other "life events," each separate and glowing and yet a part of the overall multidimensional reality of the source self. William Blake, the eighteenth-century poet and mystic, speaks of descent into the generations. Rob and I have no children "this time." We say that this is our last incarnation. Since all lives happen at once, this is our way of saying that this is our leaping-off point. For the centuries are no more real than the moments. So many, like Blake, speak of descent *into* this life, just because it's so difficult to conceive of our coming *out* into three-dimensional living from an inside that is not physically perceivable. We come from within, not from above. We also seed other earths with our probable selves; these never happen at our intersection point, though they may spring off from it.

Here is a very simple diagram (Diagram 6) representing reincarnational lives, using a reincarnational living area instead of a private one. Each reincarnation self would have its own focus personality in its own time and space period.

The focus personalities are confined to time-sense experience at their own living areas, and at that level they are unaware of their connections with other "reincarnational" selves. Other quite legitimate experience goes on adjacent to the living area,

Diagram 6. Reincarnational living area

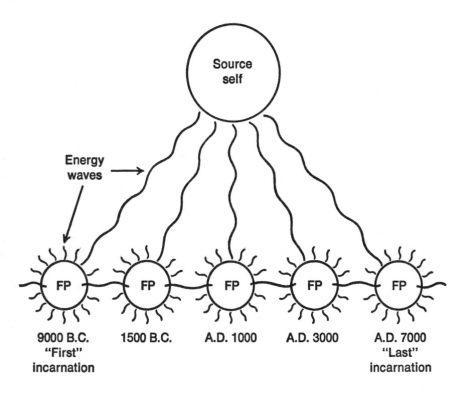

The source self is "broken down" into separate focus personalities, simultaneously incarnated in time on the living area.

however, and here free awareness would offer connections between all of the focus personalities at unconscious levels. Since all lives happen at once, "splashing" or spreading out from the source self's point of intersection with our field of reality, then a final reincarnation simply represents the individual's decision to break the circuit. You can do it "at any time," from any point of intersection. In normal time terms, that wouldn't mean that another future life wasn't in the offing.

For that matter, I believe that we have the innate capacity now to handle more than one set of memories at a time, at least in flashes of recognition that slide into consciousness much like our ordinary memories do. These are in the background just enough, off-focus enough, so as not to interfere with our here and now privacy.

It is that extra significance, that specific intersection of inner events with the space-time living area that causes our now. Memories flutter about this area, never lighting, yet psychologically visible and illuminating our daily lives, bringing to them added richness and depth. Our memories endow the moment with the additional dimensions of events not present in direct sense terms. Future memories, I think, operate in much the same way.

Yet, again theoretically, future lives or past ones would bring memories that would seem not our own; not happening on our accepted living area, and outside of what we think of as the boundaries of selfhood. And would they always be just memories? Since all lives would be lived at once, what about an "earlier" self looking freshly through our twentieth century eyes? And since Aspects interact, what about a sudden rush of consciousness into the free awareness field where one focus personality meets its counterpart in another time? More, what if they communicate to each other?

Now, I think that this is what happened in our living room when Nebene and Shirin "met". (See Chapter Five.) There was no mistaking the living quality of Shirin, and by hindsight it was easy to see that Rob and Sue had always reacted in many ways to these two Aspects of themselves. If Shirin was looking into a future, Sue was looking into a past, but each of them saw that the terms of time were basically meaningless.

Since then, Rob has been aware of Nebene at times, and Sue has sensed Shirin. And—all four have changed. Nebene, through Rob, has become aware of the free nature of creativity; Rob understands the tendencies toward over-discipline that he "picked up" for his own reasons from Nebene, and has largely dispensed with them. Shirin's attitude toward Nebene changed for the better as through Sue, she (Shirin) relates to Rob. And Sue sees the reasons for the feelings of defiance that used to baffle her.

Aspects of multi-personhood? Human personality getting a glimpse of its own entire nature? Perception, no longer boxed into a before-and-after time sequence? For surely in both old age and childhood there are bleedthroughs, when we almost see who we "were" in a past life or who we "will be" in a future one.

By using our normal experiences in the living area as balancing points, and by realizing that we recognize only one series of events as real and ignore others, I think that we can become aware of our own greater reality. If you believe that events are closed, not open at both ends (or all ends!), then it will never occur to you to use them as stepping stones to other events that are not physically focused in the same way.

It certainly seems that there will be correlations between past life experiences and our "current one," not only in terms of characteristics and tendencies, but perhaps also in the type or kind of events chosen. Any one event in this life may well be transparent if we understood this: we might move through it psychologically into other life experiencing.

This could be what happens in some of the reincarnational dramas we have done in my class. Such memories or events, however, are often clothed in symbols, imagery, or dramas that make sense to the current focus personality.

But in daily spontaneous living experiences, such memories come to us frequently, I believe, and are blocked out because of our beliefs. They are also directed into art productions—a writer dramatizing a past life of his own in a historical novel, for example, and without ever knowing it consciously.

But in any case, such memories could not be translated literally into immediate experiencing, displacing our time, our moment; they would have to be interpreted *through* our experiencing. Just the same, they could sometimes be as alive as our usual memories, and sometimes attain that quality of nowness that Shirin and Nebene showed while couched in a moment of our time—in which two nows momentarily seemed to merge.

14

Events and the Focus Personality. Omens, Moods, and Free Awareness

Let's look at *this* life, though, and the ways in which we can react to events from the free awareness field—and without being consciously aware of them. Such perceptions make sense, and are possible, only if we think of events as transformations of the psyche, projected outward, perceived and experienced in highlighted form—and isolated from all the other inner psyche events—while, in fact, not leaving them at all. The sensate world is the exteriorized aspect of our interior living, personally and en masse.

Look at it this way: Events *are* psychological motion, as alive in their own framework as animals. We react to them and they react to us. They move, without observable shape. They possess an impetus that is ours. Yet forgetting this, we often react to them blindly, swept willy-nilly by emotional storms that *seem* to erupt despite us. Actually, events are *our* projections, personalized and directed outward by our beliefs and desires; telekinesis in action. They are objectified mental states, constantly interacting, formed automatically by conscious energy's intersection with the three-dimensional field.

Until we understand this, and learn to trace the steps between subjective and objective experience, we'll feel at the mercy of events that will always seem imposed upon us from without; and never comprehend the power of our own consciousness or creativity.

Yet our private experience of an event is still only one Aspect of it: The entire event would include the participation of all the other people involved, and even its "effect" upon others whose lives it touches, even though they may have had no active connection with the event at all. But even the most seemingly spontaneous happening is a part of others that, in our terms, preceded it or will come after. So trying to decide where any particular event begins or ends is tricky indeed.

Yet we structure our lives by following what we think of as specific events, holding them in focus and ignoring others. To this extent, we decide what events of all the known ones we want to make personal. In other words, from our own bank of interests, abilities, and opportunities we make an endless number of decisions—some large, some minute—but all of them determine the focus of our attention, and the kinds of events we will perceive.

We will effectively block out some possible experiences and choose others. A sportsminded person will find the sports page of the newspaper significant and seek it out. Another individual might hardly realize the sports section even exists. The same process goes on in all areas of life. A steady discrimination results in certain choices that bring about our personal reality, and the experiences it will contain.

Again, prejudiced perception for our reality is characterized as much by the kinds of events it excludes as by those it embraces. And what makes me, me, and you, you, in this level of actuality is the difference in our subjective experience; the vast interplay between accepted and denied possible events. Between these lies our daily living.

Yet there is shared experience that does not sacrifice the private aspect of events, but enriches them, as when we share any happening with someone else. But besides this physical sharing there is an inner sharing, far more extensive; in which, however, privacy is still maintained and choices are made. Here we are dealing with an inner order of events, and the significant communications going on constantly beneath words or recognized sense data.

For here, events are open; not physically stuck in space or time and not limited to living area experience. The inner events are like roots from which physical events blossom. Then they appear at the living area. Above or below that level of experience, our perception is not bound to the what-happened-when kind of reasoning.

Free awareness is constantly bringing us information from this pre-perception field. The difficulty is that we've been taught to ignore such data—even though some of it might be important and necessitate action on our part. This information, being free from the space-time framework, might confuse or disorient us when we try to respond and act in-time. Yet often we feel like reacting to a sensed situation, when we have no normal sense data to support it.

Ever since my own psychic initiation, I've gone overboard trying to be objective, until I'm finally forced to admit that true objectivity also means granting the validity of subjective feelings, whether or not you can find any supportive physical evidence for them. You can decide to act or not to act in response to such feelings, but trying to wish them out of existence is certainly not being objective.

Often, I believe, we become aware of events that are not happening at our own living level; that is, we don't meet them directly in space and/or time. Yet in an odd way we sense their happening, and even react—appropriately. For example, one day when my mother-in-law was already ill, I began a short story about a woman in her position. The old woman in my story ran away from her son's home and made her way to her former neighborhood in another town, where she discovered that her family homestead had been sold. She'd sold it herself, but couldn't remember.

At the time, Mother Butts was living with one of Rob's brothers. I took it for granted that I was imaginatively using that situation for creative purposes. I wrote the story in great bursts of energy, twelve pages in one sitting, hardly stopping to rest. Yet, writing, I grew very sad, and when I was finished I was near tears. Natural enough under the circumstances, I thought. Still, I couldn't shake the mood. I stared at the written pages: Odd, for that matter, that I'd taken time from writing my book to do a short story to begin with! In fact, I hadn't written a short story in about three years. For a moment I wondered if I was "picking up something" about Mother Butts without realizing it. I decided not. Yet the deep mood of sadness grew. It stayed with me all day.

In the early evening Rob's brother called, saying that Mother Butts would have to go into a home for the aged: Her behavior was unmanageable. He specifically mentioned her desire and determination to return to her old home, and the fact that she'd completely forgotten that she'd sold it. Again, natural enough. Yet as soon as the call came, my mood lifted. More, a kind of relief came over me: I had something tangible to connect my mood to; I wasn't reacting . . . for no reason. We're taught that we can't react to an event before it happens, yet I'm convinced that I reacted either to Mother's condition or the phone call ahead of time.

As the days passed, I forgot the incident. In the meantime, Mother Butts was moved to a home near Rob's other brother.

One night about three weeks after her move, Rob and I went out dancing, returned in excellent spirits, and went to bed. Suddenly we heard the weirdest noise, and woke up. Rob turned the lights on. It was summer and the screened bedroom windows were wide open. I shouted. A bird was flying furiously around the room. It kept making great long figure eights in the air, swooping low where Rob stood, and just brushing his head. Rob kept ducking each time the bird passed. There was no question how the bird came in: He must have entered through the unscreened kitchen windows by the oak tree.

In the old Irish neighborhood where I grew up, birds in the house meant death. Silly, I told myself. It was a simple enough event. There was nothing strange about it. Yet I remembered that a bird had flown through the house years ago, when my grandmother had died. Yet, I reminded myself, both of my parents had died in the past year—and no bird. So why did I feel that *this* bird meant that Mother Butts was about to die?

Thinking all of this, I stayed in bed. The bird kept swooping back and forth, and Rob opened the screens, hoping it would fly out. For about five minutes we waited. Then the bird headed out the window.

Involuntarily I thought: Mom isn't going to die right now, then, because the bird is escaping! But it meant the beginning of the end. Exhausted by this time, Rob and I fell asleep, too tired to discuss it. Not till the next day did we realize that we couldn't identify the bird, even though the lights had been on. For one thing, it flew so fast! We agreed that it had been bigger than a sparrow and smaller than a robin; and all grey. But we'd never seen a bird like it, even though we have feeders all around outside the place, and keep track of the birds all the time.

I was uneasy all the next day, but again I told myself that my knowledge of Mother Butts' condition caused me to remember the bird-death superstition when we found the bird inside; and that was the end of it. Just the same, feeling silly, I closed the unscreened windows as if I could keep my mother-in-law alive if no more birds came in. So I rushed about, checking the windows and trying to keep death out. I kept on telling myself that though Mom's mind was bad, there was nothing physically wrong with the rest of her. But the words didn't ring true.

Two days later we received another phone call about Mom, our first since I'd finished the short story. My sister-in-law phoned to say that Mom had been critically ill and had been expected to die. She'd suddenly developed a bad infection. They'd taken her to the hospital—two days before—but luckily she'd pulled through and now they hoped that she would improve.

The next few days were very busy. We had some visitors coming. I made a huge pot of spaghetti sauce, put it on the stove to cook, and sat down to do my writing. Suddenly I heard a bird, or thought I did. I stopped, fingers on the typewriter keys, and listened. It sounded like a trapped bird, wings flapping, I checked, and found nothing. So I decided that my imagination was working overtime, that the sound was caused by the spaghetti sauce spattering on the hot burner, or the pressure of steam against the pot lid. I did make a note of the time and my impressions, but then I promptly forgot the whole thing.

Two days after, another call! This time my brother-in-law phoned to say that Monday afternoon, around three, Mother's condition had grown much worse again. It was Monday at three-thirty that I'd thought I'd heard the bird and connected it with Mother Butts. Rob's other brother was supposed to have called Monday afternoon but for several reasons he hadn't been able to. He didn't have to, I thought: In my own way, I got the message. At the same time I thought crossly: I can't prove any of this. It just sounds like a string of coincidences.

Two weeks passed. Mom recovered and was returned to the home for the aged. We were relieved that the danger was past. Then on a Thursday morning I awakened feeling terribly depressed. Despondency tinged the entire day.

This time I questioned my mood, wrote down the way I felt and scribbled: "Is Mom Butts OK? Am I somehow picking up a mood of hers? Is she worse?" I thought that if anything was wrong with Mom, we would have heard. Yet again, I couldn't seem able to shake the feeling of almost crushing despondency.

Friday we heard nothing. I felt better and relaxed. Saturday I felt uneasy again and finally called my sister-in-law. She said, "Mom got through the operation OK."

"Operation? What operation?" I asked, shocked. Again I found that Mother Butts had been in a crisis on the same day I'd felt so poorly and connected my mood with her. Thursday she'd fallen and broken her hip; she was operated on the same day. Once again, another member of the family was supposed to have given us the message and hadn't; yet the message *did* get through, at least partially.

I'm mentioning these experiences precisely because they are so ordinary, in a way; they didn't involve visions or voices, but represent the kinds of happenings that often occur when families are involved with the seriously ill. You can't *prove* that you knew what was going on in another place, without any physical way of knowing. You can't prove that your mood was a reflection of someone else's. You only have your feelings to go by; and we're taught to mistrust our feelings if we can't immediately relate them to physical fact.

Yet my feelings made sense and were quite appropriate once they were connected up to their physical-event counterparts; they fit, then, only if I took it for granted that I'd been aware of the events ahead of time. Certainly my unconscious knowledge had been foggy enough. No clear details were involved. Yet enough information came through to affect my moods drastically.

The bird episode is somewhat different. Certainly I used the bird as an omen of death. If it hadn't entered the house, perhaps I would have seized on another living creature as a symbol, to bring unconscious information to the surface of my mind. Once its symbolism was established, then a real bird wasn't even necessary, for in the incident that followed I perceived the sound of the pressure against the lid of the sauce pot as the sound of a bird's beating wings. A faulty, distorted perception by physical standards, yes; but a perfect symbolic perception of another event that existed in a different order of activity.

For again, where do events begin or end? In a very real manner of speaking, the mundane fact of the steaming sauce pot was connected with my mother-in-law's critical state in ways that were subjectively valid.

A few days after the last of these episodes, we went to visit Mother Butts. By then I was beginning to see a pattern between my moods and her condition—a somewhat disturbing one.

I accepted the existence of telepathy, though I didn't necessarily think of it as "reading minds," and I vaguely recognized the existence of psychic transference of moods. But now I wondered how often this kind of thing happened generally. I knew that my desire to know Mother Butts' condition played a part in the entire affair, and that this was probably the key-in.

I was led to question even further, though. How private *were* events; and how stuck in space and time were they? What about the event of death, for example? I was thinking about that when we visited the hospital, and as soon as we got home, I jotted down the following notes:

> *We visited Mother Butts. Since last week, she's suffered a clot in the lung. They're giving her oxygen. We just stood there as people do when faced with inevitability. Mother couldn't speak, of course. Tubes were in her nostrils, and her mouth was open. It looked like a gaping hole into darkness or eternity. The sound of her labored breathing, by contrast, reminded me of how beautifully and automatically our breathing usually works. With what splendid Godlike ease we keep ourselves alive; and how unconscious we are of the precise mechanisms involved.*
>
> *Mother Butts isn't dead yet, but Rob and I and his brothers and their wives have been reacting to that death for two years, at least; and so has Mother Butts. The physical death is only a part of that event, the portion that can be pinpointed in space and time.*
>
> *For one thing, a vital relating aspect of Mother Butts is dead. To her, physical relationships are peripheral, and the actual event of her death has been happening for some time. I've been aware of Mom's points of crisis in ways that appeared opaquely in my own living area. Something happens that doesn't show. We always rise to life out of an inner order of events, but at death particularly, we try to pretend that it doesn't exist. At least we don't trust it; because, of course, in our terms it "takes" the living.*
>
> *At death, though, our entire experience moves over to that inner order of events, and near death our experience approaches this inwardness; we're focused in and with our bodies for one thing, and the events we perceive are off the living area rather than on it. Episodes out of the past can supersede our usual here and now, for example. Again: Things happen that don't show. Who can*

tell? For a muteness falls upon the dying and those who care for them alike.

To begin with, I think that consciousness turns more and more away from the living area level. The time limitations of its focus no longer apply. At our end, we say that the dying are having delusions or hallucinations if they can't keep their times straight or their events in sequence. It seldom occurs to us that their vision of reality might be truer in basic terms than our own.

More and more, I kept trying to look for the underside of events, to turn over "what happened" to see what might be underneath. Again, the living area is only a representation of experience in space and time; a life of physically perceived events. But many normal experiences don't show there clearly. That is, they aren't objectified to others, though they are quite real to us. In fact, without them, events would make no sense at all.

I'm referring to thoughts and emotions. They're felt directly enough. We try to communicate them, and our bodies reflect them through motion and gestures, but they aren't objectified in the same way that, say, the act of throwing a ball is. They hover about our exterior experiences. In the same way, some other subjective activity remains just off the living area, only sifted out from usual consciousness while operating as a supportive framework for it.

We know that multitudinous inner events happen before we experience an objective one (the psychological "atoms and molecules" within the "solid" happening). It's here, beneath objectivity where multidimensional events occur in a strata that remains invisible but ever-shifting, to erupt in what we perceive finally as a physical event. Ordinary events have a sharp focus only because we experience such a small portion of their reality—the part that surfaces.

It would take a multidimensional consciousness to experience all the aspects of one event; being aware of its probable variations, seeing each as real as the other. Such a consciousness would literally have to straddle realities unknown to us in order to discover what was happening to *which* who in *what* when.

In which when?

To which you?

How easy it would be for us to get lost in the full dimensions of an event, lose the thread of ourselves, and perhaps never find our way back to the established living area with its protective illusion of continuity.

Are some forms of insanity due to this? Do some consciousnesses simply stray too far away from the precise point needed to focus here clearly? If so, everything might be distorted to them just enough so that the world lost that dear stability or semblance of stability upon which the rest of us all agree.

For we are not all here, of course. We flicker and waver about the focus of our own reality, dipping in and out of it like bees about flower petals. In dreams, daydreams, and alternate states of consciousness we tune out here to some degree and tune in some UNwhere else. But wherever we turn our focus, there *is* something to perceive, for the light of our consciousness constantly transforms undifferentiated areas of reality into significance and endows them with life.

For in certain terms our consciousness *is* energy interacting with other fields of energy. And while we are ourselves, individual and relatively freewheeling, certainly our individual consciousness forms mass energy fields also; some that hover just around the living area, and others that exist adjacent to it, in which all earth consciousness from our species and others exist despite their time periods.

I've sensed this in various trance states, and Seth insists that all of this is theoretically available to us through the window of our present moment; the point of our being in space and time. We would only have to open up that channel. Perhaps Seth represents one such multidimensional consciousness, and the Sumari, en masse, represents the sensed hosts of consciousness projected by our own source selves (higher dimensionalized ghosts of ourselves) on the one hand, and on the other, represents consciousness united and whole drawn from the earth's entire existence.

But earth would have no end in those terms, any more than it would have a beginning. The true and only "beginning" is this now from which experience splashes out to make a past seemingly behind us and a future ahead; forming ripples that spread out in terms of years from our now. But there would be other earths, probable to us, with different intersections with space and time; other living areas and other historic pasts than ours.

Yet all of us, inviolate, retain our memories, and we are not lost but free to explore our own realities from this particular dimensionalized nest of space and time that we call earth. Yet I'm convinced that in some probable earth-like world, I am not writing this book. I may not be a writer at all or I may live in a civilization where reading is unknown. My potential as a writer, there, would remain latent.

And—most probably, in some probable world you are not reading this book. Before you picked it up in our reality, your reading it or not reading it were both probable events. Your reading the book actualizes one of these probabilities, but on another level of activity the non-reading "happens" to a probable self who made another decision, or put himself or herself in a position where the book was never even encountered.

As I wrote the first draft of this chapter, I knew that this book was somewhere already finished. I hadn't begun the first part of the book at that time, or the last portions. Yet I knew that all parts were somehow being "written" simultaneously, even though at the living area level I must write it day by day. At the ordinary level, I didn't know where the book was leading me but went ahead (as with the square and the paper analogy) on faith, believing in my capabilities at another level.

I didn't want to skip all the days until the book was done, though: I knew that each one was secret and significant and vital beyond all description; dear precisely because of the sense perceptions that showed me an ordered dusk and dawn even while that sequenced reality hid portions of my own book from me for a while.

But that "while," I knew, was only relative. For if we're aware at all of our own multidimensionality, then it acts as counterpoint. Our dreams spring to life. We find ourselves sometimes brilliantly awake in our sleep and discover shining hints of our own other knowing. And all of this is like a rich underlay adding to our daily creative experience, putting it in another, odder, broader perspective that is surely somehow unique.

Yet even with this, how opaque we can be! Though I should certainly understand the nature of inspiration to some degree, still I found myself at times worrying over my writing schedule, hassling myself to make sure I got my daily five hours in, and railing at any distractions. Then I noticed that often I did my best work after hours when my "responsibilities" were done, and I was just playing around with ideas.

While writing books requires some labor that definitely takes time, inspiration itself is between "times." It opens time up. Two hours of inspired writing is worth ten hours of dry forced conscious-one-line-thinking kind of writing. But there is a subjective knowing involved; a prime moment or moments when inspiration is available and invisible realities suddenly coincide with the usual one. That knowing comes in its own time, but its time and ours must meet, of course.

I think that this strangely opaque kind of meeting happens whenever we receive information from the inner order of events, whether through inspiration, precognition, hunches, or whatever. According to Seth, the recognition of this greater reality turns on what he calls the spacious mind, and adds a different, wider cast to our perceptions. In other words, the spacious mind increases the power of normal perceptions, plus allowing us to become more and more aware of events that are not happening directly in our living area. To varying extents, the focus personality becomes acquainted with data previously closed to it because of its own beliefs. The information must then be assimilated as any sense data is.

In our terms, the person has more to deal with than before. Living in the usual world, he is also aware of some events that occur off his own living area or at other points on it than his private one. His vision is wider. The spacious mind acts like a platform just above the living area, letting the person perceive a greater range of activity, just as in an airplane we see more of the landscape at one time than when we're moving along the ground.

The information must then be put into living level context to be practically useful in our terms. All of this involves a kind of spontaneous training as the consciousness of the focus personality learns to handle not only here-now perceptions, but events outside of that framework.

Because of our cultural training, however, we're very leery of sensing events that we cannot correlate immediately with physical evidence. This causes many of us to inhibit information and to resist even spontaneous use of such abilities. Certainly I could have had clearer data about my mother-in-law's condition in any of the incidents mentioned if I hadn't held back to a certain extent, out of the fear that I might be exaggerating a mood or letting my imagination run away with me. Using the bird as omen gave me a physical handle, connected up the inner information with physical reality in the moment, and somehow made it more respectable.

Respectability to the focus personality is no small thing: It must somehow wend its way along the living area, fitting its great energies into a prefabricated structure. Our ideas of reality are its ideas. Our beliefs will allow it more freedom and leeway or inhibit the use of its freedom. The focus personality is the part of the psyche we usually indentify with. But like events, the psyche, has an invisible Aspect out of which the focus personality rises. To get a glimpse of it we have to examine ourselves and the events we experience—in and out of time.

15

The Inner Order of Events and "Unofficial" Perceptions

I was really astonished one night to hear a cello rendition of my Sumari "Song of the Creation." Wade, one of my students, is a musician; he transcribed the song from tape. The music was lovely. "A musical composition," I kept thinking. "Where did it really come from?" I'm trained as a writer and sometimes I paint as a hobby, but I don't know the slightest thing about musical notes or composition, and I've never taken any kind of voice training, much less singing lessons. Yet here was a musical piece that sounded terrific, at least to my untrained ear. And to Wade—and his wife, who is also a musician.

With musical training, could I have been a composer? How many such compositions are lost, I wondered, because the individuals who might produce them are unaware of their own ability? Are the songs just there for the taking, like the books? Like everything? And as I listened to the cello, I thought, "Why, *I* come through me as easily as that song did; and my students come through themselves in the same way; and everyone does. Our own individuality is always coming through us easily; our finest moments, our greatest talents, our physical vigor—are all

coming through us that naturally. All we really have to do is go along with the selves we feel within us."

My original singing of the song and Wade's rendition of it were both exterior events, yet the musical composition that I sang so effortlessly sprang from the inner event that produced the song to begin with. And as I listened to Wade's rendition, I saw again that all exterior events come from inner ones, from an inner order that makes sense in its own context and at its own level; and that we translate events from one order to the other constantly, often without recognizing it. The "Song of the Creation" showed me this so clearly because I was so aware of my musical ignorance at usual levels.

But how real are internal mental events, and in what order of reality do they exist? Since our attention is usually directed outward, we usually look *through* the contents of our minds. These contents merge so smoothly into exterior events that often we aren't aware of them. Instead, the mind gets lost in its own contents and we never examine them at all.

When we do, we can trace some of the inner data outward into the physical events that seem to happen to us. Yet other inner contents remain in a different order of existence. Their reality is sensed. They may even take up a good amount of our "thinking space," yet we can't follow them out into events in the same way. They seem to exist in their own mental realm where they must be accepted or denied in their own context. They don't usually appear as exteriorizations.

This inward world of activities, symbols, and experiences seems to be as extensive and varied as the outside world, despite its much more private nature. The ordinary correlations we all agree upon aren't present, or rather they aren't easy to find. The inner world *is* populated by symbols, ideas, and personalities. Yet from our physical focus, they have a shifting quality and aren't easily captured. They seem to go on just beneath our notice, and when we suddenly become aware of what is happening, they vanish.

Dreaming is a good example of this inner order of events. We *are* conscious, but in a different kind of experience in which the usual rules don't apply. A completely alien psychological framework sometimes seems to exist, in which our thoughts and actions often seem to follow no pattern. Yet if we begin to study our dreams, we soon discover that our dream activities are not nearly as chaotic as they first appear.

For one thing, time is out of context in dreams, and this confuses us when we look at dreams from the waking state. Yet we quickly discover another kind of organization, though it isn't the one we concentrate on when awake; and it certainly isn't the way we order daily events.

We spend a good amount of our time asleep and dreaming, so these inward focused events must be important, and I think they possess a kind of continuity through the years. That is, as we have a waking history, we may have a dreaming history as well—but a history in which past and future events are put together; pieces of probable happenings tried out, chosen or discarded, until finally a model for physical events emerges.

Our mental reality in dreams is not limited to our living area physical perception. Events are experienced *as* physical, yet do not occur in the focus personality's usual focus. The process of dreaming takes time, but in that framework the mind experiences without the usual confrontation with space and time. The meeting of the focus personality with three-dimensional reality is opaque in the dream state, and it has relatively greater freedom.

Yet this different order of experiencing can also intrude into the waking state, particularly if it is consciously encouraged. When this is done and according to circumstances, we learn to switch from one reality to the other—to perceive the inner order of reality, while letting the exterior one momentarily recede into the background where we are only peripherally aware of it.

When I do this, I often use normal time and events quite purposefully as reference points; I remain adjacent to them, while I'm focused quite intensely at this different order of existence and primarily concerned with the characteristic kinds of events that happen there.

Again, reality itself has Aspects, and I see our reality as only one of these. Each one is a specialized version of a basic creative undifferentiated reality—an ever-present field of latent activity—that happens or springs into being as consciousness or "conscious-ized" energy encounters it, and patterns it according to its own perceptive focus. Each Aspect of reality is as legitimate as any other. Certain of these, I believe, can be glimpsed through altering the focus of our usual attention; and others probably cannot. We can, however, expand the nature of our consciousness by allowing it to perceive as many other Aspects as it can; while learning to hold its own balance, as it perceives and interacts in more than one order of events simultaneously.

The following example of what I mean was mentioned briefly in Rob's notes in *The Nature of Personal Reality: A Seth Book,* but I'd like to discuss it more fully here. At the time Seth was producing that book, and I was writing my book of poetry, *Dialogues Between the Soul and Mortal Self in Time.* One day I was in a particularly high period of inspiration, and ended with a verse in which the soul tells the mortal self about a "double light that unites both our worlds."

Rob and I expected company later in the evening. After dinner he went to the store for wine and crackers while I cleaned up the kitchen. It had rained all day, and when I finished the dishes, I opened the kitchen window, wondering if it was raining too hard for me to take a short walk.

Suddenly I stood transfixed. The night was dark-velvet soft, but all shining as the streetlights glittered on the wet side-walks. A puddle directly beneath the window caught my attention. I stared. The raindrops seemed to rush *out* of it as much as in. It was a living creature, shooting raindrops like porcupine needles. Street lights were drawn irresistibly into its fluid silvery skin. It looked like a bush of rainy stems and light blossoms, and as I watched, it stood up and walked—one of the most astounding things I've ever seen.

I knew that in the usual world, only a flat puddle lay in a parking lot. I also knew that through my physical senses I was somehow seeing this other Aspect of reality in which the puddle was a rain creature, alive, alert, and filled with energy. I *saw* it walk, form itself from the puddle and thicken. It was ridiculous to ask which was real, the creature or the puddle. Both were. But the creature was far more intriguing.

While I was fully perceiving the rain creature, though, I knew that anyone else focused in the usual state of consciousness would only see a puddle; and I knew that in the usual world, puddles don't stand up and walk. (In that framework, if I said they did, I'd be considered mad.) But as I looked at the fantastic glittering creature, I also knew that the puddle was a flat, colorless, unimaginative rendition of something else quite as valid. I also knew that if I went outside, the rain creature wasn't about to chase me down the street because the two realities, while connected, were separate, operationally.

As I stood there, really dazzled, something else happened. A sudden, round, unmoving yellow light appeared waist-high in the air in front of me, by the refrigerator. It hadn't come from any place that I could see. There was no lightning, for example. But there was no physical counterpart for it, as the puddle was the counterpart of the rain creature. The light was physical, but in our terms it had no right to be there. It was a perfect, flat circle of light; large, wider than the refrigerator. It didn't bleed outward at the edges or illuminate the rest of the room. Light— in a different order of existence. I was so startled by it that I leapt back involuntarily, and it vanished all at once.

Quite honestly I don't know where it came from. I'm convinced that it wasn't a reflection or hallucination. I think that in some odd way it was an event from that other order of reality; that symbolically it represented "the light that unites both our worlds." Both events, the rain creature and the light, ended up in *Dialogues*. They were used as creative material, which is an excellent way of correlating perceptions that transcend any one order of events. Art, it seems to me, is certainly a method of uniting various Aspects of reality and presenting them to our world.

Writing *Dialogues,* I moved constantly bewteen the two orders of events, using the state of usual inspiration as a connective. While immersed in that other reality, for example, I've found that it's difficult to communicate, and the creative inspiration serves as a bridge between both worlds, allowing for artistic translation.

Once when writing poetry, for example, I sensed huge figures standing around the rim of the world, their waists treetop high and their shoulders far above in the distance. I didn't rush out into the street yelling, "People, look at those giants." At the same time I knew that they represented benign consciousness, giant-sized by comparison with our own. And as that feeling swept over me, I couldn't continue with the poem because the events themselves went beyond that kind of awareness. This episode is discussed later in this book.

The thing is this: It's extremely important that we recognize that two orders of events *are* involved in such cases. Most likely, the faces seen by my students around the ceiling in class one night (as descirbed in Chapter One) belonged to this inner order. They were valid: They *did* exist, but in reference to . . . something else, some other reality that we translate into sense terms or pseudo-sense terms in order to perceive it at all.

If I'd insisted on the *physical* existence of my rain creature, for instance, and tried to superimpose its reality over the reality of the puddle in our world, then I would have been in trouble. If I'd run out into the street to encounter it more directly as an entity in our fact world, then I would have been forced to fit it into a world in which it did not belong. If I had paranoid tendencies, I could have projected upon it all the scorn I felt directed against me; I could fear it would attack me. Or seeing a neighbor, I could try to convince him of the rain creature's reality, insisting that it was REAL. Of course it was real, but not in our recognized order of events.

Some people find it easier than others to change the focus of their consciousness in this way and to perceive these "other" events. Few seem able to correlate them with normal life, however. I've only lately begun to study them myself, and so far all I'm sure of is that these events are distinguishable precisely because they don't fit into the recognized sequence of official reality.

I do know that when we confuse the two kinds of events, we're in trouble. We become disoriented in our world, our behavior becomes inappropriate. Perhaps I can explain what I mean more clearly by giving two examples of such behavior. Both involve people who were in mental institutions briefly; both had read the Seth books and just about every other "psychic" book on the market.

The first episode concerns a young man I'll call Ed, from the West Coast. He called me on the phone one day to tell me that he was Christ, and that the world was going to end in a few days. He'd just been released from the mental institution, where his parents put him after he'd seen visions and heard voices that told him he was Christ.

His stay at the hospital was brief. Ed was sane enough to figure out that he was there because he said he was Christ, so he stopped saying it. Instead, he agreed with his parents that he'd been exhausted from his college studies.

So he was released, but he was still convinced that he was Christ, reincarnated. He said that the world would end on February 2, yet he asked for confirmation from me. Had Seth said anything about it? And since he was sure that he was Christ, he took it for granted that Rob and I would drop everything and fly to the state in which he lived to meet him. In fact, he let me know that I was lucky to have such an opportunity.

I tried to tell him about the inner and outer order of events, to explain that he may have received some very vital private information from that inner order; that he'd then symbolized it, and now was trying to make the symbol literal. In Christian terms, each person *is* a part of the Christhood. I suggested that he'd had mystical experiences in which he felt that oneness, and recommended that he leave it at that; recognize his personal Christhood as subjectively valid—see it as a reality in one order of events that could be stated only symbolically in our world. I further suggested that he live his Christhood by being kind to himself and others, but not by trying to impose a literal Christhood upon physical reality. "We have to treat the orders of events differently," I said.

"But the inward order and the outward order are one. There's only a unity!" he exclaimed impatiently. Astute comment, and quite true. But he was trying to superimpose one kind of reality over another kind, and interpreting one kind of information from the inner order *in TERMS* of the outer one. He hung up, still convinced that he was Christ. Maybe he was a mite less sure than he had been. Obviously the world didn't end when he said it would, though, so maybe that made him think twice.

Ordinarily, the focus personality picks up one main station, but by turning its perceptive abilities just slightly off its living level (or home station) it can pick up other realities. The living level, representing the focus personality's direct intersection with the space-time field, is the strongest station. Other signals must be interspersed with the home signals or appear as meaningless "static," so these other perceptions color or tint our usual experience. The difference between normal events and other events is what gets our notice. The unofficial perceptions tell us that something different is happening, but the data are still coming through our home station, superimposed to some extent on our "program." When this happens, the resulting translation gives us events squeezed out of shape to some degree, like objects trying to fit into a space too small or cramped.

A sort of dimensional dilemma results. The new data push events as we know them slightly out of shape, even while they must be imprinted or impressed on experience as we understand it. Since the focus personality is involved with its living level home station, the information comes through the local program, altering it to some extent. But the creative material that's being changed is the psychic content—the beliefs, symbols, ideas, and intents of the conscious mind that interprets the data.

The second episode is a case in point. This young man, whom I'll call Arnold, telephoned and said, "I've had experiences like yours." Then he told a fascinating story. In a period of two days and nights, he'd seen vision after vision of "spirits" who spoke to him mentally and began what he said was a series of studies that were to develop his psychic abilities.

One face materialized on the ceiling and mentally introduced itself as a vision of Plato; and Plato from that moment became the young man's "teacher." He was told, however, that he must follow instructions completely and obey without question. On several occasions he found himself floating in the air outside of his body. The second night—while in his body—he was ordered to go out and walk for exercise; and when he did so, his footsteps "carried him away"; he couldn't stop walking. Dogs followed him, yapping, gazing at him "wild-eyed," until after five hours he finally banged at the door of a strange house, asking for help. The police were called, and Arnold was put into a mental institution.

This young man was also sane enough to learn the ropes. He stopped speaking to Plato when other people were around. He quit talking about the out-of-body experiences (which sounded quite valid to me, by the way). He was allowed to leave. Plato, he told me, gave him information that didn't check out, when he predicted certain dire circumstances for various members of his family. And Arnold still spoke to Plato, though he was now more cautious, and no longer blindly followed the latter's instructions.

Plato had always been the young man's hero, so Plato becomes his teacher—that's OK, in the inner order of events. But externalized as literal data, such a psychic encounter must then follow the ways of the exterior order, where it does not belong. It becomes a collector of projections. There's no doubt that Arnold's view of reality had been expanded, but no one taught him how to interpret the data he was receiving.

I don't know how many St. Pauls write to us, each with his own psychic credentials, received through automatic writing, dreams, Ouija boards, or trances. Personally I know of two separate groups in different sections of the country where all of the Disciples are meeting in reincarnated form. Unfortunately, the one Christ I talked to was unaware of these people. Maybe I should have put them in touch.

It's easy enough, God knows, to be facetious about all this: How gullible can people get? Usually the automatic communications in themselves or of themselves show no particular philosophical or literary quality, and only rehash dreary dogmas of gods and demons while encouraging the weary individual to be of good faith.

Yet many of these people are intuitively and psychically on to something. They aren't as bound as others are. They *do* live lives made richer through imaginative creativity, and they *are* picking up data from the free awareness field. The trouble is that they clothe valid experiences in the garb of very limited ideas.

Often such people have out-of-body experiences, for example, and become acquainted with the psyche's luxurious activity. But they often appear downright silly, deluded, or hopelessly gullible, because they don't know how to interpret the information they're receiving, or how to make the inward order of events fit into the outward one. And they believe that this must be done. Actually they're too literal-minded, attempting to transfer the vision unchanged into practical terms. Instead, that may be the easiest way to standardize the vision, and freeze it so that its true creativity and mobility are denied.

I'm sure that creative artists or craftsmen are more familiar with the ways of translating psychic material; of bringing it to birth in our world by a kind of transcendence that's true to the vision—actually truer to the vision *because* they don't try to make it fit into our usual definitions of fact. They know that the vision is more important, that facts can come out of it, but that the vision itself is essentially beyond that classification.

What fascinates us about art is its odd mixture of life and not-life. Physically, art doesn't live. The smallest flower will grow, but the greatest poem will never have more or fewer words than it had to begin with. The letters on this page will not sprout. They are dead. But something is contained within or between the letters that not only is alive in a different fashion, but can have what almost amounts to a superlife. Or call it a translife: A living quality that rides through the dimensions without lighting; that doesn't touch down in time and space as we do, but affects them; a quality that produces seeds none the less real for being nonphysical.

We're taught to check every perception out in the physical world because we've believed that no perceptions could come from anywhere else. When we run into an experience that is basically uncheckable in that fashion, then we really get worried. Again we ask: Is it true or false? Yet I think the vital part of our being lies in a realm of events that is equally uncheckable within three-dimensional reality, because it is too big to fit into that frame of reference. Again, that's the part of our being I call the source self, with the focus personality the portion that deals with the exterior order of events.

When we come into contact with the psyche, with the source self, in whatever way, we might well personify it as a great "dead" teacher, philosopher, artist, or religious leader, precisely because we would instinctively sense its multidimensional nature. Symbolically, the representation could be quite true. This sensed portion of the source self, according to Aspect psychology, would actually be the basic prime Aspect mentioned earlier, and would also represent our own idealized selves. The personification would be developed, however, in response to that multidimensional part of ourselves that can't appear as itself in this reality, but from whose existence our present being springs.

Such personifications may run the gauntlet from cardboard-cutout-guide personalities that mouth simple "goodyisms" to personagrams—personalities like Seth who reach out from the private psyche into dimensions still unknown to us, and whose reality even here is considerable. They may appear in visions, in dreams, or other states of consciousness. But their basic reality lies in another order of events, that becomes enmeshed with ours but exists apart from it and may serve as the source of the world we know.

When we interpret these personifications literally, as coming from people who are dead, as coming from great personages of history, or from gods or God, then they must be encountered and dealt with in the normal world of people and events. They must be good or bad spirits; they become tinged with the entire bag of concepts and beliefs held at any given time, and the initial vision simply turns into more baggage. The valid, perhaps vital, data are gone.

16

When Aspects Speak, "Unofficial" Messages, and Apprentice Gods

When Aspects of the psyche speak, their language is often poetic and dramatic and by its nature confounds the common-sense world. I receive calls and letters from people all over the country who mentally hear the voices of gods or otherworld intelligences, receive communications from beings in outer space, and see UFOs in every stray light:* They're convinced that their revelatory material will change the world for the better and help transform the race of man into a more spiritual condition.

The exaggerations in such cases are often so glaring and obvious that I'm at a loss trying to understand why they aren't apparent to the people involved. And such experiences happen to individuals in all walks of life, including adults who hold excellent positions in the sciences and other fields.

Just today, for example, I received another such letter, this time from a man convinced that he'd seen a UFO. Following that, he began receiving mental messages from a "colleague of Seth's." This material was of utmost importance and would save

*I am not referring to instances of UFO sightings that seem to have a *definite* objective basis.

the race from destruction. The man had also read my books and many other "psychic" books. He had a good job, and was in a position of responsibility.

All this man actually saw was one distant bright light. Why couldn't he realize that one light minus any other data didn't necessarily add up to a UFO? Yet as I thought about it and about the nature of Aspects as they appear in the psyche, certain things began to make sense.

The exaggerations in such cases are probably one of the most important elements, waking the focus personality out of its usual orientation by presenting it with a dramatic, exciting symbolic event. Most of these people *are* creative and explorative by nature, even if they haven't realized it. They've been dissatisfied with official beliefs, looking for something for years to give new meaning to their lives, and striving to release and express their own buried creativity. They yearn to unlock the deep psychic energy and power that has been blocked.

No small, innocuous event is going to do this. It must be literally earth-shaking; it must turn the ordinary world upside down, and it must have some *authority* to do this. Since most people don't understand their own inner reality and have been taught to mistrust the self, then the revelatory material must erupt as if it came from an outside source.

Often this presents them with an irreconcilable dilemma because they must prove that the outside source—god or spirit or spaceman—really exists, or lose faith in their source, and face the fact that their information is not infallible. And, generally at least, infallibility is the word here. The information must be all right or it is all wrong and meaningless, and their experience a fraud.

So on the one hand, often there is great pressure to make others accept the validity of the exterior source, and at the same time, a near-shattering suspicion that no such source is involved. I can certainly understand such reactions, with my own experiences. But somehow I walked mentally around them, viewed them with a fascinated but not awed air, musing, "Ah, now what does that mean? Mmm." And I kept a certain respectful distance until I had a better idea of what was going on.

When Seth first said that his material would be published, I thought, "Great, all the world needs is one more egomaniac out to save it from itself; one more visionary blinded by a vision, determined to force it on everyone else." I admit I *may* have gone overboard in my reactions in that respect. Yet I was free to pursue my psychic life because I knew I had to view that part of my experience as clearly as I tried to view any other part.

Instead of going "overboard," then, Rob and I embarked on the long series of tests explained in *The Seth Material* in an effort to discover how perception itself worked, and how reliable the Seth Material was in those areas that *were* checkable. But I never took it for granted that Seth was a Superbeing in literal terms. I struggled with the question, but I didn't accept *a priori* answers.

To most people working with current beliefs, though, such trance personalities must be gods or nearly, or nothing but the creations of a "deceptive subconscious." Again, this leads to great pressure as such a person tries to prove the validity of his or her source. But such messages are clothed in symbols. The inner language is not literal in our terms, and yet we often take the symbolic statement as literal truth in the most limited of true or false terms.

The exaggerations in such communications are probably in direct proportion to the person's previous inner desperation, and represent the tormenting need to free inner energies. These, then, take on the cloak of any ideas or persons in whom the individual has confidence, and thereby allow a belief and acceptance of concepts that the recipient would be afraid to entertain on his or her own authority. After feeling that life itself is meaningless, such a person is not only important enough to gain the notice of gods or superbeings, but they need his or her help to save the world.

Yet potentially what a therapeutic situation this can be! Such people often feel renewed zest, greater ambition, better health. They have a new sense of their own value and worth. On many occasions they solve problems that have bothered them for years.

But often, also, this does not last because the over-compensation is accepted literally. For instance, the person may now see himself as super-important. While before he didn't know what to do with his life, now he is to help save humanity from disaster almost single-handedly. A superhuman task is bound to make any human being feel a bit inferior and not quite up to it. Besides, others may not believe in or accept the superbeing or spirit to whom the individual may by now have transferred his own sense of worth. If the outside source isn't accepted, such a person often feels misunderstood and sees the world as against him. This may lead to further exaggerated claims on the part of the superbeing; offers to show proof and so forth, often followed by excuses when such proof in our terms doesn't develop.

The entire framework—the visions, mental communications, spirits—is highly creative, however, in the deepest meaning of the term. The emotional power represents the psyche's original impetus and forms a pattern meant to couch the inner events. The exaggerations are *not* lies, if understood in their own context as rich creative guises *meant* to dazzle and astound the limited nature of our daily-tuned minds; meant to make us question, wonder, and look upward into the further reaches of our inner skies.

The prosaic mind wants its truths labelled, parcelled in neat packages, with clear-cut contrasts for easy handling. It believes in good or bad, true or false, black or white, and is a stickler for authority. Many people who follow Seth, for example, haven't read my novel *The Education of Oversoul Seven,* because it is fiction and therefore "not true." They are precisely the kind of people who will mistrust their own revelatory data, and insist upon structuring it in conventionally accepted ways. Yet they are creative despite themselves.

They will most likely, however, be hardest on themselves in examining any of their own automatic writing, Ouija board material or whatever, for the exaggerations will have to be accepted as true and factual, or as lies. Here again, our religious concepts and rational true-or-false approaches can compound matters in a different way, for such a person reasons that if there are good spirits, there must be bad ones. Then many of the psyche's inhibited fears can also erupt, dramatizing themselves as demons, devils or evil visions that give orders of a destructive nature.

In such cases the focus personality never views its own psychic contents directly. Instead, the psyche's original revelatory message is played out in the pageantry of an already structured drama. The focus personality never looks beyond the personifications of the inner morality play for the greater meanings beneath.

Even this is of great import, providing an inner excitement, a quest for truth, however misguided, a new surge of meaning. For that matter, often such events come with their own "sign from heaven." The light seen by the UFO observer, for example, served as an exterior signpost saying, *This is important. Pay attention!* The light operated as an omen, highly important psychologically and symbolically. Linden, I'll call him, was certain that a UFO was involved and nothing could shake that belief, though he sighted no craft. But the inner statement was correct: On an inner level he *was* sighting something different and of significant importance to him. An unknown "object" was floating through his mental skies, and the inner world of the psyche was making itself known.

Often under such conditions (and in Linden's case also), odd things begin to happen. Outcroppings of valid, previously unofficial knowledge suddenly appear. Instances of telepathy or clairvoyance frequently accompany such experiences. Sometimes these are followed by out-of-body episodes—all richly evocative of a world beyond the usual one. For perhaps the first time, the focus personality sees that while it usually operates in space and time, the psyche from which it springs is free of such limitations. To some extent, data from the free awareness field becomes psychologically visible.

Please reread the material on personagrams earlier in

this book. Realize that I believe such revelatory data can be very valuable; the best of it coming at the very least from trans-dimensional portions of the psyche. Often it does contain information that is supernormal to us as we concentrate on the living area.

The Seth Material, I believe, offers the deepest insights into the nature of reality, and Seth himself is what I would call a trans-world entity, straddling inner and outer events. But I do not at this point define that in our ordinary terms of spirithood or personhood. I've spent a good deal of time and energy getting this far and learning to recognize various levels of reality. Certainly I hope to learn more.

The mail and phone calls do upset me, though, because I see so many well-meaning people trying so hard, without learning to distinguish between the validity of their own vision and its exterior symbolic clothing. Such Ouija or automatic writing messages, trance manuscripts and so forth *can be* extremely important. They represent the encounter of the focus personality with the vast power of its own psyche in dramatized fashion, and with the source of its being.

Each individual *is* responsible for the world, and each person's actions are intimately connected with the survival of the race. It's one thing to recognize this intellectually and quite another for the focus personality to be struck with an almost blinding personal recognition of this fact and presented with the importance of itself in the universe. This is none the less important because it comes in dramatized form.

In one way, each person *is* at the center of the universe and at the center of the psyche. I am not saying that there is no superbeing in such cases. I *am* saying that the psyche *is* a superbeing, existing outside of the time-space context, possessing knowledge that we desperately need at the living area of human experience.

I am simply asking that we no longer clothe revelatory knowledge in old guises. Actually, such experiences present us with nothing less than the opportunity for a direct confrontation with the psyche or source self, but most people immediately back away from the original naked vision. The psyche instead is cloaked in the guise of the master teacher or spirit or Indian guide or whatever; and denied the originality of its own nature and voice. The personagram becomes a puppet.

This may be a handy way of working with such material, but in the long run it's extremely limiting. Instead, a journey into the psyche is demanded. Does it spread out into an even more extensive self? Into a kind of consciousness that almost defies our present ideas of personhood? I strongly suspect that it does. Only a personal commitment to the study of the private consciousness can help us find any answers. Stripped of the juvenile symbolism that we usually throw upon it, the psyche or source self may surprise us with the original power and creativity that have always been behind the images, symbols, stories, and dogmas.

In a way, these guide personalities operate as private junior gods, reflecting in a far lesser fashion the mass "history" of the gods as they've shown themselves through the ages through visions and revelations. And left alone and understood for what they are, they might serve as man's true guides to his own greater reality. It's too bad we allow ourselves to cloud that vision.

For where do our personified gods come from, and what do they represent? What is behind them? In the following poem, I think that I sensed a part of their reality as they are reflected through the psyche and serve as guides, teachers, and representations that are themselves only shadows of what they really are, and we really are.

Apprentice Gods

In April the gods rise
as all religions teach
in their tales for children.
In winter the gods sleep
and close the million leaf eyes
through which they peek,
the green peepholes

through which they look
into our world.

In winter the gods take their voices back,
but you can hear their soft murmuring
far off before they speak
through the green tongues of the grasses
through which the gods secretly
send their messages.

In April the returning gods
bring festivals,
local magicians delighting the populace
with their apprentice god tricks;
divine troupe of conjurers,
earth-tuned, earth-bound,
wandering Apollos and Athenas
grown up since the world was young,
dazzling spirit bogglers,
turning winters into summers,
dying and returning,
shouting, "I'm here. . . . No, here!
See I died and yet I live
and you can too."

They play hide and seek with us
through the centuries,
perform disappearing acts, wear masks
miraculous in their complexity.
"Look, I'm here," and a white robed god
appears on a mountain top.
"These are my commandments,"
and apports of clay tablets
swirl to the feet of Moses.
"No, I'm here, bearded,
triumphant with my sword."
"No, I'm here, drunken with joy,
playing flutes in the dizzy hills,
beguiling the grapes with my abandon."
"Here I die on a cross,
dear children, cry,
but ah hah, I rise before your eyes,
no strings, see, and float into the sky,

*so rejoice and dance the spring
into its million resurrections."*

*What tales they spin,
what dramas glowing
in the theater of our minds,
as returning the gods roll out
the props of the centuries;
devils, soldiers, kings and queens,
churches, priests and alchemies,
rich and poor, murderer, thief,
and civilizations that seem
to rise and fall.*

*All this for us? Do we play roles
while wandering earth gods direct
and others watch?
Do they clap their hands
and thunder rolls across the skies,
shout, "Let there be light,"
and curtains rise,
reptiles flash their whiplike tails,
and smiling fish rise up from seas?
Do apemen and apewomen squat
in caves just put there in the dark,
offstage, but soon to move to center place
when a stagehand says,
"Let there be men?"*

*Yet I think not,
for how like us these earth gods are,
yet next to us, superstars,
bigger than life counterparts,
dramatizing us beyond degree
and running off with the show
as vicariously we watch
them play our parts.*

*How dear they are and how we love them,
our giant children,
projected out into a universe
with powers that are ours and yet are not.
How we follow their pursuits,*

shouting for our favorites
as they go racing through the ages,
cavorting among the stars,
blessing our friends for us,
confusing our enemies,
fighting our battles,
praising cardinals, gurus, and saints.
How we write their histories,
proclaim their sacred books—
Indian, Hindu, Christian, Jew,
each singing with the breath of truth.

Yet how were they born?
From what loins and womb?
What great uterus stretched
open between universes
dropping out our world,
you and me and gods and all?
What cosmic parcel,
Pandora's box
or surprising apport fell
from other worlds to this?

What master magicians
taught our gods their craft?
If you look behind the sleight of hand,
and refuse to be distracted
by the tales,
then other images emerge behind
the gaudy guises our gods wear.

17

From gods to "God," The Speakers, and God as an Event

So I believe that these gods are representations of something else, rising out of an inner order of events. I also think that in one way or another, we're in communication with that inner order and rise out of it, and that though we often distort the "inner voices," they have a meaning. But who are we, and what is our relationship with the gods, the "daemons," the muses whose messages bridge physical and nonphysical reality?

Each of us is aware of this inner reality to some extent. Each of us at some time or other is struck by a moment that is timeless, in which we "know what we know" in a way that has nothing to do with words, in which the focus personality almost stands at the summit of itself and views the inner skies of its own soul.

When people write me, often they speak about wanting to "possess" knowledge. To my way of thinking that's the quickest way of losing it. Or they want to learn the secrets of the universe in Giant terms: No tiny funny truths, but just the big important spiritual ones. And that attitude, I think, can close us off from the humble but divine voice of nature that's here all the while.

And what about our ideas of God? Where do they fit into all of this?

Our ideas of personality and personhood make it difficult for us to consider a multidimensional God. Even our species orientation and loyalty hamper us in this respect. We're sure that man is more spiritual than a cat or insect; and usually we insist that only man possesses a soul. God becomes superman (and not even, for example, superwoman, so closely do our religious concepts follow our social, cultural and biological conceits).

God is usually thought to reside outside nature, rather than inside it; as apart *from* his creations. Our religions have always tried to explain the opposites that appear in human experience. Seldom have they searched beneath these seeming opposites for the source of all appearances.

Yet from the inner order of events, all physical experience springs into experience. Here is the source of being, so difficult for us to conceive. For certainly God is not a person in our terms. If "His" existence can be explained at all from our point of view, the idea of a multi-personhood would come closest. Even here we're limited, though, by our own concepts about the nature of consciousness itself.

God would be a superconsciousness, but if this wasn't endowed with love, wisdom or understanding or some counterparts to these, then at least to us the idea would be meaningless. I'm convinced that the reason for our being *is* our being. This doesn't make sense to us either if that being is preceded and followed by an annihilation or by a nirvanic merging and loss of individuality, however joyful. I find it difficult to believe that individuality exists only to be destroyed, and I insist that in our belief in personal identity, we may be closer to God than we realize.

For God must honor individuality, since even in our reality all things, even snowflakes, are unique. And if a God created the universe, then a part of the creator must be within his creations: in you and me, stars, animals, insects, and rocks. As an event, God must still be happening; as observable or unobservable now as he was in ages past, for in some way this world itself is a materialization of his creativity, and that creativity constantly continues. We exist in God's newness and nowness, whatever our definitions.

And whatever God is, he is not static or unchanging. To the contrary, such a concept of God denies him even the natural limited growth enjoyed by his creatures. What a cramped dimension in which to exist—perfect beyond all change or fulfillment; almost like a senile god with no place to go but down, living through his children and their accomplishments.

Sometimes we're so earnest, so intent and determined to *know,* that we cut ourselves off from our own inner knowing. And we always expect mystic experience to be solemn, shattering, awe-inspiring—and to fit in above all with our private concepts of good and evil and morality. Many of us, also, have the idea that to know God is to lose ourselves, to fall willy-nilly into an overpowering solution of cosmic love in which all individuality is dissolved. To those so anxious to lose their individuality I say, "Lot of luck." If God gave us individual selves, he must be rather astonished to find so many so willing to throw the gift in his face. And without so much as a thank you. Just, "Take me back, Lord, I'm sick of being myself."

So I've never had that kind of mystic experience, so lauded by many, in which a Jane dissolves into God. But I do believe that God "dissolves" in all his beings, and that we rise into consciousness and song because our individuality in itself is a part of any Godhead. To throw away individuality is like throwing the baby away with the bath water.

But no, the variety and freshness of even our own experience hints of an ever-changing source of energy and expression.

Here I'd like to discuss an experience I had two years ago. It's mentioned briefly in Rob's notes in *The Nature of Personal Reality,* which Seth was dictating at the time. One day in a state of inspired creativity I wrote a poem called "The Speakers."

As I wrote, the inspiration outdid itself. I could tell that the inner symbols were becoming exteriorized. It was then that I sensed through the window the images of massive beings; they were ringed at the end of my personal eye-level horizon, seeming to rise so high that only their trunks were "visible." Their shoulders would be in space far above.

These images were not three-dimensional. I knew that I must be projecting them outward, and they blended with the houses and trees and scenery. I saw them just as I was writing about "massive relatives." I could no longer write. The vision had escaped the poem. It was becoming real.

We were expecting important company. I called Rob, told him what was happening, and decided to take a brief nap. As soon as I lay down, though, a startling series of events began. In the meantime, Rob left the house to meet our guests at the airport, so I was alone.

I'm going to quote from my original notes, written just afterward:

> *I made an attempt to nap . . . . Suddenly one idea sprang out at me, literally shocking me. We are IN God. We were NEVER exteriorized. The realization just isn't contained in those words, and they do little to explain my feelings. For suddenly I felt being-in-God as being in a house. Everything we imagine being outside, in the three-dimensional world, ourselves included, is inside. There is no outside. I felt claustrophobic. My eyes were open. I saw the bedroom and bath beyond, and my vision was altered in some funny fashion so that while I saw everything as being normal, at the same time I saw everything as being inside an inside that was itself inside, ad infinitum. I felt dwarfed for an instant . . . .*
>
> *Almost immediately, however, came the oddest feeling of fantastic security and I realized that being inside God, everything we saw WAS God, regardless of form, and that we were literally made of God-stuff and therefore were eternal. Next came the feeling, again difficult to describe, that this inside was so inconceivably vast that within it was all the ever-expanding space possible; and that only an inside could possess those characteristics of constant expansion. Next came the realization that this "God's" thoughts*

became alive, endowed with the various kinds of dimensionality that then bring forth others of their kind . . . .

The next experience happened almost at once, but was not included in Rob's notes in *Personal Reality* because it wasn't pertinent to the discussion at hand. It is very pertinent to *this* discussion, though. As I lay on the bed, staring, seeing these versions of insideness, my eyes must have closed. My body suddenly felt literally massive. I grew slightly frightened, but reminded myself that there was nothing to be alarmed at. Then I felt myself expand in some new way, grow very light, and begin to rise.

From my notes:

At some point the massiveness stabilized. I was still lying flat, but not on the bed. A man emerged from my skull, and he instantly gained giant size. He began to stride over mountains that suddenly appeared—these might also have emerged from my skull; I'm not sure. My consciousness entered the man, though I was not his consciousness; he had his own. Yet from within his giant form I felt his massive legs striding over the mountains (exhilarating to me, but quite normal to him!). I was very aware of his leg motions, the huge thighs, the spring of the earth beneath our feet. His steps were gigantic in our terms.

At one time from within him, I felt "us" bend down. Again, to me, "we" were so impossibly tall that bending down that far was startling, to say the least. Beneath, in a small hollow of the earth was a fire, small to him, and inside it miniature people were writhing and burning. (To me, the people were normal-sized.) As my massive companion bent down he seemed mildly astonished, reached into the flames and lifted the people out, tossing them gently into the air. Anyway, he'd freed them, and I knew that this was a symbol of hell in religious terms, and that there were probably other such fires into which people stupidly blundered. The fires were just there, having no moral overtones at all. His attitude was merely a mild astonishment, and wonder that these beings could be so silly, much the same way that I feel when I see an ant crawling in the sink beneath the faucet just when I'm ready to turn the water on. (Sometimes I get the ant out first or scare him off or whatever.)

I wasn't sure what happened to the people, but knew that

they were free, and had changed form. I saw them through his eyes though, and after he freed them they were like a glowing group of fireflies, bright for a moment in dark space; then he forgot about them at once.

It was then that the giant took one or two steps upward, and this brought us from the earth to a star or other planet. We were walking along the surface. There were other beings like him suddenly all about us. One had just died. The others laid him out flat on the ground. He was literally huge, laid out that way. Through the giant being's eyes everything was normal-sized, of course, but as I looked out separately through his eyes, I viewed everything as gigantic. In a ceremony I barely remember, the others surrounded the dead one, turned his body around several times in certain directions, until finally he started to rise, still lying flat. Then he began to spin very slowly. The spin grew quicker and quicker, and his body began to rise faster at the same time until finally, as I watched, he began to disappear above in space.

In some way I've now forgotten, his giant form changed as it spun, and he came to rest in space as a planet. I was still on the surface of the same star and visually I couldn't see—though I looked—where the form came to rest in space. But I saw all of this very clearly through the giant's mental images. The dead giant's consciousness roused again, and as it did, the planet began the process we'd call evolution. That is, his thoughts turned into emerging life's beginning forms.

In that experience I think my source self was personified as the giant being, and I tried to view our three-dimensional existence and this universe from that framework. The earlier feelings of being-inside-God and never being exteriorized were then acted out as my own consciousness, still itself, was later experienced through the giant's. It's as if a cell within my own body were suddenly aware of its position, viewing my reality through its own eyes and then, suddenly, through mine; being now and then aware of my intentions as apart from its own.

The revelatory information was experienced in ways that I could understand, symbolically and psychologically true, and carrying great emotional impact. The entire experience *was* a trans-world communication; a message from the source self to the focus personality, using sense data that did not intersect with our usual space-time coordinates in our world. But my consciousness was not blurred: Instead it was heightened and illuminated, aware of its unique separateness as well as its part in a greater organization.

The entire episode was dazzling in its emotional intensity. Yet I didn't suppose that I'd *literally* been taken to another physical planet, and I certainly knew that in this system of events no giant being emerged from my skull. I didn't say to my students: "Yes, there are giants because I've seen them. One came and took me on a journey to another planet."

I believe that the whole rich, dramatic event was an interpretation of something else, dramatized so that I could understand—to some extent at least—certain concepts that may lie beyond words and images as we know them.

As I rose and dressed, the birds were singing, and I *knew* that these were the gods singing. This wasn't a symbolic or artistic intuition, but sudden known fact. I was listening to the gods singing, and found myself laughing at the incredible sweetness of their song. At the same time I saw my nails were chipped, and touched them up. And my motions were as natural and blessed as the birds' songs; and my laughter was the laughter of the gods too.

Yet in this system of events, how do you say, "Listen, the birds are gods. There are fifty million gods out there, people. Listen to them"? Because in our world, then, people want Super-people-Gods who give commandments and yell about hellfire and help us wage war against our enemies.

Even while I greeted our company, I was still caught up in that revelatory knowledge: We were never exteriorized. The words kept running through my mind. Yet soon the immediacy of the feeling vanished, and I could only try to remember it. Later I thought: Does that mean that we aren't really objective creatures in space and time? Sometimes, even now, when I recall the experience I get the oddest claustrophobic feeling as if there's something to get out of, or as if we're still unknowingly in some cosmic womb, not even half born. And I think: Who wants to be a dream in a god's mind?

Yet *then,* at the time, I felt the greatest freedom: Space itself was born from within, and this within was literally endless and capable of all kinds of expansion. There was no outside! *Then,* I thought: Of *course.* And it made brilliant sense. The whole inside-outside, subjective-objective affair was meaningless.

Later I thought: No outside? And my mind blurred around the edges.

At the time, it was impossible to ask where God was not, for what he was was everywhere and everything. When the birds were singing and I knew they were the gods singing, I also knew that the gods were what God is. There was no contradiction. Later, all kinds of silly questions came to mind. Do you capitalize "God" and put "gods" in small letters? And surely there's a difference between a . . . god and a bird. What nonsense. What was it that I thought that I knew?

Yet stubbornly I insist that I did know, and that the knowing is still there, untouched by the seeming contradictions that appear at the living area of experience. The trouble is that God doesn't make sense to us unless we can personify "Him," "Her," "It" in some way, so we try to imagine what God would be like—in our terms.

Writing this, I remember my rain creature. It was a puddle in this order of events. Was the rain creature the spirit of the puddle? And was the light I saw in the kitchen really *my* spirit in that inner order of events? Was I the physical counterpart of it that I looked for, and couldn't find? For how different that inner world might look from this one, and so who would guess that they were each a part of each other?

So a god might appear in one guise here, quite commonplace. He might appear as everything we experience, including you and me, giving reality its fantastic patterns and individuality. Yet within these selves of ours in the inner order of events, in the hidden insides of ourselves, we would know this greater reality from which we spring. And we would send messages from there to the selves that we know.

Out of this inner sensing would come all the personifications of God, the dramas and sacred books, as we tried to relate inner events in three-dimensional terms.

Maybe our desire to know who God is puts us in the same position as some hypothetical unborn child who wonders where its mother is, and wants to see her face to face: We have to get born first. We may be inside what God is. The child's birth puts it in the presence of its mother in objective terms, while removing it from its mother in a basic way, so that the child can grow on its own. So perhaps our seeming exteriorization is the same thing.

So if we are inside what God is, conversely God may be inside what we are, though we never come face to face with "him" in our terms. I think that all "mystic" visions, revelations, inner voices, and automatic writings are our interpretations of greater truths about ourselves, messages from multidimensional Aspects of our being to these selves in space and time.

When we hear or sense such messages, what do they really mean? The following poem, "The Speakers," is the one I wrote that day in which I tried to examine my own experience and find at least a hint of an answer. Who are the Seths, the muses, the voices? As I wrote, the poem outdid itself; the answers came as symbols and the symbols became real, until finally they emerged as the experiences just mentioned in this chapter. The poem says things that can't be said in prose, and as such it represents the clearest statement I can make so far about "revelatory information" and its source.

The Speakers

*Let me then as a speaker speak
with these voices that issue through me,
mine, yet not the me I know
who struggles in the marketplace for bread,
or turns despondent at a dreary day. Instead
these voices, daemons, with their own ancient
yet new powers leave their mark on me
as surely as ink on the pages of a book.*

*I'm holy, but only as the leaves are,
and miraculous but only as the wind is
that rushes through the open window of my mind,
filling it with times and places that spring alive
and open up the geography of my brain,
adding continents, rivers, soft arching valleys
not there before,*

*completing my inner skies, in which
new stars and planets appear
to astound the shepherds of my thoughts
who acclaim new births unendingly
and stare upward, hands lost in the wooly fabric of the earth,
eyes in awe mirroring the ever-changing universe.*

*Into my mind come voices that speak
with the eloquence of ancient oaks given speech,
and so their gracious wisdom and wonderings rise
with a wild yet restful resonance
that rides far above my daily-tuned ears.*

*And others speak with smaller yet even fuller songs,
sung before the sounding of the first word,
as if the atoms and molecules each yearn for speech
and through me express the deep
belonging that casts them into form and changes them
with such swift tenderness that they fall
through one image into another, loving each,
yet staying only long enough in one
to animate its magic motion
with biological songs that sing each thing to be its own,
yet a member of its kind.
So now I let these voices speak*

and listen to what is said
through the whirling patterns
of my dizzy creaturehood.

"Muses? Earthgods? Spirits?"
The weary intellect like a traveler alone at night
trembles and shouts out, "Who's that?"
and fearfully turns his head, suspecting the worst
from such unconventional company.

"Where are your credentials?
From what honest school of knowledge do you come?
Why bother me with your silly tales
when I must be on my way
about the sober details that concern my life?"
So asks the intellect, frowning, pausing unknowingly
on the threshold of himself from which
though he's forgotten
the muses first came.
Now like aliens they seem to confound him,
adding their own whispering
to the constant chatter that he carries like a bag
of rattling groceries in his head.

One voice says: "The fruits of your thoughts are rotting.
They are too old, their sticky juice
is good only for catching flies.
The bread of your endeavor is soggy
and heavy in the basket of your mind."

Another voice says:
"Why are you so hesitant and lonely
and so frightened for your dignity
that you refuse our company?
Surely you remember us, the voices
in the nursery that spoke
through sunlight, shadows, furniture;
the names you knew before the speaking of the words
diagramed your listening
and you became so particular
about what you allowed yourself to hear?"

I am a vortex
spinning myself in the magic web of my being,

weaving the seasons thread by thread,
night by day.
The weeks glimmer
in the translucent nests of the months' intersections
through which I move
and extend myself.

My vocation came upon me suddenly
when my adulthood met the ancient child,
and in an instant my hour spoke its own alphabet
and formed a magic word
that echoed
through the yellow daisy fields of my cells' knowledge,
called together all the lost
parts of me who'd fallen off in jigsaw images,
or crumbled like the edges
of rich continents, breaking apart
in small jagged islands of forsaken thought.

The word called the east and west
and north and south together,
and like a magnet drew
the furthest reaches to one tune,
the discordant wound into symmetry.
My breath is an airy river
carrying me inward and outward
into worlds so rich that I wonder
at the shallow eddies in which I walked;
The river—the rhythm of my naturehood
in which I feel my place and hear my tone clear,
yet merged with all things else.

Invisibly beyond the edge of touch I feel
realignments triumphantly assembling,
celebrations as long forgotten prodigals come home.

My eyes chant a new language,
my hands join like stars forming a new galaxy,
an alliance in which their wisdom
speaks joyfully their double five worlds.
The shadows of my fingertips
fall out on inner landscapes,
conjure magic from the forests

and form paths across the centuries
upon which my brothers walk.
My body knows its holy flesh focus
in this place and time,
and feels its own song sing itself
through the substantiation of this form.

And other speakers, tongueless,
speak out through my fingertips,
dream in hidden caverns of my blood,
doze within my creaturehood,
who once walked the earth as we do now
and spoke, and will again.
Even as I give them tongue
so will they in their turn speak for me.

A little village once in Spain
may for a moment nest within my hand,
forming now a tiny cell
of friendly atoms and molecules
instead of houses, barns, and fields,
enclosed by mountains of smooth bone
beneath the brilliant moon of brain,
and each small structure hold intact
the memory of king, knave, housewife, fool or thief,
each alive and in its place,
standing in the doorway of its soul,
so dear—
and tongueless for a time.
Each shape my body knows
inside or out this magic flesh,
carries memory of hearth and fields and wood,
and once again in different form
will speak for me who give them voice.

I am consumed
yet born again from a different womb,
remade
from an earlier self who even now
fades into memory and becomes
an atom in someone's hand,
a leaf fallen into fresh ground
to be itself born again,

or a dust mote floating past my cheek,
now unrecognizable
and gone from me.

Who speaks?
Yet speaking for the tongueless,
I find my voice
and no longer stutter
through bleak silences,
for these voices
which are not mine
fly on my wings and I on theirs,
until there is only
flight.

Do the speakers live?
Their massive lives straddle ours,
and through the pupils of their eyes
we look out upon a universe.
All that we know or see
is but a detail in a scheme so overpowering
that now, writing, I grow weak
and cry that what I sense
falls through my words which cannot hold
such inner evidence,
for I am left with gaps so huge
that what is unsaid is all—
and there—what I cannot hold—
is what I am and what you are.
My thoughts are as incapable as my cupped hands
to grasp these meanings,
and our lives
are like the shadows of my fingertips.
So are we
sent out by other ones,
massive relatives, in a family so vast
yet in which each member
basks.
So I speak words
that are not mine or yours
but theirs,

and so give nature speech
in what humble way I can.

True or false?
These voices live in realms
where true and false are meaningless,
and rise up with a fire
that never finds final form,
but speaks the spirit
with a flame
that forms all worlds,
and is behind
the truths we know.
And so I hint
of truths beyond life or death
in which the birthbed and the grave
dissolve
in a magic calculus in which
each has its place.

18

Sphere of Identity. Events as Invisible Structures

In "The Speakers" poem, I spoke of "massive relatives." It's almost impossible to explain what I mean by that in ordinary terms; not physical giants certainly. Perhaps giant consciousness comes closest to expressing it. Are we embryo consciousness then, infants in that respect, being spoon-fed one reality at a time? Are we leashed to our living area of physical experience, with only dreams or visions giving us a small glimpse of what is outside?

I think there's more to it than that. I think each of us has a "sphere of identity" that we've hardly begun to explore. First, though, take a look at Diagram 7. It shows the focus personality as I've described it so far.

The circle represents the focus personality at a moment of our time as it moves along the living area. The living area is our physical experience level, because only here do events intersect with space and time. The inner level of experience is composed of probable events or banks of actions from the free awareness field. From these, we choose according to our desires and intents. The probable events we accept are actualized as physical experience on the living area. All experience actually happens at once, but the properties of the living area form an apparent past and future

Diagram 7. The focus personality as described so far, surrounded by its inner level of experience

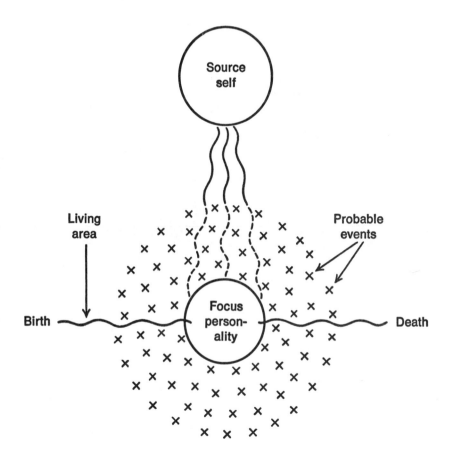

The x's represent probable events that serve as banks of action from which we choose physical experience.

Diagram 8. The sphere of identity with its inward order
of events

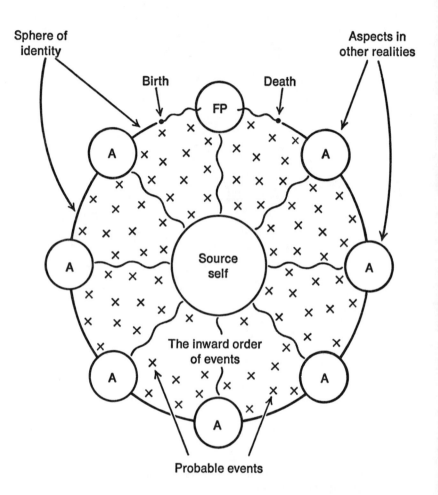

An inside view of the focus personality and its living area from the standpoint of the source self. The outside circle represents the source self's identity in the inward order of events, from which all probabilities emerge.

Diagram 7 represents the source self and focus personality as if the source self were positioned *above* the three-dimensional field. Actually it would be *within* it, in the inward order of events. Diagram 8 is an attempt to show an inward look from the source self's point of view, as it "faces" our reality.

Here the large circle represents a sphere of identity coming out of the source self. This sphere of identity would be in constant motion and ever-changing. The small circle on the living area represents the focus personality in physical life.

This diagram actually shows the living area in a truer light, as a curve, rather than as a straight line, though our physical perception makes it seem straight, leading from birth to death. (In the same way, our senses tell us that the earth is flat—we don't fall off.) But this curve of physical existence also has peaks and valleys in it and depths not usually explored. Theoretically you could live "eternally" in one life span, still rooted firmly on the curve by exploring these "moment points"—the peaks and valleys that go off from any instant.

As in Diagram 8, the focus personality is *that part of* the source self's sphere of identity that impinges into three-dimensional reality. The focus personality's experiences, then, are the result of the "friction" as inner events are sparked into physical ones by this intersection.

The focus personality attracts inner events that rush toward actualization. Actually I see the focus personality as the psychological opposite of a blank hole, for through it inner events rush into actualization, mass and weight appear, time spins outward into experienced reality, and a universe of objectified phenomena comes into being.*

*Physicists postulate the existence of black holes in space. These are remnants of giant collapsed stars that have become so unimaginably dense, with such enormous gravity, that nothing can escape from them, not even light. They are invisible spots in which time and space have lost their meaning, and matter disintegrates.

Some physicists have also theorized that the energy "lost" in black holes turns up in another universe as a white hole.

We fall through this "psychological white hole," experiencing the plunge of time and the change of events in one direction. It's at least possible that other consciousnesses fall "backward" from a source on the other side; and perhaps despite all we think we know, other people are plunging backward through time as quickly as we seem to be plummeting through it.

Even physically we are events in this universe, composed of the same stuff as it is. We may be white holes ourselves in a certain sense, but if so, we wouldn't be aware of it. As time disappears in a black hole and matter disintegrates, so, through psychological white holes, time would be built up and matter formed at rates that *inside* would seem perfectly normal and logical.

Psychological white holes would be finite. At death, a reverse would take place. Then we might turn into psychological black holes, in which time falls apart and matter dissolves into its components; weight and mass disappear and light is not emitted. The light might be present, but from outside the black hole it would not be apparent. Later we'll carry this analogy a bit further, examining what might happen to the nature of consciousness under such conditions.

For now, let's look more closely at the nature of events as we encounter them. Generally the focus personality's experience involves specific space-time events, but as precognition shows, some events are perceived in an out-of-time context. Such an event still won't exist for the perceiver as an ordinary one. A future development "seen" now will still happen in the *future,* and not at the time of the perception. For example, if A sees a vision in which B dies on a certain future date, and if this probable event does occur, then it will happen on the future date, and not in the now of the perception. For the perceiver, the event may seem to happen twice; but when it does, it will be in its own space-time intersection.

Such an event may be occurring in the free awareness field, at the inner order of events where it is in a probable state (from our viewpoint). As mentioned earlier in this book, I believe that cells are "precognitive." (Seth has always insisted on precognition as a cellular characteristic.) Certain correlations may be made automatically at deep body levels in which, for example, our cells may know when our parents will die. Sometimes this data may rise to consciousness. I don't believe in any kind of pre-destination; and I see events at any stage as being plastic. Such "cellular death calls" might frequently come and pass, then, reflecting changing conditions, the triumph over diseases and so forth. But at certain levels, our cells may well reflect the health or illness of our children and parents, in a way that has nothing to do with heredity in usual terms.

Strange thought: But could the cure of one family member also help cure another one who might be suffering from some malady quite different? The symptoms of any disease are only the surface portions of the disease-event; the roots may have far different connections than we've supposed.

Let's look at the composition of events. Again, they're composed of energy just as objects are, but so far we haven't learned to isolate their components. Events, it *seems,* must be personally experienced to be meaningful to us. Yet a tree falling in a forest *is* an event in the world focus level, whether or not any one hears or sees its falling. Our hearing or seeing the tree fall are potential ways for us to perceive what happens. The tree falls whether or not we know it. The ground reacts to the sound waves in its own way, without needing ears. The ground's recation is a part of the event, as our reaction to any event is a part of it.

While we think of events as definite and concrete, apart from the perceiver, as psychological objects almost, stuck in space and time, then their true nature and relationship escape us. We can't see the atoms and molecules that make up a table, but we know they're there, within the solid-seeming surface. We *can* learn to sense the "atoms" of an event, though, by looking through the obvious happening for all the minute multitudinous events within or beneath the surface. The physical event is just frozen motion that seems stuck in time, if only for a moment. Free will is possible, I believe, because of the true plastic nature of events, and the existence of probabilities that always cluster about any space-time action.

Certainly our body's integrity rests securely in this plastic medium of events, and at certain levels the cells deal with immense calculations simply to maintain body stability. Keeping other probabilities out is as important as choosing the "correct" one in this context; and a constant juggling of probabilities underlies the body's condition in any moment of our time. Seth discusses this in *The Nature of Personal Reality*.

As mentioned earlier, events also show their other faces in the dream state where, I believe, we often deal with their larger probable versions, mixing and matching possible combinations and sequences, choosing our physical tomorrow in a state of consciousness that works intimately with the inner composition of events. Some dreams, in fact, may already be translations of other experiences that we never catch, dealing with perceptive levels above or below both words and images as we understand them.

Images are basic to physical perception. They are also necessarily stereotyped ways of experiencing "reality." Our senses present us with a lovely package of the world. We hardly ever realize that it's a do-it-yourself kit; that at other levels we put the pieces together, assemble the ingredients then present the entire box to our conscious selves, pretending it's a surprise and something entirely apart from us or our creativity. We experience events the way we do because of our senses, then. We're programmed to perceive the world in a certain fashion, but there isn't any basic reason why it couldn't be experienced differently.

If we turn the focus of our attention away from the living area even to a small degree, the world looks different. It feels different. You realize that reality can be our way—and other ways too. For that matter, the utilization of images could even follow different associative patterns than the ones we use; and appear quite differently to others who were programmed differently.

Some kinds of consciousness might perceive an object at once as it changes through time; see the old chair and the new one, simultaneously for example; or see a town, say, as one object with many moving parts. Others might see images formed from sound, while not seeing our objects. They would see a musical note as an image, but a table might be relatively invisible except for sound values that we wouldn't be aware of.

In such frameworks, what would happen to events? In a different kind of reality, when we thought of Uncle Ellis, we might see all the objects connected with him at once. These might change in the next moment, to be replaced by an entirely different set of objects connected with Aunt Ellie.

A sudden shift in focus conceivably could result in someone's experiencing yesterday in everyone else's today. We say that someone lives in the past, while obviously they share part of the present with us through their existence in our now. But certainly the same kind of shift takes place sometimes, in which events from the past literally override the present ones. (On several occasions, for example, I watched Mother Butts in her old age, react to a "past" event in *our* present.) In such a case, I'm convinced that the powerful motivating forces of personality would have moved just off the living area.

The point of all this is the fact that our experience of reality and events is the result of a delicate tuning-in of our consciousness to a particular "earth program." Any straying away from that home station may well present an entirely different picture of reality.

Usually, however, most of us experience events from our recognized sense-focus framework at the living area in which body integrity is firmly rooted. Sometimes illness or drugs operate to scatter our usual focus and give us a glimpse of other alternate realities, other ways of perceiving and organizing data. We see events out of shape, elongated or shortened, squeezed, magnified, or shrunken. Unless we know what we're doing, we can lose our fine orientation.

Such unofficial perception, however, makes us question the nature of events in general. We usually take it for granted that actions must occur simultaneously in time and space, for example. We find it difficult to imagine an event happening in space but not in time; or in time and not in space. Yet all events, I'm convinced, happen outside of both, in that inward order from which time and space themselves emerge. What we perceive as an event is only one blossom from invisible rooted events that intertwine through the universe.

Three weeks ago Rob had a very brief dream in which a strange man and woman were asking for our rent money. Rob was going through our accounts, trying to find old rent receipts in the dream. He told me about it in the morning, then we both forgot it. Two days later we received a letter informing us that a new real estate agency would be handling the house in which we have our apartments. Rent was to be sent to a new address. The letter also mentioned that the real estate people would be around to check the apartments and discuss the new arrangements.

The house has changed hands only once in the twelve years we have lived here, and the same agency has handled it since the original owner sold it. When we got the letter, we realized that at least some of the dream's contents were true: Rob had received definite information that checked out in daily life: Strangers would be asking for our rent. We thought that was the end of it.

A week ago however, we received a call from the new agency: They hadn't received our rent money, though Rob had mailed them a check. Rob found himself searching for the check stub which served as our receipt. As he did so, he recalled the dream again. And that wasn't the end of it. Yesterday two strangers came to the door, a man and woman, checking the apartments for the real estate agency.

Rob's dream was precognitive, but what does that mean? Is a precognitive event one happening in time but not yet in space? If a physical event is only one version of a greater one, is a foreseen action an event picked up out of context, blurred, perceived off focus, before it's clearly differentiated in space-time intersection?

In Rob's dream, again, a strange man and woman asked for our rent, and Rob was going through his accounts, trying to find rent receipts. These events happened at once in the dream, but in actuality they were strung out in time, over a period of three weeks. The first part of the dream, connecting strangers and rent money, seems to refer to the change of procedure on the part of the landlord, which would have happened before the dream itself. Our physical notification came with the letter. The other events were seemingly dependent upon the dream's first statement.

The dream condensed these events, mixing past and future into one. Physically the events were played out in time, in serial fashion. I'm convinced that in such cases, we tune into the free awareness field in the dream state and perceive events from a different perspective.

Energy fields surround each event, but only when these coincide with three-dimensional reality do we recognize an event as physical. Even here, however, there is a great difference in time distinction. We know little about the time sense of animals, much less that of insects, trees, or plant life. We know that it must be different from ours, but it still lies within our dimensional context.

It's as if we are all plugged into a huge switchboard. Lights flash off and on as the inward series of events intersects with this space-time webwork and clicks "on." The network itself automatically transforms inward action to exterior events, and turns each light on. We are all connected to this switchboard while we are alive; indeed our nerves and cells would be a part of it, both receiving and transmitting constantly.

Each of us is an earth event, transformed through the network into physical actuality. We are turned on, broadcasting. The body is the living home station, and through it all physical actions must come. We are constantly clicking off and on, though our earth-tuned consciousnesses are geared only to a certain series of frequencies, and do not pick up the "off" periods. Again, it's possible that we have other home stations as well; that other Aspects of our identities are tuned into other realities as we are to this one. Some may be enough within our own range so that we can tune into them from here, where they will bleed through and tinge our events just enough to get our notice.

Diagram 9 is a representation of a hypothetical whole event. Actually, I see each event as a part of every other, so the designation is arbitrary and merely for convenience. The perceived event and the focus personality coincide, with changes in each; the focus personality becomes a part of the event, and the event becomes part of the focus personality. The event will be experienced according to the methods of reception available to the perceiver. Those methods differ, so that even in our dimension entirely different kinds of realities can be, and are, built up from the same common "stock of events".

Animals will experience an event also perceived by us in an entirely different fashion, for instance; and while we share certain stock events, our methods of perception are so various that they are used to organize systems of existence that can appear quite alien.

Any event, however, would be formed by energy's (conscious-ized) intersection with space and time at a now point; the "waves" splashing out in all probable directions, forming on the living area the apparent past and future. The further away the event from the living area, the less real it would be to us. The entire event, however, would exist in the free awareness field of pre-perception.

Diagram 10 is a representation of a mass event. As mentioned, the surface level of the living area would be more like a curve than a straight line. Mass events happen when one event intersects with the living area of a group of focus personalities. In terms of energy, there is an explosive element here, an overall change in the inner landscape at such intersection points that is quite as real as any earthquake, causing readjustments and sometimes complete reorganizations at the living level.

When inner events collide with three-dimensional reality, then, there well might be an explosion or charge as real as that

Diagram 9. A hypothetical whole event

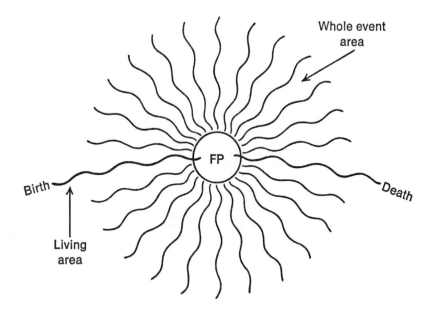

As it travels along the living area from birth to death, the focus personality perceives a portion of the event area at a space-time intersection.

Diagram 10. A mass event

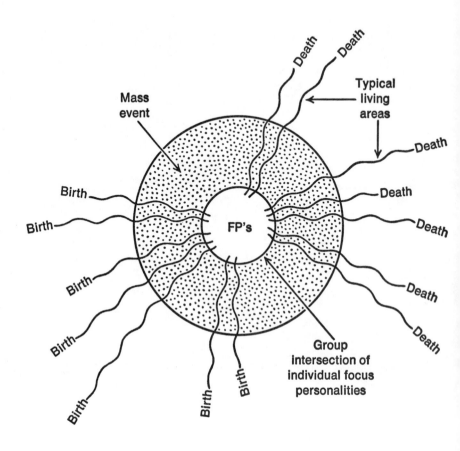

The dotted area represents a mass event as it coincides with a number of individual living areas at a particular point in space and time.

caused by colliding atoms. We're just not used to thinking about events in that way. Actually they are invisible structures, as complicated and varied as external objects. They repel and attract each other, form new alliances and combinations in the same way that cellular life does. They change as the elements do to form various mass groupings. They possess components—the equivalent of nuclei and orbiting electrons; and their reality is locked into our biological and psychological structure. Events possess great mobility, and like psychological animals for all we know, they may breed and die three-dimensionally, going beyond our space-time intersections, while part of their reality, like ours, continues to exist.

19

Earth Experience as a White Hole

I've been talking about the nature of events because our psychology is intimately connected with the way we experience reality. Not only this life, but any survival after death would involve us in an encounter with events of one kind or another. After death, I believe that we would be dealing almost primarily with that inner order of events mentioned earlier in this book.

What kind of a structured universe could explain both the inner and exterior worlds? If we consider our universe as a white hole—our exterior universe of sense—we at least have a theoretical framework that reconciles our inner and outer activity, our physical and spiritual or psychic existence; and the apparent dilemma between a simultaneous present in which all events happen at once, and our daily experience in which we seem to progress through time from birth to death.

How can the privacy of our intimate experience be upheld while at another level of reality all events, including ourselves, are united? How can our individuality maintain its solitary splendor in the face of a dazzling Overlife in which all things are ultimately connected? The following analogy at least gives us a frame-

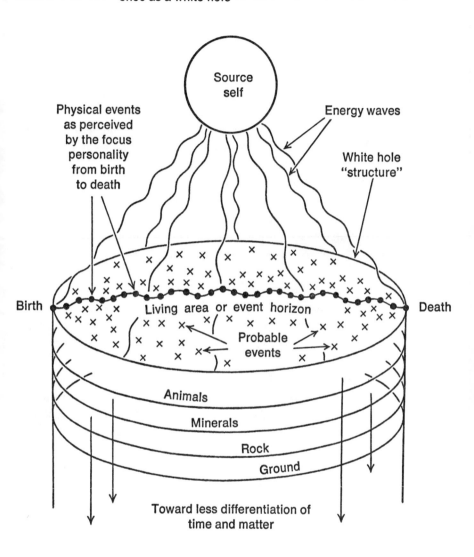

Diagram 11. A focus personality's entire earth experience as a white hole

Our most specific space-time events lie at the "top" of the white hole structure. Our living area corresponds to the event horizon.

work in which to consider such questions and, I believe, presents us with some important intuitive insights into the nature of our own physical and nonphysical reality.

Diagram 11 is a representation of earth experience as a white hole. In the inner order, events rush toward the "event horizon." They are only physical while actually on this event horizon. Above and below it is an area of suspension in which probabilities hover in a timeless fashion, in the wings, to be attracted to the event horizon or not, according to what happens there. As an analogy, the probable events rush toward physical actuality in the same way that sperm speed toward an egg. Events on the event horizon can be knocked out by constant motion and flux that occurs there, and other probable actions can then surge in to take their place. (There is also a correlation here between the behavior of electrons and electron traps.)

The event horizon actually includes several layers or sandwiches, and the degree of immersion in these determines the resulting kind of consciousness and the amount of what we call self-awareness. The particular kind of an "I" with which we identify, the focus personality, exists only at a definite position on the event horizon.

The deeper the immersion, the less conscious awareness (in our terms) and the less experience of consecutive time in a focused fashion. Further "down" there is a lessening of distinctions and specifics, and a closer correspondence to conditions that exist "above" the event horizon.

The physical body (at the event horizon) is formed by material "rising" from the lower levels, and its components possess free awareness properties peculiarly suited to maintain our kind of conscious mind, which couldn't handle the same kind of data directly and still maintain time-to-time focus.

An inner atmospheric level exists above and below the event horizon, where the inner order of events cluster, attracted toward physical actualization. There would be constant motion here as these probable events bumped up against each other like electrons; and the final actualization would be directed by the conscious thoughts and beliefs of the focus personalities who would then experience the events as real. The focus personalities collect and focus events and are conscious events themselves, organizers of activity, self-conscious events.

Here I hypothesize a "nuclear self," which would be that part of the source self's sphere of identity that forms the focus personality. The nuclear self spins outward, its motion forming the focus personality as it constantly translates itself into physical form at the event horizon, and there forms the individual living area. The nuclear self is the ever-emerging energy of the source self impinging into three-dimensional fields, and it is free of space and time. It is the energy that generates our personal level of experience, but is not confined to it. The nuclear self can perceive all of the focus personality's probable experience at once and help it make choices.

This nuclear self forms and maintains the body, endowing the cells with their own free awareness; that is, the cells are able to operate in the "unconscious" knowledge of the whole living picture, aware of future probabilities in order to maintain body integrity. The nuclear self is relatively freewheeling, then, though generally focused to the focus personality (or particle physical self). The focus personality operates almost like an electron trap, drawing and holding the energies of the nuclear self which also forms it; and attracting events into actualization.

When at death the nuclear self escapes the three-dimensional system, then the matter that composed the body breaks down to its simpler components, falling to the bottom of the "well," where it is then used as building blocks for further physical forms.

The nuclear self, while "trapped" within matter, and endowing it with self-aware energy and the I of the focus personality, still hovers at both sides of the event horizon and sees all probable events. It is not itself captured by time, which is experienced only at its own edges or boundaries; its "outside rim" being the focus personality.

TIME AND THE EVENT-HORIZON

Time is built up at the event horizon, and is experienced differently according to the position or level within it. Toward the middle it is most specifically felt, and it is less distinct at either end, toward birth or death. Time experience is also qualitatively different the further down you go away from our event horizon. We're used to thinking of time only as we experience it on our level, but past, present, and future merge to some extent both below and above our event horizon. Each kind of consciousness has its own event horizon, then, with its characteristic kind of living area and time experience.

(Unconsciously we react to telepathy constantly, and to "future" probabilities at the nuclear self level, and by changing our focus [to its horizon] we can also perceive this inner order of events to some degree.)

Again, the focus personality is the self we know in relation to exterior events. It is one Aspect of the source self as it impinges into the three-dimensional framework, but the nuclear self is the initial wave expression of the source self's intersection. It splashes out to form the particle focus personality, yet is free from it, and contains in latent form all the other Aspects of the source self which are held in suspension here, invisible psychologically, but forming the dynamic structure of the self that we know. Its action can only be perceived at all through its relationship with the focus personality; only in this way can its presence be sensed.

Even time behaves in a particle fashion at the surface of the event horizon, giving us the appearance of moments, but the further down (into the white hole) we go, the more time breaks up into longer waves; so that while we share time with mountains, insects and trees, some live for centuries and some for only a few hours. This has nothing to do with the subjective experience of time, for that belongs to the still undecipherable inner order of events.

Everything on the event horizon is materialized from that inner order and rises out of it. Less differentiation, again, exists above and below the horizon. All energy entering this system is transformed into its characteristics; these include mass, weight, matter, and space-time relationships. From within the system it's almost impossible to get a clear idea of the inner order of events, because of this constant translation of it into outer manifestation. From inside everything checks out. The laws seem to be the only ones because they're all we observe. Even our mental calculations are involved, because our brains work with matter and are composed of it.

We *can* alter our focus to some extent though, and momentarily take our attention away from the line of experience-that-agrees-with-itself, *and concentrate on those experiences that don't fit in, that disturb the official picture and contradict what we think we know*. We will, I think, end up with two separate views of the world; an objective and subjective one, each valid and real, but in a different order of events.

Altered states of consciousness can be most effective in this regard, and so can a study of dreams, but with a different attitude. There *is* an inner landscape of the mind, translated into the convoluted ridges of the brain—where things happen first, where creation is always happening now, where consciousness is bursting into physical actuality as much as it ever did in some hypothetical beginning.

Inspiration, artistic or otherwise, often allows us to perceive this inner order; and it is often called irrational because the inspirational picture is so different from the official one. No wonder people often equate genius with madness, because true genius often perceives that inner order. The two kinds of reality make up our world, but the one remains as the invisible structure for physical reality.

Diagram 12. The whole life of a focus personality

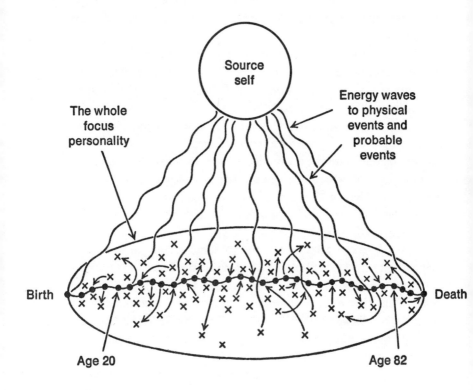

There is a constant interchange between probable events (the x's), and physical events (the black circles on the living area). The older you are, the more "past" events you have to play with.

Diagram 13. Closeup of the constant interchange between physical events, probable events, and time

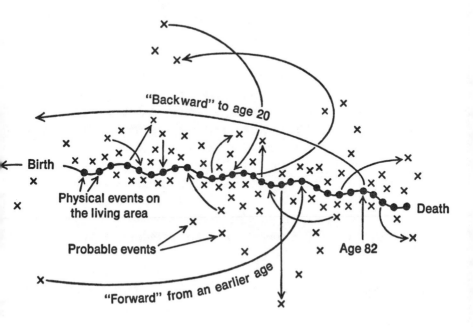

"Backward" to age 20

Birth

Physical events on the living area

Probable events

"Forward" from an earlier age

Age 82

Death

Here an event at age 82 displaces an event that "happened" at age 20. The latter event then becomes a probable one.

The focus personality is not complete except in its entire three-dimensional existence; i.e., at its death. All of its experiences exist at once despite its perception of them in serial form—but the events are ever-changing as in the life instant of impact, energy bounces out in all probable directions. This causes constant motion and flux within the entire life pattern (see Diagram 12).

A motion at say, age eighty-two, can "displace" an event that "happened" at age twenty, and the choices we make in any now completely displace other acts, knocking them off the physical line of experience and out of our focus and bringing up other events that, "until then," had been probable (see Diagram 13).

In our terms, this is more apparent toward the end of the living area when we have more past events to play with, and this is precisely when we often begin to play havoc with our official past. I think that some of my mother-in-law's experiences involved this phenomenon, but other episodes in my own life also lead me toward this conclusion. Again, since we usually follow the recognized order of events, we're not used to looking for such unofficial ones, and it takes work and energy to train ourselves to discover them. Certainly I intend to pursue this particular kind of study further.

I'm convinced, for example, that "past" events change after their occurence in space and time on the living area—after they've happened, in other words. I don't think that just our attitude changes toward them. While we focus upon continuity in terms of time, this alteration of past events in the present literally becomes invisible. Dreams involving experiences not at the waking level of events give us some clues here also, for in dreams I think that we tune into probabilities and literally organize our daily lives over their entire range from both ends of the living area at once—according to our conscious desires and beliefs.

Again; each wave of energy from the source self pools out to form a nuclear self which in turn forms the particle focus personality. These waves constantly hit the three-dimensional field,

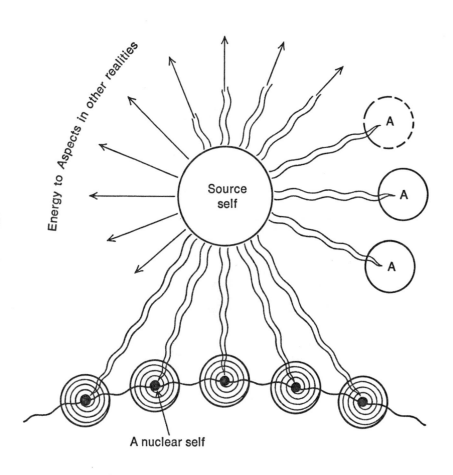

Diagram 14. The source self, from our point of view,
forming a series of nuclear selves

Energy to Aspects in other realities

Source
self

A

A

A

A nuclear self

Each wave of energy from the source self forms its own nuclear
self, which is free of space and time. Each nuclear self spins outward
to form its focus personality on the living area.

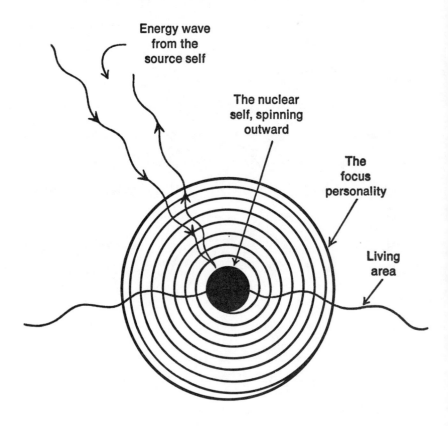

Diagram 15. The anatomy of a nuclear self as it forms
a focus personality

Energy wave
from the
source self

The nuclear
self, spinning
outward

The
focus
personality

Living
area

The outside rim of the nuclear self is the focus personality, which experiences space and time.

are attracted to the event horizon, and impinge into physical actuality (see Diagram 14). So we are in those terms really a "series" of pulsations; aware, conscious beings having a sphere of identity far greater than we usually realize.

These pulsations intersect with the three-dimensional field *at once,* though the focus personality experiences the birth-to-death sequence. The nuclear self is aware of the entire simultaneous earth-life event. To it, later pulsations occur at the same time as earlier ones, therefore events can be altered to some extent over the entire living area (see Diagram 15).

Earlier events in any present are experienced by the focus personality as ghost events, since the time-space intersection is not precise enough to form a now perception. I'm convinced that we also react to probable future events in dreams, but even then their future nature may not be apparent because they may seem senseless in the context of present experience. Doubtlessly, future memories go unrecognized for this reason, but it's possible that with a change of attitude we could handle precognition as easily as we handle ordinary memories.

In sleep and dreams we look from the inward order of events outward, but opaquely, at the physical objective world. Dreams *are* present events, not encountered on the living area in the same way as waking ones.

Probable events from our standpoint have much the same quality as dream events. Our event horizon is the only one we recognize, where for us energy coalesces into matter and events. Any events not in our "sandwich" of space and time would exist nevertheless as probabilities, physically and psychologically invisible and not a part of our recognized reality. The nuclear self would accept them, however.

Yet, in this same system there are an unlimited number of event horizons like ours, in which other probable events are actualized and experienced. Still within the same system, then, there are alternate earth histories still happening, and as "real" as our own. Any number of consecutive years, say, from 1900 to 1980 are experienced in infinite ways, not played back, but endlessly growing out of the medium of the system itself.

Since the event horizons are different, the inhabitants from one probable world are not aware of the other alternate worlds. Within each probable world, probable centuries exist, and consciousness is "born back" into the same probable system until it "escapes."

In a black hole, a million years would be felt to be only an instant. In a white one, an instant or eternal now is experienced in the slow-motion cognition of consecutive time. In this hypothetical white hole, identity becomes temporal-ized and the source self's sphere of identity broken up into self-segments, just as an eternal now is broken down into the appearance of series of moments.

Since the source self is beyond the three-dimensional field, however, it's overall identity and knowledge is held in solution, latent, in the indestructible nuclear self which forms the particle focus personality. In the white hole, individualization as we understand it is born, specialization becomes the rule, and eternal forces are broken down to local laws. The source self, however, is not dependent upon the local system.

Diagram 16 is a representation of probable event horizons. When energy falls into a white hole, it's transformed into matter, but the nuclear self's energy propels this translation, which is caused by the dimensional aspects of the white hole. The white hole also exists in relationship to the fields that surround it. Matter built up within it can't escape in its present form. But the invisible energy within it *can,* and its very appearance of material stability is caused by the energy constantly bouncing back to itself (through the sphere of identity, through the nuclear self to the source self).

Again, at death we may turn into a black hole, where space and time are meaningless and matter disintegrates. The nuclear self, retaining our individuality and memories, would then

Diagram 16. Probable event horizons (and living areas)

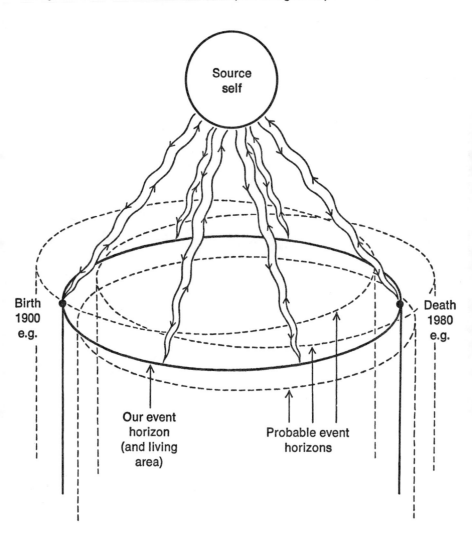

Any number of consecutive years in our system would be experienced differently in other realities, utilizing probable events and alternate event horizons.

emerge—into another white hole and a new system of reality. To all intents and purposes, the "inhabitants" of the separate systems would be unaware of each other—except in the inward order of events.

20

The Focus Personality and the Senses, Some Questions, and Surrender to the Self

Psychological white holes or not, we're focused in physical reality; we manipulate objects and seem to move through time. We're caught between the knowledge of our certain physical death, and the inner revelations that tell us that death is just another state of being.

Rob and I were talking last night, and I was looking at his face in the light of the small electric candle that sits on the bedside table. It was almost as if I saw his face come swimming out of darkness into our reality, so full of life and expression, the most fantastic miracle of consciousness—a self forming itself from the universe, alive with brilliant focus—yet bound to vanish as mysteriously as it came. Like us all, I thought. For we're caught between the triumph of our existence, and the anguish of our ignorance about what comes before or after. And if we exist forever in any moment, then why can't we realize it?

Yet even then I realized that our determined clear physical focus is, to some extent at least, dependent upon our forgetting. How can we experience the dear privacy of the moment if we're aware of all of those other equally valid moments? And would we savor our hours in the same way or become glutted with them, drunken with excess?

And I was led to think: How valuable the physical senses are! They create the theater of perception through which we experience reality. They organize, categorize and pin down vast fields of raw data to form a three-dimensional living picture in which we are so intimately involved that we are *in* the picture we see, even without recognizing ourselves within it.

Our beingness is directed constantly by the senses: That much is clear. What isn't so apparent is the fact that we experience physical reality from within (within the body, which is itself within the picture), though reality appears to be "out there" beyond the skin. We even form what reality is, even while we perceive it as something that happens outside.

The senses cleverly and beautifully create physical reality and our most meaningful experience of it, yet it seems as if reality has always been *there,* exteriorized, regardless of our perception of it. Sounds certainly make it seem that there are noises *out there* to be heard. My eyes make me certain that there is a world of objects out there to be seen.

But our being-in-the-world and our feeling of being rooted in it, secure and alive in it—all of these are dependent upon the senses within the body itself (within the body which is itself within the picture). We aren't consciously aware of this inner relation upon which our whole experience with the world rests.

For example, our aliveness and responsiveness to the world are dependent upon feelings of inner balance that align us with "exterior" conditions, but actually this inner sensing creates those conditions. We say that a day is warm or cold, according to how the air feels as it hits our skin. But the air is neither warm nor cold on its own. Only our inner thermal senses create the sensations.

Objects seem to be all around us in the same way, because our physical perceptions organize data in certain patterns, and then we respond to the apparent reality. The body is a unique reality-forming organism; one that not only projects a three-dimensional picture outward, but is itself within the living picture of reality that it is constantly creating. The feedback is so flashing, so instantaneous that this escapes us.

The body continually creates itself from within this system of interrelatedness, throwing out from itself physical representations in three-dimensional fact which it then experiences— creating, for example, the space through which it moves, the time through which it grows and ages, and all of those exterior conditions to which it then responds.

Its corporal aliveness, of course, arises from layers beneath usual consciousness. On those layers we are constantly responding to qualities of temperature, air pressure, cosmic rays and tidal motions of which we are unaware, but upon which our reality depends.

It's easy to see how a tree grows out of the ground into space: Its limbs or roots, while able to move, are relatively stationary. If you think of our bodies from that perspective though, then our bodies grow out in space in all directions as we walk up and down the street, fly airplanes or dive underwater. Motion and growth are just different aspects of the same thing: We grow in space and move through it as we grow and "move" through time. We're just not used to thinking of it in that way. These motions, if we could perceive them at once, and if they left "paths" in space, would show us acting and reacting—"growing" in all directions at once; exploding in space like some odd animal-flower, blooming in many places at once, appearing here, then there. Your body would seem to appear to grow at the corner of your street; ungrow there, and emerge at the next observable point, and so on. We are rooted to the earth and oriented within it.

Enjoyment of physical sensation with its natural being-with-itness is one of our greatest delights and one of the best uniting devices, bringing body and soul firmly into their rightful relatedness. Physical joy and corporal motion set things right, putting the conscious self (the focus personality) in its proper position as it feels its soul alive in flesh, securely anchored in the support of its own creativity. In this relationship, thoughts are as physical as body cells; body cells as mental as thoughts; both uniting to form corporal expression.

The senses within the body create dimensions of space through which the body can then express itself; enjoy, explore; dimensions of agility and motion with limitless possibilities for action, manipulation and performance; an equally limitless and always unique opportunity for tactile experience and expression. Besides this, there is the taken-for-granted corporal triumph of being a body three-dimensionally equipped to act within a system in which it is peculiarly suited to exist.

Watching fish swim in water, for instance, you can see how beautifully equipped they are for their environment, and sometimes you can sense the fish in a different way, as a part of the water's environment; each moving through the other. So man moves as naturally within space, with his appendages as suited to it as a fish's fins to water, and the organism naturally takes basic joy in this interrelatedness. If you look at it in this way, then man can be seen as a part of space also, moving through it as it moves through him.

This feeling of corporal creativity as happening within the body brings a sense of physical aliveness, of corporal happening and gut-level relatedness that gets lost if we overemphasize the mental aspect of thoughts. At least for now, thoughts rest on the cells' physical life. That much should be apparent. While we have bodies, thoughts are a physical expression, growing out of our brains as flowers grow out of the earth.

This doesn't mean that thinking can't exist without a physical body; it means that while we have one, thinking rests firmly on the foundation of earth-body relatedness. Our thoughts *have* to follow our physical expression as selves in flesh, for they interpret the data perceived through flesh, and created by the senses. Thinking apart-from-the-body, outside of the three-dimensional system, would be far different (I *think*), since the necessity to organize perceptions within time and space would not necessarily exist.

We can't see inside the body, but it has an inside landscape or fleshscape as vital and living as the one outside the window, in which tree branches wave in the wind, people walk down the street and flowers grow. The cells certainly are not "little people," but they are minute consciousnesses and they respond to their environment as we do to ours. All of this activity is us; is me; is you; creating and then responding to the life in which we presently have our being.

I believe that the body is basically a self-clearing and self-regulating system. As the cells form organs, the thoughts form belief-systems that are just as alive and vital as organs. Within the belief-systems, thoughts come and go. Both organs and belief systems retain their own "place" or position. Belief systems are needed just as physical organs are, for they direct the unconscious health and vitality of the body and form its experience in corporal terms.

Seth's book, *The Nature of Personal Reality,* stresses the importance of personal beliefs in the private creation of daily reality. He emphasizes that it's important not to be afraid of thoughts or feelings, particularly of aggressive ones. Expressed naturally and easily through body motion, gestures, and activity, these are a necessary part of corporal reality. Only when we fear them and impede their natural expression do they back up or become dangerous.

The body, using its sense data, becomes more aware of itself; and more fully alive as it constantly creates and then perceives its life. The freer and more extensive our physical expression, the more leeway we allow our mental and emotional life. The more the body is used and enjoyed, the greater its responsiveness and its sense of being-in-life and within-the-world; and the greater the feedback and stimuli for further physical and mental expression.

I don't believe that we become more spiritual by denying the flesh, or that we can expand our consciousness by *not* using the kind of consciousness we have, hoping that if we close our eyes to this world we'll see another world more clearly. Instead, we must begin by learning to use the great flexibility available to us—a consciousness that *we* can turn in many directions while still keeping our earth focus clear and brilliant. Exploring our creaturehood and all of its abilities may teach us some basic truths about the really valid mystical elements of nature that we seem to have forgotten.

For reasons beyond the scope of this book, our religions have emphasized repression, restriction, and penance rather than benediction, expression, celebration, or love. They have generally failed to help us love "God," but have taught us to distrust ourselves and our physical existence instead. They have consistently taught us to deride our creaturehood; and nearly all religions, Western and Eastern alike, have shown a suspicious willingness to surrender the conscious self—the focus personality—either to a bland heaven or nirvanic blessed imbecility.

Seth maintains that this tendency has to do with the development of our consciousness more than anything else: Sometimes we find the freedom of conscious decision and contemplation too much, and yearn "back" toward what we imagine to be unconscious bliss.

If God is individualized in us, then it's precisely that God-given identity, that God-knowing-Itself-as-us, that we want to throw off. Even in our terms, we're a combination of conscious and unconscious activity. Are our cells blissful? Why do we seem to think that self-consciousness can't contain the experience of bliss, while it seems to have no trouble feeling the greatest kinds of horror?

No wonder so many of the poor saints were nearly insane, forced as they were in their system of beliefs to interpret their revelations through such a dark mirror. Attain godliness by mutilating or denying the body; that miraculous manifestation of spirit made flesh in the world of time and the seasons? Self-surrender? Far better, surrender *to* the self and the joyful development of its abilities.

The focus personality *is* whatever godhead there is, individualized in earth life. Perhaps we'll find a god we don't have to crucify, and a concept of selfhood that doesn't see perfection as dependent upon its own annihilation. But neither of these developments can occur until we trust our own nature, and no longer find our individuality a burden. When we let ourselves be ourselves, we many discover that when we think we are sacrificing ourselves, we actually have nothing to give. Even a god would suspect a gift so desperately offered.

And to what great acts and heroism have such ideas led us?—to fanatically held concepts of Good for which we have gladly killed; to dogmas based on the premise that we are damned by reason of our creaturehood, by the very fact that we are alive. Many of our greatest crimes are committed when we think we are most in the right, yet seldom do we question our ideas of right and wrong.

When we think we're wrong, at least we often stop to consider; we're hesitant and sometimes even humble. Yet when we're self-righteous and feel ourselves justified, we often become cruel and unthinking. Certainly we've run rampant across the planet with little respect for it or other kinds of life, because we've believed we were given a mandate from God to use the earth as we see fit.

Yet, often we trust nature but not ourselves. As I type this, for example, the shadows are lengthening. It occurs to me that this happens with no help from me. Last week my cat, Willy, sustained a bad wound; the injury healed itself easily, in the same secret way that the evening comes and goes or the light changes and the shadows lengthen. I took it for granted that the cat would heal himself. And most of trust the seasons in their coming and going. Why do we find it so hard to trust ourselves in the same way?

I stew and fret, and sometimes it seems I never give myself a moment's rest; yet I know that my breathing in and breathing out is as natural as the tides' rhythm and that life is breathed in and out of me all the time, without my knowing. I know that my existence is as inevitable and right as my cat's; and that all of us ride on the great given breath that sustains us. I know that my personal life rides on the same sure order; my life opening up to a particular time and place in the same way that a leaf opens. Surely leaves trust the tree, and Willy certainly trusts himself; his every motion in bathed in the knowledge of the rightness of his being.

If a cat trusts the universe, why shouldn't I? Why shouldn't you? The cat trusts his catness; his leaping and his chasing of birds, his appetites and desires. And these qualities of catness add to the universe, and I bet those characteristics are reflected through it in a million unknown ways—as they are in our world, with the panther and kitten and my specific housecat.

So why don't we trust our peoplehood? Or, more to the point, why don't we trust our specific personhood as it's reflected through our unique individualities? Why can't we trust that in nature's greater order, all of our private characteristics have their place, and that even the meanest of them are somehow redeemed? The cat in killing birds does no wrong, but fulfills himself and in so doing, helps nature regulate itself.

I'm certainly not trying to justify murder, but most of us have the idea that, left alone, our natural feelings are somehow wrong, and that left alone we'll ruin everything for ourselves, privately and en masse; that all nature is right but us; and that we're the one blight on nature, the mistake that still survives.

Yet some part of me insists on my right to that same grace; to sleep and waken with the animal's supreme innocent trust. And my cat, Willy, incidentally, doesn't have to pray, "My father who art in Heaven." He doesn't have to imagine a cat god or do sacrifice or homage.

I can't begin to explain our atrocities or our cruelty to one another, yet I can't see why nature would be right—in every other respect showing order and rightness—and be wrong when our race emerged. Are we an experiment gone askew, to be destroyed, its parts disassembled or loaned out to others, distributed safely, defused, to a thousand other species? Are we never to happen in the same way again?

Everything in me shouts out against such condemnation.

Then why do we condemn ourselves? And how can we look at our history and not condemn ourselves? I don't know. But as I sit appreciating the deep sensual integrity of this particular moment, I *know* that the kind of creature who can have such perceptions can't be something to condemn. Right now I thrill to the shape of my hand on the white paper, the shadow of my pen and arm on the card table, the mountains of light and shadow piled on the white walls. And no creature with that kind of appreciation can be bad. Maybe the universe needed us to appreciate it. Maybe we're nature's mirror.

But . . . but then why do we kill and know it's wrong and condemn ourselves? And if our killing is as natural and right as a cat's killing of a bird, then why a conscience that says it's wrong?

Do we appreciate the individual more than the rest of nature does? Does its own creation of us surprise a nature that cared only for life forms—and not the one form—any one form? Were we accidents of a nature that outdid itself with a creation that stepped outside it; still on a leash, but exulting in a new kind of individuality? And is that individuality so unique in its way that we're still only half-sane, half-mad, driven to attain true divinity or be less than nature's least?

Are we nature evolving, half-finished creations; our self-condemnation our salvation, leading us on? And have we done all this before?

I don't think that we can avoid such questions, but I believe that the answers lie within the psyche and not in the objectified universe. That is, I see the psyche—the source self—as having a reality that straddles the world we know. This source self, as explained earlier, has Aspects of itself that are immersed in different fields of actuality. Earth life is just one of its environments. There are basic portions of our focus personalities that correspond to these other Aspects. They combine to form the self that we recognize as ourself. Usually they are psychologically invisible, but they do "communicate" through revelatory statements, dreams, visions, and other unofficial perceptions.

Much of the time the Aspects serve as inner guides in the guise of the "inner voice." Sometimes they become "isolated," relatively free-acting, forming personagrams—personality structures that actually bridge realities. These rise out of the basic Aspects of a focus personality but they represent another kind of consciousness, or another type of being whose prime existence is outside of our system. The resulting personagram as it appears *here* will be colored by our own ideas, and its communications will be given in a way that makes three-dimensional sense.

Of course it's natural for us to interpret such information according to "the facts" as we know them. From this standpoint, our ideas about the nature of consciousness itself, and personhood in particular, are very limiting, I believe. On the one hand we try to protect the ego or focus personality at all costs. On the other hand, we think that the focus personality must be sacrificed if we are going to expand our consciousness. Proponents of religious and drug experiences often stress this dying-to-the-self.

Instead, our consciousness itself has many channels or "stations"; each, I believe, belonging to these other Aspects of the source self. With our official home station earth consciousness, the focus personality perceives physical life. The other channels simply blend in the background, while the focus personality's perceptions predominate.

We can turn our consciousness in other directions, though, tuning into these other stations. When we do, we can view reality from an entirely different viewpoint. Then we see that our official "newscasts" are just local programs presenting only a part of the truth about existence. Other stations (other altered states of consciousness) bring us into contact with different

Aspects of the source self of psyche, Aspects that can give us information not only about the part of the psyche from which they originate, but also about the kind of reality in which they have existence. To some extent, we can then view physical reality from other vantage points.

Such information can automatically increase our knowledge, lead us to ask other, wiser, questions, deepen our usual perceptions and broaden the scope of the focus personality. But since all data must come through the "home station," it will be distorted to some degree. Look what can happen, for example, when we try to translate a book from one language to another.

Revelations, visions, hunches, and other unofficial knowledge may all partially represent bleedthroughs from these other channels—acting as messages of various kinds from one portion of the psyche to another as well. Unfortunately, it seems to take some finesse to extract the messages from the static. Besides this, the messages will be couched by us in terms of our own beliefs. We project these upon the revelatory information so quickly that we hardly ever catch ourselves in the act.

We're used to putting the picture of the world together in a certain way, so turning to these other stations does require a willingness to suspend the usual beliefs, judgments, and assumptions of our world. Such alterations of consciousness require an unprejudiced perception, the ability to let the usual world picture momentarily dissolve as much as possible.

As I see it, the difficulty is that we only identify ourselves with one limited focus of consciousness. Yet we have only to broaden our view, and learn to consider these other facets of awareness as other stations of existence also available to *us*. The self we know doesn't have to be sacrificed—in fact, we dare not do so, while trying to maintain psychological stability and corporal composure.

I believe that the Aspects represent the usually unconscious elements of personality, the great sources that insure our physical survival, the exuberant trust of being within us, upon which the focus personality rides. Literally, I see the source self or psyche reaching from cellular experience to Divinity—whatever we mean by that term.

In personal terms, when these Aspects are working harmoniously within us, we're healthy and creative. When we emphasize some to the exclusion of others because of our beliefs, then the psyche itself tries to bring about therapeutic adjustments. In the future, I hope to discover more about the normal workings of the Aspects as they balance out in the personality, lending their various characteristics and abilities as raw material for the focus personality. I have some insights already as to their importance in health, and I can see an Aspect therapy in which people learn to mix and match the portions of their own personalities for greater creativity and effectiveness. Such a discussion is beyond the scope of this book, which is only meant to serve as an introduction to Aspects in general.

Socrates said that a happy man was "well daemonized." I'd say that he was well-aspected.

I agree with Seth that we make our own reality, choosing from an infinite source of probable actions those we will experience as physical, and I've suggested a theoretical model of the universe which explains how probabilities become physical events.

I see the conscious mind making such choices through its beliefs, though the actual mechanisms that bring about reality are unconscious. In this system at least, the nature of events and the nature of the psyche who experiences them go hand in hand. One can't be considered without the other.

The most important parts of this theory came to me in altered states of consciousness as I tuned into other stations of my own, and viewed this reality from other subjective standpoints. I tried to be as unprejudiced as possible in interpreting the information. Please realize that I consider these other subjective states as doorways into other valid realities and kinds of existences. I've barely dipped into those areas. To that extent I'm still a tourist in strange lands.

I offer Aspects as a framework through which we can view our experience in a different way, hopefully bringing us into a newer creative encounter with ourselves in this reality and those that we are only beginning to sense. Our consciousness is certainly our birthright. I believe that we've hardly begun to use it, to shine its light in all directions, into the psyche itself and into those unknown dimensions in which it also has its greater being.

APPENDIX I

In the first few chapters of this book, I studied the nature of Seth's reality from my usual state of consciousness. As mentioned, much of Part Two was written in altered states, and there, particularly in the material on personagrams, I looked at Seth's reality from another viewpoint, at a different level of awareness.

"The Speakers" poem, written in a high state of inspiration, showed me the reach of the psyche from cellular to "divine" existence and gave me new insight into the reality of the "daemons, muses, and the voices." Though Seth was not specifically mentioned, it was my experience with him that initiated the poem, and my intellectual questions about his reality that were creatively answered.

Here I want to include some of Seth's own statements about his existence and his relationship with our world, by quoting large segments of the class session of January 29, 1974.

This session was very briefly quoted in Chapter Two, and it is particularly significant for several reasons. In it, Seth speaks about his independence on the one hand, and about his representation as a part of the psyche on the other. The way the session was given also reinforced this double element (of independence in one sphere, and representation in the other), for in a way difficult to describe there were "bleedthroughs" from Seth Two and Sumari, almost as if, speaking for himself, Seth was speaking for them also.

In fact, further on in the session he does state that he is speaking for Seth Two, and some of the vocabulary he uses is more characteristic of Sumari than it is of Seth's usual wording. Seth's delivery was also rather extraordinary in that he seemed to have even more energy at his command than usual. In some places, his voice really boomed out as if he were speaking not only to the class, but to the world at large.

Remember when you're reading the words here, that this was a spontaneous monologue in which Seth was quite active; looking around the room, gesturing often, and sometimes commenting to one particular student or another. As mentioned in Chapter Two, Seth began speaking when one of the students wondered aloud whether Seth had actually appeared in one of his dreams, or whether some kind of projection was involved instead. The question led students to discuss the nature of Seth's reality, and Seth interrupted, smiling.

CLASS SESSION: TUESDAY, JANUARY 29, 1974

"Who is Seth? I put this question to *you*. And what magic is worked here that *you* work, and that we all work together? Now, I will tell you this: On the one hand, I am someone you do not know, lost before the annals of time as you understand it. On the one hand, that is what I am: And that is a loaded sentence.

"On the other hand, I am yourself . . . so through me do you view and meet the selves that you are, and so I rise, in your terms, from the power and antiquity and the glory of your own being, projected outward into the world of time from a universe in which time is meaningless.

"So I am what each of you are individually, and I am what each of you are, en masse. And I am what the world is, individually and en masse.

"So when I speak with my voice, with this voice, I speak with all of your voices, and with the knowledge that each of you have, and with the knowledge that the world has. And so, what you know is translated into the area of space and time that you presently recognize. So I bring up within you, great rushes of emotion and being that arise from the knowledge of your own existence. I allow you to reach portions of your own reality that exist beyond space and time. Each of you, then, do project upon me those characteristics that are your own in other terms, and so I am a multidimensional being as *you* are multidimensional beings . . . .

"I am myself, but apart from that, I am also what you are. If all of you at this moment denied my reality, I would still be what I am, and you would be less. I would be less also, but I would still be what I am, and you would still be what you are. And you might find other ways of contacting what you are. You would not be lost. Nor would I.

"Through me, you sense your reality, beyond the reality that you presently know. Through you, I remember my reality in your terms, and yet I can never count on it—it is not done and finished, for as you grow, I grow. Seth Two grows. You grow beyond me, beyond my reality even, into other worlds that you do not presently know, and I grow into other existences where we cannot meet. But here, we meet . . . .

"I return you to yourself. But beyond that, here is indeed a new framework in your terms, ladders that you can climb, that lead you not from mountain to austere mountain of dogma and denial; not from Nirvana to Nirvana of denial and nonbeing; but instead I offer steps, alive and glowing, that lead you to the furthest reaches of yourself. These are not steps created by a god or devil or guru, but sent out and projected by you through the

centuries; steps born of your living selves, that lead into the knowledge of your ever-growing beings.

"And so, therefore, with joy do I speak to you, with
the joy that is alive and knowing. I speak with the voices that, in
your terms, come from centuries yet unborn. Yet these are the
voices that you, yourselves, have whispered from the fossils of
your being, when you were (in your terms, now) unthinking selves
on sunlit cliffs in worlds unknowing. And projected by your desire,
these voices then speak to you and urge you to your own fulfillment . . . .

"You have allowed 'something' to become transparent,
so that you can step through yourselves. Use the energy of this
voice as a lifeline, and as a road and as a message, and follow it
in whatever way you choose, into your own experience, into your
own greater reality.

"I will suggest certain images, but if others spontaneously come to you, then follow those. But imagine—those of you
who want to—a pyramid. See it reaching into unimaginable distance, and realize that it is a channel into the antiquity and future
of your being. Within it you will find selves that are so 'advanced'
they seem alien, and selves that are so spectacularly simple that
you cannot relate to them.

"For there (in the deepest reaches of your being), is
a greater reality that knows your present existence and looks upon
it with the fondest, the dearest, the most familiar of memories;
a reality that has grown, in your terms, into entities indescribably
vast; realities that form worlds more complex than the one in
which you now dwell.

"And yet also, through that channel of being you will
also find fossil cells that are not yet selves, that have not [yet]
grouped into complex organisms, but that lie filled with the desire
of being, filled with the desire of God, for fulfillment and thought
and complexity. These lie inert in the history of your craniums,
still to be born in the knowledge of your being—selves in your
terms still to be realized, wandering in the bowels of unknown

worlds—selves that will become entities; fossils of yourselves that still, in certain terms, contain memories of the selves that you are.

"As they wander in what seems to you to be a dark world, as they seek toward a sun that is your brain; as they journey over unknown cliffs, seeking recognition; so do you wander within worlds of greater selves that you are, seeking for the rays of other suns that are the brains of your own greater being. So are you all one, and so is my voice speaking from your own greater being— from which you are forever born and always reborn.

"Even in your secret and most private dreams do you form new selves with desires that lie latent in unknown worlds, and rise, groping toward new probabilities. So are you couched tenderly in the soul of your being . . . .

"Return now to your selves as you know them. Experience the divine privacy of the selves that you are. Those selves are the corner of your being in which all intersections occur, and in which your privacy is forever maintained and unique. Do yourselves just honor, and in so doing, you give directions to cells not yet born, to fossils that are thoughts still unfreed from your own minds. Enjoy your selves and the gods of your being, in which you are forever safely couched."

We took a break in here, and class members began discussing their own experiences as Seth was speaking. All of them were caught up in feelings of transcendence, and to one extent or another each of them sensed the private self as a hub, a chosen point of focus around which other realities spun in spontaneous order. Rick, one of the students, said that Seth's statements reminded him of something he'd read about Vishnu, a Hindu god. Seth interrupted:

"You dream of Vishnu, and dream dreams of the god as the god dreams of creation. So all are one, and all are individual, for the cell dreams of the god as the god dreams of the cell. And you dream of your entities as they dream of you. The smallest cell in your toe dreams of your reality and helps to create it, as you dream of the smallest cell's reality and help create it. From the power of your being springs all its developments, and all gods, and all realities, and the power of the present."

Rick turned to get a better look at Seth, and Seth spoke to him directly. "You move your hand and touch your face, and what realities do you stir, and what seasons do you cause to fall upon other worlds—and how, as you lift your finger and touch your face—do you stir ponds of reality? What frogs sit by the ponds that you have stirred, and what winds blow with the power of your thoughts? How your reality stretches out from this moment to touch all worlds! For you are, and because you are, all being is. Your lips curve and tremble, and the muscles move across your face, and as they do the wind blows in other universes.

"Your reality is now, and your thoughts are footprints in other worlds. You leave messages when you so much as lift your head or say 'Hello.' And listening, others lift their heads and say, 'What a strange wind blows.' So do you, hearing my voice say, 'What a strange wind blows. From whence come these winds'?

"Listen to me now and in so doing, listen to yourselves. You 'come through' as I come through. You are not nonbeings in a god's dream. You speak and the god listens. You are the god that listens. From you, that god, that All That Is, learns what is happening in your corner of reality. You send messages 'backward' through the fabric of time and space which is also, in your terms now, the fabric of that god's being. As again, the smallest cell in your finger or toe sends messages to you, and you, even if unconsciously, make adjustments in response—so in those terms and using that analogy, do you send messages to that god as to what is happening in your corner of the universe. And that god makes adjustments accordingly.

"In your present state, you are not aware of the intimate alive being of the cells within your body. But the godhead of which you are a part *is* aware of your reality, and takes your messages seriously. So there is a constant give and take in which your being changes the experience of the godhead of which you are a part . . . .

"Within yourself is a history of all being; the birth of consciousness, in your terms, ever being born. The grace with which you sit before me is so secure, so nonchalant in its physical integrity, yet what small selves uphold you? And yet how you ignominiously ignore the cells within you, as minute, and grant to them none of the functions of creativity and development that are your own. But let them flicker out one by one, and what happens to the proud physical moon of your brain? In your terms, their existence is as sacred as your own. And through the scrutiny of *your* eyes, and the beauty of *your* mustache [*Here, a smiling Seth pointed to Jerry, who has an elegant mustache.*] do the gods know themselves, and live through the smallest hair upon your head.

"And indeed, through me now is Seth Two given voice, a voice that you can understand; and a lifeline is being thrown to you that you have thrown down to yourselves from a time in your terms not yet born, and yet have you created it . . . . I am the voice of your world in its past and future as you think of it. Because of that, I am your own voice in its past and its future.

"The rocks cannot speak words that you hear, and you do not listen when your cells speak to you, and so I speak humbly for them, and translate for you the archeology of your being. Here then, the fossilings within your spirit speak."

During the session Seth's voice sometimes thundered out, and sometimes fell to a whisper. The sense of extraordinary energy had never been more apparent. Students experienced their own reality in ways impossible to describe, and equally impossible to forget. If you consider Seth as independent in one reality, and as a representation in the psyche at the same time, then the session is an excellent description of the psyche from the inside; given by a prime Aspect as well equipped to look inward through the psyche as the focus personality is to look outward.

Here we catch glimpses of an interior world of the psyche that is as complicated and rich as the exterior one is; one, in fact, from which the world of sense springs.

I call Seth a "trans-world" entity, a personagram, so for me the subject of his reality is twofold—his separate existence in his own dimensions, and his existence as it is reflected in the psyche. Seth's personality as expressed through me would only be a part of his reality. Beyond that would be his own nature.

Again, I suspect that Seth's greater identity somehow includes Sumari, Seven, and Helper, and that they are further expressions of his overall reality, also operating as Aspects. Seth often directs Sumari, for example, answering a question in his own way and then stating that a Sumari explanation will follow.

So far, I can only get the Seth Material through Seth. Again, though, in other terms Seth is an aspect of me; and does he speak for me in other worlds?

APPENDIX II

Here I'm including a brief class session in which Seth did not speak. Class sessions are recorded, then one of the students mimeographs copies. Here, in response to a student's remark, I began to speak as Cyprus—who is a character in my novel, *The Education of Oversoul Seven*.

As mentioned earlier, as soon as Cyprus appeared in the book, I knew I had been speaking and singing as her since the beginning of Sumari. Here, though, I started speaking in English, went into a Sumari song, and then translated it on the spot.

I'm including this because it shows how questions asked at one level of consciousness can be "answered" at another level; and also because I remember my own joy: skipping steps of consciousness just because it was such fun, so that even old questions look new.

Later I did make a few changes in the translation of the Sumari song, and the final version is used here. Remember, this song was sung first, before it was written down. Then I translated it at once for class, but did not sing it in English.

TRANSCRIPT OF CLASS SESSION
TUESDAY, JULY 3, 1973

Jane and the class were discussing the dimensions of an event. Carlos said that he'd like to "travel through" an event, and mentioned the beginning of the world. Jane said, "It happened tomorrow, Carlos."

CARLOS:	"Pardon?"
JANE:	"It happened tomorrow."
CARLOS:	"It happened tomorrow?"
JANE:	"Right—the creation of the world—it happened tomorrow."
JEFF: [another student]	"Cyprus." (Meaning, Jane is speaking as Cyprus.)
JANE:	"Read it in the *Times*. It has all the news. Yes, Jeff."
JEFF:	"Cyprus!"

A Sumari song came through, followed by this translation by Jane:

Out of the memories of your being
emerge the flowers of other centuries.
Out of the unknowing splendor of your present
come your pasts and futures.
Unfolding like mirror flowers,
the petals of your selves forever open.

Your future memories become your past tomorrows.

The cells within the present
  fossils of your bodies
speak as songs in times you do not know.
The miracle of your flesh unfolds
where flesh is not known.
The surprise of your understanding
is in the pupil of your eye.

The pupil of your eye grows
in the medium of your being.
It sees realities that do not appear
to the sight that you assign it.

The eye looks inward,
and looking inward, creates its vision.

> JANE: "And yes, Jeff, this came through Cyprus, who is—don't forget it—a fictional character, as you know."

APPENDIX III

A Comparison of the Altered States Discussed in This Book

WHEN AND HOW

Seth trance

Sessions by prearrangement twice a week; otherwise spontaneous, with my permission. Seth is "here" or I turn into what he is.

Seth Two

Feeling that I "go out" to make contact which happens somewhere between where my body is, and where Seth Two is. I seem to go up through a chute or pyramid. Spontaneous, with my permission.

Sumari
(Cyprus)

Spontaneous, with my permission.

Sumari
poetry and
"math"

Just comes, when I'm alone, with my permission.

Sumari
(for translation into
English)

Usually when I'm alone though sometimes on the spot, as in class session.

DESCRIPTION OF STATE

Accelerated state; vigorous and active, though sitting; definite personality characteristics; excellent response to others.

Body slack, inactive.

Accelerated state; speaking in Sumari, singing, mimicry; voice dramas. Many gestures; excellent response to others.

Mind and body passive. Mind waits for words to drop in.

Mind at alert passivity. Feeling I go down beneath sounds.

SENSATION AND "PRODUCTS"

Feeling of "other" additional energy, beautifully focused into the session. "Products": books, a personagram of great merit.

Feeling of remoteness and distance. Haven't utilized this to the fullest by a long shot. "Products" so far: further alterations of consciousness that I haven't learned to translate.

Feeling of "other" additional energy. "Products": musical dramas that communicate by disrupting usual verbal patterns; utilizing rhythm and sounds.

Intense inner listening. "Products": poetry, some evocative material on mathematical principles.

I hear inner silence turn into inner sound. This may get too fast or too slow, so I readjust the focus of my consciousness often.

WHEN AND HOW

"Seven"

Seven's material comes to me in
my normal state of consciousness,
flowing into it easily from "someplace else." It is not my "own"
normal inspiration in the same
way that "I" am inspired when
I write poetry.

Helper

Sometimes I'm spontaneously
aware of Helper; usually I send
him to help others.

Special
State

I go into this from any of the
other states; never "cold" from
usual consciousness. It's a far
stronger version of the
Sumari states.

DESCRIPTION OF STATE	SENSATION AND "PRODUCTS"
Normal state, but slightly altered, taking down dictation sort of thing; smooth flow.	Seven so far "produces" fiction of very good quality. Though Cyprus supposedly wrote *Oversoul Seven,* she did it through Seven, through me. I consider Seven my playful creative self, but he also gives me advice about creative areas of my life—through writing when I request it. I don't concern myself with the nature of his reality.
I think Helper operates exclusively on the inward level of events. I go into a slightly altered state to reach him. I say "him." Actually I think of Helper as personified energy.	He seems to have assisted people in various troubles; I still have a lot of work to do here in understanding how Helper operates.
Here I feel that a vast amount of data is available but it is in some kind of "cosmic language" that has to be translated through the nervous system; I keep making adjustments that I don't really understand.	I feel that the data is not verbal, perhaps electromagnetic. I may take a minute to get a syllable or the flow may be too fast for my own nervous system, and I try to slow it down. I'm still learning here and feel this will develop in its or my own way.

Comments on Altered States

I consider the state of creative consciousness or high inspiration as normal for me, and therefore not as an altered condition. It's always been the basis for my poetry, for example, and probably includes a particular way of looking at the world. During such periods I'm in an accelerated mood, "lost" in whatever idea I have, intellect and intuitions working together, full blast. I'm caught up, and nothing else matters. In all of this my "I" enjoys itself as itself. Sometimes I feel that the idea or poem is after me, and I allow myself to be found; mentally feeling cagy and triumphant as a fox who catches a prey by laying low. Other times I feel as if I'm on a great chase, with the idea like some divine animal galloping ahead of me in the mental distance—and I'll never catch up—but I swear I will. Or sometimes the strange creature will stop just long enough for me to grab a hold; invite me to ride it if I dare—and off we go. I guess I consider this art, fun, sport, religion and "truth-seeking" all at once.

In a Seth trance, though, everything changes. The "I" that is so filled with excitement in the usual creative state, steps aside. I open the door and the strange divine animal comes prancing in to perform all by itself in the creature arena of my mind. I'm tempted to say, "Forgive me for the analogy, Seth," except that I'm sure he understands. For I've "caught" the inspiration. It's here in the open. It speaks. And what do we make of it?

But thinking of Seth in this odd fashion, as some kind of exotic species, as a divine animal, opens up ideas that are invisible if you consider him as a spirit. He *is* a different kind of species; whether mental, creature, or spiritual. And, in my terms at least, he brings gifts. Because his books just come; they're just here, with him. And they come from whatever he is, as apart from what I am or consider myself to be; though I'm necessary. I'm the one and the only one who can "milk" this odd divine animal. In that respect I feel the product is Seth's, not mine, though I am an indispensable intermediary. In that regard, he needs me as much as I need him.

Seth and I merge in sessions, I think. Seth doesn't turn into me; but I may partially turn into Seth, becoming more in certain terms than I usually am; letting the personagram imprint its messages on my psyche, and not, for example, imprinting *my* messages on Seth's psyche. Funny, if the personagram might be some kind of psychic species go-between, connecting our creaturehood with a spirithood that we don't yet understand.

In many dreams, I'm being "imprinted"; at least I'm being given Seth Material, often night after night. I'm quite aware this is happening. Sometimes I get tired of it and yell out, "OK Seth, cut it out for a while," and he does. Yet the passages of the book or whatever vanish when I try to recall them. I know that they reappear in book dictation. So I'm being programmed.

In some sessions, the program is simply played back; Rob takes the dictation, and that's that. In other sessions, Seth is right there, with material I know he hasn't given me before. I'm aware of being inside what he is, to some extent basking in his exuberance, energy, and wisdom. In one way or another, though, Seth comes into my home station. Whatever his reality elsewhere, during a session he is "alive" and immediate.

With Seth Two, everything shifts again. Then I feel as if I leave my body to travel to some lonely frontier of consciousness, waiting for signals or messages that I can barely decipher; a peaceful enough "place" but not a warm, human, emotional environment; more like a waiting area between worlds. I feel as if I journey upward—this could be a symbolic interpretation though, since I doubt that such directions have any meaning as far as states of consciousness are concerned. I'm not as sure of myself here, and a few times I felt as if I was caught in an elevator between floors of reality. I wasn't frightened, only uncomfortable. From where I was, I couldn't get my body working, or go further ahead on my journey. So I just waited. Each time, Seth "came along" and helped me back. I'm not sure how. I didn't see him or anything. He just animated my body and spoke, and that brought me back.

The immediately previous material described my natural states of altered consciousness—I say natural, since each happened spontaneously, without being induced, and none of the states themselves involve strain. I believe that each person has his or her own states, all merged into normal consciousness; each representing an Aspect of the source self, and operating as components of the focus personality, adding to it their own characteristics and abilities.

I don't see any particular need for others to "speak" for their own Seth, or to isolate the Aspects *in the same way* that I am doing. I do think, however, that our own personal talents and natural leanings can give excellent clues as to the nature of Aspects, and that an understanding of them can help us balance the components of personality in a more effective way. Certainly, though, when the Aspects are isolated, they cast brilliant light on the dynamics of the psyche as it expresses itself through the focus personality. I've only begun to explore those avenues.

I also believe that the Aspects are responsible for the birth of civilizations, as through revelations of various kinds their knowledge is transmitted to the conscious mind. I believe, therefore, that the Aspects serve as built-in impetuses to civilized behavior, providing basic knowledge of mathematical, "scientific," and mystical nature that can be translated in any of numberless ways to form any number of cultural systems. These would vary according to the reality system in which the focus Personality found itself. Any system may be more or less sophisticated than ours, from our viewpoint.

I'm not saying that a child left alone in a forest is going to develop his or her own mathematical, mystical, or "scientific" system. I'm saying that a group of human beings, starting from scratch, *would*, and has, and will. I see these Aspects with their revelatory information as natural psychic components of personality—as valid as the cells are, with *their* built-in impetus to physical growth. The Aspects provide the inner psychic thrust; the blueprints for cultural growth, and the means to achieve it.

As such, a study of Aspects can tell us much about our past as a species in historic terms, and provide hints as to the further development of our consciousness as well. Despite their general applications, though, the Aspects are each unique, and not just stereotyped psychic patterns out of which individuality is formed.

APPENDIX V

*Divinity is
a give and take
between unknown participants,
in which miracles occur
beyond the reach of each alone,
yet always happening—
a dizzy secretness
of relationships.*

GLOSSARY

Aspects   The reflections in the focus personality of other Aspect selves. These operate as "trace elements" and form the basic components of personality as we understand it.

Aspect-prints   Messages from one Aspect self to another; usually to the focus personality

Aspect selves   Each source self sends projections or Aspect selves into various fields of reality. These are Aspects of itself peculiarly suited to exist in specific dimensional environments.

Basic source aspects   The most prominent Aspects in any given personality, operating as huge power centers and organizing forces.

Event horizon   The psychological area separating probable and physical events.

Focus personality   The source self's earth Aspect self, focused in our space and time; the known self.

Free awareness   Our potential perception, as apart from the usual three-dimensional orientation of sense data.

Living area   The "paths" our lives follow from birth to death.

Nuclear self   That part of the sphere of identity that forms the focus personality and is responsible for its physical survival.

Personagram   A particular kind of trance personality; a "bridge" personality, straddling realities.

Pre-perception   The basis for our physically focused sense perception.

Prejudiced perception   The propensity for organizing undifferentiated data into specific differentiated sense terms.

Probable self   A version of the focus personality who chooses
          events that are probable from our standpoint.

Reincarnational drama   A spontaneous event in which two or
          more people perceive what seems to be a shared episode
          from another life.

Source self   The "unknown" self, soul or psyche; the fountain-
          head of our physical being.

Sphere of identity   The psychological and psychic area of iden-
          tity connecting the source self with its Aspect selves.

INDEX